Born in remote British Columbia with an insatiable appetite for the *raison d'être*, Chelsea Haywood has travelled the world independently and as a fashion model since she was sixteen. She is currently deciding where to call home. This is her first book.

90-DAY GEISHA

90-DAY GEISHA

My time as a Tokyo hostess

CHELSEA HAYWOOD

PEGASUS BOOKS
NEW YORK

90-DAY GEISHA

Pegasus Books LLC
80 Broad Street
5th Floor
New York, NY 10004

First Pegasus Books cloth edition 2009

Library of Congress Cataloging-in-Publication Data is available.

ISBN: 978-1-60598-071-3

10 9 8 7 6 5 4 3 2 1

Printed in the United States of America
Distributed by W. W. Norton & Company, Inc.
www.pegasusbooks.us

This is a true story. Everything that happens in these pages is an account of what really took place, according to my perception. For reasons of respect and gratitude certain names and details have been changed, but these are real people, real conversations and real events. Unless of course you happen to be my mother, in which case everything in this book is a figment of my imagination, none of these people exist and none of this *ever* happened.

Itadakimasu.

90-DAY GEISHA

ONE EYED JACK

The yellow line lay obediently at my feet. A shiny canary yellow, it was impossibly perfect. You couldn't have painted a more perfect, candy-coated line, unless you were a robot. It *must* have been a robot's work, but then again, maybe not. Everything around me had the same quality as that yellow line. The antiseptic voice broadcasting in high definition through a spotless ceiling. The orderly lines filing like clockwork through a row of identical counters. Everyone perfectly groomed. Perfectly poised. Perfectly patient. The way I was summoned to step over that yellow line. A quick flick of the wrist. *Come this way, please.* No translation needed. It all had that same immaculate polish.

He looked startlingly young for the crisp severity of his uniform, every strand of a symmetrical bowl-cut glistening under fluorescent lights. He was the first immigration officer I'd ever seen whose eyes sparkled. A slight bow brought his pin-straight hair falling forward and I nodded slightly in return, surrendering my passport into a starched white glove.

'Good morning. What is the purpose of your visit, please?'

'Ummm, tourism,' I smiled innocently. My response was automatic. It might have been inaccurate, but I doubted I would get one step further if I told him the truth.

'And where will you be staying?'

'The Hotel Sunroute, Shinjuku.'

Flipping through my passport, the immigration officer stopped briefly to look up and compare the live version of myself to the colour photo on page 2. I smiled again. Satisfied, he flattened a sticker precisely onto the lower-left corner of page 8:

JAPAN IMMIGRATION INSPECTOR. LANDING PERMISSION.
Date of Permit: 30 AUG 2004. Until: 28 NOV 2004. Duration: 90 days.

⸺

'Nathan's in a meeting. He'll be with you when he's through.'

The room reminded me of an old vaudeville theatre. Slightly run down, slightly done up. It was the deep-buttoned velvet decor. Brass poles on a mirrored stage. The way the ridiculously low lighting buffered the edges, the faces, made everything soft and threw the corners into darkness. It was a mood that permeated even to the waiters, handsome but gaunt as they were.

The club had yet to open and there were maybe ten men in the room. Some Japanese, some Caucasian. I shifted my weight on the bar stool, sitting up straighter to focus on two suits in conversation at the far end of the room. It was for one of them I was waiting, and with little else to do I watched the smoke gather in a faint haze above them.

Thirty minutes passed. The two men disappeared, and soon I was joined by a nervous Israeli at the next table. Hopeful-job-applicant-of-the-evening #2, she had long raven curls that overpowered her delicate bone structure. Her English was laboured and difficult to understand, so we sat in silence as bottle-blondes began to strut in on four-inch heels, clutching designer handbags beneath acrylic French-tipped nails. They were the first to arrive of the reported seventy hostesses who worked at One Eyed Jack – Tokyo's most prestigious international hostess club – and I watched as they gathered in groups to chain smoke the elasticity of their skin away.

These tawdry glamour girls were nothing like my memories of the girl I'd met on top of a mountain in Nepal. I had been sixteen and it was my first trip overseas. She had been travelling around the world for years on her own. She was beautiful. She was intelligent and carefree. But most intriguingly of all, she was funded by the most unlikely of benefactors: the male Japanese customers of a Tokyo hostess club.

Since then I'd met other girls who'd hostessed in Japan. Their stories were just as fascinating. I'd noticed that they'd talk it up at first, but mid-spin they became jaded. I wondered what had caused almost all of them to leave Tokyo with an unpleasant aftertaste of everything Japanese. Was it one drink too many, one gram too much? Was it the men? Even more intriguingly, what caused them to go back? Because many of them did.

These ambitious young women seemed to have *something* in common, apart from a First World nation imprinted on their certificate of birth. Were they the lost ones, seeking distraction from lacklustre lives, a string of bad relationships, or the reality that they'd spent four years earning a degree they didn't know what to do with? Perhaps they were the adventurous ones, looking for something different. Or was Tokyo just the best thing going at the time?

For me it was a conscious decision. I am thoroughly prepared. I am rock solid, and I must admit, I have a bit of an agenda. Since the early eighties, I would guess that hundreds of thousands of women have come to Japan to temporarily work in Tokyo's lucrative hostess clubs. All of them had a motive. All of them had a story. Yet a person's desire to hear these stories could not be satiated by even *one* personal account. No one had written about their experiences. Why not? Well, this may sound brash, but from what I could tell, everyone who might have had the inclination had just got too fucked up. So I'd decided to do it myself.

Another thirty minutes passed. *Where the hell was this Nathan?* There wasn't a speck of dirt left under my fingernails. I'd surveyed the entire room from top to bottom. My second complimentary cranberry on ice was now just ice, and a scratch was developing in my throat. I was just about to consider walking out when he walked in, on a direct path towards me.

Immaculately dressed, Nathan wore a suit you couldn't buy at a department store and shoes that shone like polished marble. His hair was spiked and glossed. His eyes were sharp, his eyebrows perfectly shaped. A commanding, utterly confident air oozed from his every molecule. In the realm of first impressions, the man was a machine. 'Excuse me, I'm sorry to keep you waiting. I'm Nathan. Please come with me.' He shook my hand firmly but briefly as his eyes locked onto mine, and I followed him across the room to a circular, thirties-style lounge. Sliding around to the back, he undid the only button on his suit jacket and straightened the points of a stiff collar in what seemed like one motion. Then he glanced over the application I'd been left with an hour ago.

It covered all the basics, plus the statement:

Anyone working for One Eyed Jack Co. must obey company rules and all Japanese laws. Anyone underage or without proper permission may not work. Anyone participating in illegal acts will be immediately dismissed without pay.

Curiously, 'Do you have a working visa: Yes/No' had already been circled 'Yes'.

'Okay, Chelsea. You're interested in working as a hostess. Where are you from?'

'Canada.'

'Oh. I was guessing the States. I grew up in New York. My father, he's Italian-American, but my mother, she's Japanese. I've been in Tokyo the past eight years. It just grabs hold of you, sucks you in. I love it, and there's absolutely nowhere I'd rather be, but sometimes you have to wonder what the hell you're doing here. How old are you?'

'Twenty.' I shot a look at the form in front of him and he stopped to read it this time.

'You're a fashion model?'

'Well, yeah, I . . .'

'And you're looking to work part-time to supplement your modelling income?' He'd cut me off with surgical precision, but that wasn't my answer.

'No. I came specifically to hostess. I'd like to work full-time.'

Nathan's head cocked slightly as the edges of his eyes narrowly creased. 'We're open six nights a week, but most girls work five,' he began. 'Let me explain our club's system to you. All our new girls start off on two-thousand yen an hour, which can increase later depending on your ability. Our best girls are on three-thousand to thirty-five-hundred yen plus drinks, which means they can make up to sixty American dollars an hour when it's busy. Working hours are from 9.00 pm to 3.00 am. Drink backs are five-hundred yen for every drink the customer orders you during the night, up to a maximum of twenty-five. That's four or five every hour; most girls can do that easily when it's busy. Drinks do not have to be alcoholic, you can order juice, but it's still fifteen-hundred yen to the customer. We don't pay for requests, which is when a customer asks specifically for you. It's a base hourly wage plus drink backs. Got it?'

I nodded and let him continue.

'We pay three times a month. The 10th, the 25th and the 15th. The 10th is for the second two weeks of the previous month worked, the 25th for the 1st to the 15th. On the 15th we pay you for your drinks. When you come in to work, the girls will explain anything else you need to know but that's the basics of it. I'll give you my card with my number on it. You don't have a phone?' He tapped the space I'd left blank on the form.

'No, not yet. I just got here two days ago.'

'All right, get a phone, then ring this number tomorrow, around seven. I've got a few other interviews tonight and I'll be able to tell you by tomorrow. A lot of girls are coming back from their summer holidays broke and they expect to work here. Give me a call.'

Nathan took out a napkin and pulled a silver pen from his breast pocket. 'I'll give you the names of a couple other clubs you can check out tonight. They work on a different system than us. Some girls do better in a different-style club . . . they pay a higher hourly wage, but you're not paid to drink.' He scribbled out *Greengrass* and *Outline*. 'Both of these are looking for girls. When you go outside, turn left and go past Velfarre. On the right you'll see Seventh Heaven, it's one of our other clubs, a strip club. Don't worry, I'm not sending you there. There's an elevator past the entryway. Greengrass is on the sixth or seventh floor. Then go check out this one.' He underlined Outline. 'Once you leave Greengrass, you ask the black guy downstairs and he'll tell you how to get there. It's pretty close but I don't know where exactly. I don't get out much. I just come to work and I go home.' He smiled a cool, ironed-on smile. 'I don't hang around.'

'Okay. Good. Thanks for your time, Nathan.'

'No problem. Any questions, call me on the number I gave you. And good luck.'

Nathan ended the conversation with a firm shake of my hand and disappeared.

—

My black pump drew back as quickly as it hit the pavement. One stride further and it would have been under the tyre of a jet-black Lamborghini Murciélago, so close I could see my reflection in its über-buffed paint job. Its state-of-the-art sound system breathed heavily into the humid night air as it tried to bully its way down the narrow alley like a stallion on a tether. It was a wickedly impressive beast — surely the chariot of choice should the devil come to town — but here its presence was hardly acknowledged.

As twilight fell, neon signs everywhere were awakening from dull and dusty sobering disappointments of the day to scream out '*It's better than ever!*' as their kaleidoscopic gases seeped into the veins of the city, infecting them with a euphoria that heightened the senses and brought lustre to the underneath.

This was Roppongi. It screamed to be seen. *Irashaimase! Komban wa!*

—

Even though I'd never heard of Greengrass, I thought I should check it out, and so in the name of a good backup plan I made a beeline for the corner, where, at the end of a second, darker path, I could see the glowing sign of the strip joint. *Deep breaths. Keep your head up* and *walk towards the light.* I dodged erratic taxis and a blacked-out Mercedes-Benz, trying to watch out for potholes in the beams of their headlights. I passed two enormous Pacific Islanders flanking the sweeping red staircase of a towering Yakuza-owned mega-club, and not much further was the entryway to Seventh Heaven, blocked by another bouncer as intimidating as the last pair.

'Hey, hey, hey! Where you going, girlfriend? You lookin' for a job, sweetheart?' He had to be the guy Nathan had mentioned.

'Yeah, sure I am, but not the kind you're thinking of, thanks.'

'What you tellin' me, you not an exotic dancer, honey?' I grimaced as he looked me up and down. 'Crying shame, man, I would be your best customer. You would make a lot of money, I am telling YOU!' He pinched his fingers and gave them a loud smack, like an Italian telling

Mama that her spaghetti bolognese was the most succulently delicious in all of Italy. I smiled coldly.

'No, sorry. Not interested.'

'Okay, okay. I understand. Don't worry, girl, I am your friend. You looking for a hostess job, am I right? Okay. That is sweet.' His posture softened as he extended a hand and engulfed mine in it. 'I am Solomon. From Nigeria.' As he nearly dislocated my shoulder, I added his name to a long list of the street hustlers who'd already tried to recruit me that night. Once free, I made towards the elevator.

'Hey, girlfriend!' Solomon shouted after me. 'You ever change your mind, you know, 'bout dancin' in my club, you just come see me!'

That wasn't going to happen any time soon.

THE SILENT LAUGHING MAN

Coming out of the elevator on the sixth floor I thought I must have got off at the wrong stop. In front of me were two giant ornate doors plastered with studio shots of some very handsome ladies. Posing seductively in lingerie, they were all smiles, Adam's apples and silicone boobs, with a few manicured man-hands clutching the overflowing breasts of fellow Y-chromosome cohorts. There was certainly no subtlety here. Even the door handles outdid themselves. Of Dionysus-like proportions, they were golden penises thicker than you could get your hand around and a foot in height. With disturbed amusement, I turned to the other side of the narrow corridor to see a plain door with a discreet sign next to it: Greengrass. This *was* the right floor after all.

Inside, I stood in semi-darkness. Eric Clapton played softly in the background. My pupils dilated, and when the room came into focus it was surprisingly small and demure. The walls were hung with prints of tasteful masterpieces and lined with turquoise, deep-buttoned seating. Still, it lacked the grungy feeling of Jack's. Everything was low to the ground, hard-angled and decidedly masculine.

A dozen tables skirted the perimeter of the room, each with round, cushioned stools beside them. There were no windows. At one end, a karaoke machine lay dormant, the wall behind it dominated by a large audio system. It made me distinctly anxious. An unobtrusive bar occupied the opposite side of the room, and it was here that three men in pressed white shirts were sitting. I must have startled them with my unannounced appearance, as they dropped their three cigarettes into an ashtray like schoolboys caught smoking, but when the oldest stood and solemnly gestured for me to approach, the smoking resumed.

I was taller than him, but without heels we were probably the same height. He wore a peculiar black bow tie and his hair was unnaturally shiny, as though freshly sprayed on with aerosol paint. His face was heart-shaped. Kind eyes, tiny mouth, bad skin.

He looked at me expectantly, his hands clasped behind his back.

'*Komban wa*,' I bowed. 'Nathan from One Eyed Jack sent me to your club. I'd like to find out about working here.'

Nodding, he motioned towards a tiny table between two liquor cabinets filled floor to ceiling with bottles. The absurdly low table was no higher than my knees, and as we sat across from each other I felt like a Girl Scout at a secret powwow. With both hands, he presented his name card. An inscription read 'Nakamura Nishi' beneath three large *kanji* characters. He was the club's manager.

Normally, hostess clubs are managed by a *mama-san*, an older woman who is typically an ex-hostess herself. She maintains relationships with the customers, cataloguing their personal preferences while simultaneously presiding over the girls like a mother hen. In the case of Greengrass, however, it appeared that Nishi had been installed as a kind of male *mama-san*.

I made my introduction and formalities mostly in Japanese, and he smiled without parting his lips until I couldn't think of anything else to say. Finally, he spoke.

'Prease, I am Nishi. Nakamura family name. You speak Japanese berry well.'

'Thank you, but I don't really. Just a little. *Chotto.*' I held up my thumb and forefinger measuring just an inch in the international sign for 'just a little'.

'My Engrish not so berry good. I am sorry.' Nishi's head bobbed up and down on his shoulders as he laughed without noise. He placed a piece of paper in front of me that seemed to outline the club's system – a jumble of paragraphs about wages, bonuses and the conditions to be met in order to receive them. It was surprising that you were fined twenty-five-hundred yen for being sick and ten-thousand yen for not coming to work, but from their point of view I suppose it was necessary. Each point took Nishi several minutes to explain, a combination of his poor English and incredibly slow and humbled manner. With an endless stream of clarifying questions on my part, I slowly began to grasp the differences in his club's system that '*some girls do better with*'.

The hourly wage was higher, but guaranteed hours were shorter. The bonus system sounded promising, but it required the building of continuous relationships. I wasn't sure about that. It sounded awkward and made earning potential a lot more complicated than showing up and knocking back as many standard drinks as you could every night – the paradoxical advantage of Jack's.

Here, in order to earn a decent wage, you had to be popular. Customers had to ask specifically for you, and to achieve your bonus you had to reach a quota of a certain number of *dohans*, which were pre-arranged dinner dates with customers before escorting them into the club. Otherwise, you were on the minimum-wage wagon.

Greengrass certainly fit my preconceived notion of a traditional hostess club, closer to the geisha system from which it stemmed than the high-flying One Eyed Jack. Instead of a mirrored stage and half-naked cabaret dancers, here the karaoke machine and its catalogue of songs provided the secondary entertainment. Hostesses were valued for their conversational skills (otherwise known as ego pampering), rather than just as drinking partners who could hold their liquor and look hot in a skirt. However, the biggest distinction between the clubs was how much *more* money you could pull at Jack's for doing essentially the same job. A couple of hundred dollars a night multiplied over three months becomes a dynamically decisive factor. If I could work at One Eyed Jack, I would.

When Nishi had finished, there was only one crucial thing I had left to know. 'Do I have to sing karaoke?' I was definitely *not* going to sing karaoke. That was my worst fear, but Nishi's head bobbed silently up and down.

'No, no. Chelsea-san not singing. Only customer. Some girls sing. Some girls sing *too* much, give me berry bad headache. You come Friday night, okay?'

Today was Thursday.

'Ummm, can I let you know tomorrow? I need to think about it.' I didn't tell Nishi it all depended on whether Nathan from One Eyed Jack said yes, and I wanted to discuss it with Matt. 'Can I call you tomorrow after, I don't know, seven o'clock?'

'Okay, tomorrow. I wish for you to decide Greengrass. I wait for your call. If Chelsea-san say yes, I will be berry happy man.'

~

'Hello, is Nathan there please?'

A soft female voice instructed me to wait, so I waited. And waited. I kept waiting until I worried my phone credit would run out. Just before the sickly sweet J-Pop oozing into my ear started to cause irreversible cavities, a man picked up. 'Nathan is not here.'

'Okay, I was in last night. He told me to ring at seven about working there.'

'What's your name?'

'Chelsea.'

'All right. I don't know anything about it, but he's not here and he won't be here until Monday.'

'Monday?' I repeated in disbelief. *But Nathan had been so specific about tonight.*

'Yeah, that's right.'

'So should I call back on Monday?'

'Uh . . . yes, call on Monday.' I hung up and pulled out Nishi's card from my wallet. It was all a bit mysterious. Monday was three days away and somehow I suspected I wouldn't get an answer even if I waited until then.

Ring, ring. '*Moshi moshi.*'

'Hello, Nakamura-san? This is Chelsea, I came into your club last night. I've decided I'd like to work for you.'

PINKS, YELLOWS AND BREASTS

'Hey girlfriend, you lookin' fine tonight! You work here now? All right! Where at, Republika?' Republika was the building's all-Russian hostess club.

'No, Solomon. At Greengrass, on the sixth floor. How's it going tonight?' My hand disappeared inside his again as he pumped it up and down.

'Good, good. I'm doin' good, girlfriend. Pretty busy tonight, you know. Friday night!' He dropped my hand quickly to wave a glossy flyer in front of some briefcase-toting Japanese salarymen passing by on the street. 'Sexy girls, topless dancers! Beautiful girls!' Ignored, he shouted after them. 'You don't like sexy girls? What's wrong with you, man?'

'Have a good night, Solomon,' I laughed in retreat.

'No, no, *you* have a good night, sweetheart. Don't you worry 'bout me.'

While Solomon shouted at passers-by, I studied the posters on the brick wall next to the elevator. A backlit group of Filipino girls with near identical haircuts, miniskirts and bobby socks smiled at me collectively above names like Rose, Julie and Jenny. Four noodle-limbed Japanese hostesses kneeled submissively in lingerie, faces covered with the backs of their hands. The advertising was somewhat disturbing, far more unsettling than the nondescript Las Vegas-style poster for Seventh Heaven, all pinks, yellows and breasts.

Luckily, Greengrass had no poster; it was just a name on the floor guide. There was nothing for the lady-boy club next door to it either, but with such a distinct niche the golden-penis-gated ones probably didn't have much in the way of competition.

Alone in the elevator, I pushed six and the doors closed. Okay. *Asphyxiate the butterflies. Make them go away.* Greengrass didn't welcome its patrons with phallic symbolism, and I had no use for nerves. All I had use for was two pieces of information: how did it work, and how could I work it? I could do this, I told myself. Easy.

—

What we often misunderstand in the West is that hostessing in Japan has very little to do with sex, quite a lot to do with psychology and nothing to do with prostitution. It is more like being a tip-seeking bartender and a native English teacher at the same time. Cleavage with cadence. That is why it is okay, for instance, to have a boyfriend. Or to be married.

I got married in Australia. I was eighteen and he was twenty-three. Mr Matthew Brian Brennan. He completely blew me away. I'd never met someone so self-possessed, so beautiful and so consummately unique. And I'd never, ever thought that I would want to do something as predictable as getting married. But then the future just slipped into my mind — and by coincidence he was thinking the same thing. Two months later we wore sneakers and blue jeans to the city registry office with a couple of his best mates as witnesses, and it turned out to be the only type of wedding we'd ever want to have.

Matt and I have never really embraced the conventional rules of expectation. I don't care about flowers and we don't pine over calendar celebrations or token gifts that 'prove' each other's commitment, but we love each other unconditionally. Our friendship is paramount, and we've always been equals. That's why when I came up with the idea of writing this book while eating New York cheesecake in Bangkok one afternoon, Matt was almost more enthusiastic about it than me, and two days later we were en route to Tokyo. His faith in me has always been unshakeable.

This exploration into the unknown wasn't about me being a hostess, spending my nights platonically entertaining older Japanese men; it was about the experience, the opportunity to live the life and to document it. I am lucky that Matt has the emotional confidence not to be worried by the idea. As for me, I know that anywhere I want to go, I can always get there of my own ability, but that's not the point of relationships, now, is it? Matt is my elevator, and I am his.

—

It is bizarre, yes, and seems unorthodox to foreigners, but the world of Japanese hostess clubs is just another dimension of reality. Drop a Zulu in Disneyland and he'll think it's crazy, but millions of people love the magical kingdom and its weird, surreal little corner of make-believe. It's a billion-dollar industry, a part of the American social furniture.

Likewise, hostess bars in Japan are commonplace, respectable and not at all revolutionary. They're not even a recent occurrence, because long before Western women came to pour drinks and help them practise their English, Japanese men were flocking to *Japanese* hostesses. It wasn't until the bubble economy of the eighties – when international trade swelled the fortunes of the country's millionaires and billionaires to extreme highs – that English became a hot commodity for the elite, and so too did the fantasy of the blonde, blue-eyed woman. Today, Western girls remain a novelty – that maraschino cherry in your caramelised rum – and probably always will, but this is a subculture with revolving doors that ensures most of them are only here temporarily.

No less a part of the Japanese psyche than the Sunday family dinner, the hostess club exists in the business and entertainment districts alike. No one is ashamed of frequenting a hostess club. No one denies it. It is nothing like a stolen hour spent in some seedy showgirl venue. In many a Japanese hostess club, men are privileged just to be going. The more exclusive, the higher the status, and so they boast. They even use clubs as legitimate alibis for wives who dare question their endless stream of late nights out, as companies often schedule after-work meetings or leisure time at a favourite hostess club. Attendance is mandatory. Clients are entertained at the best club a company can afford as a measure of goodwill to strengthen business relations.

It is a cultural phenomenon that runs parallel to daily existence, even complementing it. It is a place where men come just to be *in the company of* women for however long they are willing to pay for it. Men rely on the hostess club, its hostesses and often the karaoke to relieve long-workday stress, to talk make-believe and have someone listen to whatever the hell they feel like saying. In Japan's workaholic patriarchal world, it's probably almost a necessity. A part of the social furniture.

And I was fascinated. Could something so untainted really exist in the eye of such a sexually charged storm? Next to pinks, yellows and breasts? Across the hall from a transsexual treasure trove? With all the other options out there, what were powerful, intelligent and obscenely wealthy Japanese men seeking in a young, Western *hostess*? She didn't take off her clothes or dance around a pole. She certainly wasn't going to suck their dick. And in my case, I wasn't even going to be chatting about current events in a set of matching bra and panties or a school-girl uniform like Rosie, Julie and Jenny. I would be required only to wear a respectable cocktail dress and speak perfect English in a polite and charming manner. I'd need to laugh at jokes, pour drinks and light cigarettes. How hard could that be?

AS GREEN AS GRASS

I opened the door to the loud '*Irashaimase!*' of one of Greengrass's two gangly waiters busily displaying his talent for bending to hundred-degree angles at split-second notice. It was startling to receive such a formal welcome, but as he snapped back to standing, his eyes expanded behind Lennon rims. 'Oh! Chelsea-san. Hello,' he laughed with embarrassment. Nishi must have told him I was coming. 'I am Tehara.' I was given a much more appropriate head bow and then ushered through to the powwow table until Nishi could come join me with his ashtray.

'Chelsea-san, I am berry happy you choose Greengrass,' Nishi whispered. He smiled and slid a single sheet of paper across the table with a weathered finger. It was a contract. Then came a second. *Tap, tap.* 'Berry important for your job, Chelsea-san. Prease read.'

Hostess duties

1) *Handing the customers oshibori (hand towels).* When a customer goes to the table and returns, hand the customer an oshibori.
2) *Making drinks for the customers.* When there is a bottle of whiskey, brandy, wine, champagne, etc. at the table and the customer's glass is empty or nearly empty, ask the customer how he wants his drink and make them what they ask for.
3) *Exchanging name cards.* As you seat yourself at a table, introduce yourself and exchange name cards (or, alternatively, phone numbers and/or email addresses).
4) *Not singing karaoke.* The hostess's duties do not include karaoke. Doing so limits the number of times a customer can karaoke. Also realise that the customers do not come to listen to you sing. Host-

esses should, however, sing alone with a customer when the customer wants to sing a duet.

5) *Apparel and footwear.* In order to help entertain customers, hostesses should realise that there are desirable and undesirable types of apparel and footwear. For example, skirts should be either a mini-skirt or a long skirt. Shoes should cover the ankle and have heels with a minimum height of 3 cm (about 1 and 1/5 inches) or higher. T-shirts, pants, cardigans, sweaters and sandals are prohibited. Be aware of the dress code, because violations will lead to a disallowable of work for that day. (Hint: party dresses are OK.) If you have questions, ask a member of the staff or an experienced hostess.

6) *Phone customers (email customers).* For example, phone a customer the day after he visits and thank them for coming, tell them that you enjoyed their visit and humour them, etc. Or, in addition, make an appointment to escort them (DOHAN), etc.

7) *On customer escorts (DOHAN) and activities outside the workplace.* Be absolutely sure to leave contact info (name of person you are escorting and a phone and/or email address with a member of the staff) before you go. You should leave contact info with the staff when going to have a drink with a given customer for the first time or accompanying them somewhere as a matter of course. Do not agree to join the person you are accompanying anywhere in which you will be alone with them (such as a private room, car, etc.). Also, be aware that there do exist persons with perverted intentions as well as members of organised crime groups who will try to take advantage of you by posing as ordinary customers. Be aware that such dangers exist. You should observe the same precautions when taking long/short trips or taking a drive, etc. on your own time (your days off).

On Saturday 21 July 2000, her day off, a British hostess working in the Roppongi club Casablanca made a call to her friend saying she was going on a drive with a customer to the Chiba coast. Chiba is Tokyo's neighbouring prefecture to the east, and the nearest seaside escape from the concrete metropolis. She was never heard from again.

Later that same year a wealthy Korean–Japanese businessman named Joji Obara was arrested for allegedly drugging and raping numerous women on separate occasions since 1996. On further investigation, police found nearly five thousand videotapes at his properties as well as personal diaries chronicling the apparent rapes of more than two hundred women. Obara pleaded not guilty to the charges, maintaining that all of the sexual relationships had been consensual. He also continued to maintain innocence as the prime suspect in the 1992 case of a 21-year-old Australian hostess from Perth, Carita Ridgway, who died mysteriously of liver failure in a Tokyo hospital after allegedly being heavily drugged and raped at the perpetrator's home.

On 8 February 2001 a dismembered body was found buried in a seaside cave in Misaki, approximately fifty kilometres from Tokyo and a strong spit in the wind away from a condominium owned by one Joji Obara. Forensics linked the body to the dental records of the missing British hostess, Lucie Blackman. When questioned, Obara claimed he had met the hostess only once at the Roppongi club and had no involvement in her death. DNA and fingerprints found in his condo were later forensically matched to the body found in Misaki *and* to Lucie Blackman. In light of this forensic evidence, and on top of the previous rape charges, Obara's trial acquired the charges of 'abduction with an indecent purpose, rape leading to death, and damage and abandonment of a dead body'. Apparently, in Japan's disgustingly twisted judicial system, the raping, killing and dismembering of a woman is a crime punishable by only three years to life.

Holy shit. At the time I arrived in Tokyo, the trial was still ongoing, and I had to wonder who in their right mind would get themselves into such a position by getting in the car of a virtual stranger? How did that happen?

(Note: On 24 April 2007, Joji Obara was acquitted of all charges relating to Lucie Blackman despite abundant circumstantial evidence that showed Obara had bought items including quick-drying cement and a chainsaw soon after Lucie's disappearance, and that he had conducted internet searches on how to dispose of a dead body the day after she disappeared. He was sentenced to life, however, for the guilty verdicts of eight other rape charges and one charge of rape leading to the death of Carita Ridgway.)

'This is change room, and *toiret*,' Tehara announced as he opened a narrow door on to what was essentially a broom cupboard with a coat rack, 'but now, you can sit there, Chelsea-san.' *There* was a spot on the low couch between a rail-thin blonde painting her fingernails by the light of a mobile phone and a curvaceous blossom of colour, all wrapped up in a dress of scattered begonias. While the blonde continued to paint, the blossom introduced herself with a lilting accent and a warm, sunny smile. 'Bianca, from Romania. Vhat is your name?' The next ten minutes of my life became a space filled with the diluted version of hers, puffed out on a long, thin cigarette.

Bianca smoked like a 1930s movie star. Elegantly, disaffectedly. *Puff, puff.* She had come to Japan on a university scholarship, and next month she'd begin her MBA at a prestigious international school in Tokyo. To pay the tuition she'd been working nights as a hostess, days as a travel agent. *Puff, puff.* Even in the dim light you could see the dark circles under her eyes. It was a heavy load for someone on a student visa, but somehow I suspected her official status to be different. The authentic-looking rock switched to her right hand might have had something to do with it, and the fact that, well, marital compromise is sometimes a small price to pay for personal opportunity. When an educated, multilingual woman working in a Tokyo hostess club just happens to come from Eastern Europe, it hints at a conscious resistance to a future spent in a struggling, post-Communist society. Even if Bianca was on a student visa, the classes that substantiated it would eventually end, or she'd burn out working night and day to fund them. Then she'd have to go back. Back to what? Bleak Town, Romania. *So, how long had she been married?* No, no, she laughed cordially. The ring was just an heirloom. Right. And mine was from the wee leprechaun down the road.

Once her nails had dried, the blonde leant across Bianca's ample cleavage. 'Hello, I am Sonja, from Colombia.' I shook her dainty hand, but before I could respond, a blur of colour flew past and flung itself over the bar.

'Am I late? Don't fine me! I'm sorry, but I haven't eaten. You don't expect me to work when I'm *starving to death*, do you? Don't think that I don't know the rules!'

Nishi puffed on his cigarette and the pretty Chinese girl whipped around. 'Oh, hi there, you're new! I'm Jamie.' She waved. I smiled. She turned back to Nishi. 'Have I got enough time for another sandwich? Huh, do I? You don't punch me in for eight minutes. I'll be right back!' And Jamie ran for the door, half a Starbucks sandwich still in hand.

Just then, a sliver of light split the darkness and a husky voice seeped from the change room as three girls – who'd slipped by unnoticed during Jamie's entrance – emerged, deep in heated discussion. Rs rolled. Words halted. Throats constricted. *What language were they speaking?* A dark girl, eyes burning with a fierce intensity, offered a clammy hand and a softly spoken introduction in English, an English that was velvety rich. She looked Arabic. 'I am Dick La. *Shalom.*' Maybe not.

'Sorry, what?'

'Dickla. *Dic-o-la,*' she enunciated. 'It's Hebrew. Israeli name. We are all of us from Israel. This is Abie,' a mousy, bony girl with a nasal American accent, 'and Levana,' a buxom, fake redhead with ivory skin encased in clinging cherry velvet. She smiled between puffs on a ciga-rette but didn't say hello. With camaraderie established, Hebrew was quickly reinstated as the tongue of choice and I was abandoned until Jamie came back.

'Okay, so I'm supposed to tell you *everything* you need to know about being a hostess. I have no idea why they picked *me*. I'm, like, the worst hostess in the history of Japan, so it's probably 'cause I'm from Canada and you're from Canada, but maybe 'cause I actually *know* how to speak English. Thank God you're here. Before I was, like, the only one. I don't really know what there is to tell you. Did they show you that list of rules, "Duties of the Hostess" or whatever? Pretty much just follow that and it's no big deal. Oh, and there's blank name cards up there, and lighters. Do you smoke?'

'No.' I took a breath, deep and quick, before she relaunched.

'You might as well start, everybody does. I really should quit, but it's just so cheap! You know how much it costs for one pack? Three-hundred yen! That's it! In Vancouver, it's like eight dollars a pack! I'm pretty bad, but the customers are worse. You should probably get one of those lighters you can just press down on and then you won't burn your thumb. I did that, burnt my thumb. Oh, and when you light their cigarettes, make sure you cup your other hand around the lighter. They get pissed off if you don't do that. It's not proper *etiquette*.' Jamie stopped to pull at the hem of a bright red Chinese dress sliding up her thighs.

'It's too short! I cut too much off, but whatever, they like it. I just don't want anyone to see my underwear. I shouldn't even be wearing a mini, look at my thighs! Did you know I've put on seven kilos since I got here? Seven freakin' kilos! That's the worst thing about Tokyo, *you get fat*. All you do is drink and eat and you turn into a big, fat balloon. I go to the gym *every day* and I still can't stop it from happening. Can you believe it?'

Hmmm. Jamie was just like any other girl I'd gone to school with: small-town pretty, the life of the party, and looking for something different from the everyday. She'd left behind her friends, obviously not settling for the steady job-slash-boyfriend, DVD escapism on a couch in the suburbs.

'So watch out. Actually, you probably don't need to watch out. What are you, like a size 6? You should model! Are you crazy being a hostess? What are you doing? Any *gaijin* can model in Japan, even fat old guys. Except for me, because I'm Chinese, *well*, mixed Thai-Chinese. They don't like Chinese. But you'd make way more than doing this, talking shit to kindergartners. It's easy, though, kinda like babysitting, and it beats teaching English. I tried that for a while, but God, was I ever bored out of my mind . . .'

'Jamie! *Jamie!*' hissed Tehara with a glare. 'Customer! You deaf? Come on!'

'What? I have to go *already*? Is it a request? *God!* Sorry, one of my regulars came in. We'll talk later.' She scooped up her clutch and teetered away.

EXPANDING VOCABULARIES

'*Irashaimase!*' Tehara pitched forward as two men entered through Greengrass's one and only door. They bowed stiffly in return, allowing him to stow their briefcases in a hidden closet and sit them next to the karaoke machine. There he presented steaming *oshibori* and lit cigarettes from one knee. Drink preferences were vocalised. Tehara's head dropped slightly. It was the same practised charade that had brought the club to full, and so by the time Tehara started to back away in a succession of miniature bows, I was aware that his next call of duty was to bring the hostesses. Alone at the powwow table, there was only me.

Nishi came. He motioned for me to stand, shuffled across the floor and indicated my place with a downturned hand. I breathed in deeply. *Here we go*. Wiping the perspiration from my palm as discreetly as possible, I sat nervously with a big, friendly smile.

'Oh! *Sagoi!*' Saliva landed on my face. Glasses were quickly taken from a shirt pocket so that two narrowly slit eyes could inspect my face.

'*Komban wa. Watashi wa Chelsea desu. O-namae wa nan desu ka.*' I held out my name card as I introduced myself and asked his name.

'Oh! *Sagoi, sagoi!* Berry beautiful *and* berry crever. So smart-o! You are like my boss! Smart man, over there!' The foreign face pointed across the table to a man engrossed in conversation with a blonde and then snatched up my card to study it intensely, inches from his eyeballs. 'I am so sorry. You are most beautiful, I forget my name. Therefore I will now introduce myself to you.' He pulled out a proper business card of his own and presented it to me. 'I am Shio. Over there, that is my boss, Takori-san. He rikes girls, but you do not need to know him.'

'Shio-san, it's very nice to meet you,' I smiled.

'Yes! Do you know, *shio* mean salt in Japan? I am Mr Salt, but that is not important. What country do you come from?'

'Canada.'

'Oh! Canada! Your Engrish berry good! Takori-san, Takori-san!' Shio shook his boss's kneecap jarringly. 'You must meet Chelsea-san! She come from Canada. Engrish berry good!'

Takori smiled, swiping away Shio's hand to grab mine firmly. 'Sorry, I cannot speak English. Shio-san speaks berry good English. Shio-san my number-one boy. Tonight is my celebration to him. This is because he recently making big company achievement!'

Shio-san beamed from ear to ear.

'Oh, really, is that true?'

'Yes, I am number 1, but not boy! I am man. Guess how old you think I am?' Shio assumed a serious expression and pointed at his face. He looked like he might be in his early thirties, so I guessed 30 to humour him.

'No! Berry wrong! Forty-two!'

'No, come on. You look amazing. You can't be 42!'

Shio obviously delighted in what must have been an often-played guessing game.

'Sank-you berry much. However, I am 42.' As he pulled out a pack of cigarettes, I held up my lighter, poised in the shelter of a cupped hand. He leant forward casually and sucked the flame up into his cigarette. 'How long you have been in Tokyo?'

'Five days.'

'Whoa!' Shio was astonished. 'Only five day! *Honto?*'

'*Honto?*' I repeated. 'What does *honto* mean?'

'Rearry. *Honto* mean rearry. Don't worry. I teach you Japanese, one-thousand yen, one hour. But,' he paused, springing up an index finger, 'you teach me Engrish, two-thousand yen, one hour.'

I laughed and made him shake hands. 'It's a deal.'

'What does it mean, "it's a deal"?' Confusion revealed the faintest wrinkles.

'It's like an agreement. We both agree to something, like we are making a trade. "Okay, let's do it – I agree." Do you understand?'

'Ahhh, it's a deal. *Wakarimashita*. Okay. You come from Canada. Do you rike ski?' Shio thrust his arms back at the elbow, pumping them side to side.

'Skiing? Oh yes, I like skiing. Is that one of your hobbies?'

'Yes, I rike ski berry much. But no time. No holiday for me.'

'What about Sunday? You *don't* work Sundays, do you?'

'Yes, unfortunately I have berry difficult job. My business sound and lightning.'

'*Lighting*,' I corrected without thinking.

'Yes, *lighting*. So long hours! Everybody need sound and lightning, so bad time for hobbies. It is so difficult. However, next year is berry big job. Famous new hotel coming: Ritz Carlton. Ritz Carlton people do not know Japanese wedding, but I am expert. Therefore I must organise for them. I will have no time for movies. I want to see Michael Moore.'

'*Fahrenheit 911?* The movie about the war in Iraq?'

'Yes, yes. War in Iraq. President Bush berry stupid man,' he spat. 'Japanese businessmen do not rike Bush. But that is another matter, not for beautiful young rady. What does it mean, fairy height?'

'*Fahrenheit*. It's a way to measure temperature, like ten degrees Celsius, only Americans use Fahrenheit, like, "*It's ten degrees Fahrenheit outside*".'

'Oh yes. I see. I want to see it but no time. Movies are too long for Japanese people.'

While I continually topped up Shio's whisky, sipped on cranberry juice and lit his cigarettes, he and I talked more about skiing, which led to a discussion of the 1998 Winter Olympics and whatever else struck his fancy until Takori-san asked for the bill. When it came, I got my first lesson in Japanese hierarchy; Takori-san refused to acknowledge its existence, and Shio obligingly paid hundreds of dollars to celebrate his own recent achievement. Out at the elevator, I handed over Shio's briefcase and bowed.

'Thank you very much for coming, Shio-san. *Arigato gozaimasu*. Have a good night! I hope to see you again soon,' I said, and Shio shook my hand with vigour.

'Okay!' he beamed back. '*It's a deal!*' Oh God. Matt was going to love hearing about this. This game was a cinch. It was so much easier than I thought.

—

Nishi didn't even let me catch my breath. One heel back in the club and he had me by the elbow, gently guiding me to an overflowing, noisy jukebox of a table that immediately magnified the lack of alcohol flowing through my veins. I gave Nishi a long, sideways look and he patted me paternally on the shoulder. 'No probrem, Chelsea-san. More smile.'

'Are they Japanese?' I whispered. They didn't look Japanese, and the disciplined politeness that Shio had displayed despite his own drunkenness was nowhere to be seen.

'Korean,' muttered Nishi, and I was left alone in the middle of a wild pop song with no one to introduce myself to. Everyone was engrossed in a slideshow on a digital camera, and the man next to me gave more attention to the cigarette lingering from his lips, half-burnt to ash, than to me. At least he knew it was there. I felt like an idiot, waiting to be noticed.

'Who's that guy? Wait, go back. *That* dude! Hah hah, that's Akira, you scoundrel!' The camera was thrust towards a man who had one hand casually draped over Jamie's shoulder. The table was littered with shot glasses. Sucked-out lemon sagged in ashtrays.

When my neighbour finally decided to introduce himself, I wasn't paying attention. He cleared his throat. 'I'm Christopher,' he repeated, flat, distant and uninterested.

'I'm Chelsea.' He nodded and lit another cigarette. I looked over at Jamie, and thumbed the crisp edge of a name card I'd painstakingly written out. '*Should I?*' I mouthed. She shook her head and motioned to put it away. Good call. It probably wouldn't have gone over well anyway: '*What the hell is that? You wanna give me a business card? Does it look like we're doing fucking business?*' He gave me that impression.

I wondered what Christopher was doing in a hostess club. Sure, my reference point was severely limited, but he wasn't even in the same ballpark as Shio. He was completely Westernised. His mannerisms. His lingo. His arrogance, virtually imperceptible in the Japanese. But maybe I was just biased. As the conversation turned to movies, budgets and healthy profit margins, Akira leant across the table, pointing a politely accusatory finger at Christopher. 'Do you know who this man is?'

'C'mon, man, stop it. Do you know who *this* man is?' Christopher countered.

'This man is the number 1 movie producer in Korea,' Akira continued. 'He is a *very* successful man.'

'Yeah, well *this* guy is one of the biggest movie producers in Japan. *He* is a very successful man.' Raucous laughter ensued, and a toast was declared.

'What are you drinking?' Christopher asked. 'Is that *juice*? You gotta be kidding.'

'Yeah, it's orange juice. I don't drink.' I could hear my voice, aristocratic in tone.

'And *how long* have you been in Tokyo?'

'Five days. This is my first night.'

'Jesus! Your first night? And you got us Koreans . . . *and* you're not drinking? Now that's madness, holy shit.' Christopher's frozen wall of ice suddenly thawed as he realised I was human. Then, distracted by the opening notes of a familiar song, he quickly stood. 'Oh, oh, that's my song, that's my song!' Someone passed a microphone and he began to sing 'Desperado' by the Eagles. Everyone cheered. He was better than I expected, and surprisingly alluring.

In the mayhem, someone forced another microphone into my unwilling hands between verses. It was Christopher. He looked me in the eyes and said, 'Sing with me.'

'I don't sing. Christopher, really, you don't want me to sing,' I pleaded, as he tried to pull me to my feet, but luckily Don Henley came to the rescue. I sat down in relief, but as I listened to Christopher's soulful voice against an eclectic murmur of backup vocals, my entire impression of him changed. He seemed accessible. Tender. Radiant. Maybe it's the second impression that counts more sometimes.

As the last notes rang out, the table exploded in applause. The drunkest one stood, only to fall back down. Christopher nudged his stool closer to mine. I was smiling ear to ear. 'Next time I come, you're going to sing,' he said. Tiny beads of sweat glistened along his hairline.

'Next time? I thought you lived in Korea.'

'I do, in Seoul. I produce movies, Korean movies. That's what I do, but we're coming back in October for the International Film Festival.' He reached out to grab my *thumb*. Why my thumb? It was such an odd gesture. 'That's when I'll see you again.'

'How will I know when you're coming? Do you have an email address?'

'Yeah, hey Jodie! Do you still remember my email?' Christopher shouted to the blonde belting out a Stevie Wonder hit. Jodie gave a thumbs-up. Her mouth was open so wide you could see the stud through her tongue. 'I gave it to her last time. I want her to come to Korea, she's an absolute . . .' Christopher stopped to squint at me. 'You know what, I'll *tell* you my email. If you can remember without writing it down, you can come to Korea. Maybe you can come with Jodie. I'll send you a ticket and show you around for a couple days. It'll be great.'

—

Gradually I became less anxious in anticipation of what might be said or done next. I still had an iron rod in my back and a tentative pitch to my laugh, but I almost felt like Christopher and I were old friends reunited after years of absence – familiar, but with that edge of formality. 'Are you okay?' he asked at one point. 'I mean, are you comfortable? Are you enjoying yourself? You're really calm, very relaxed.' I shrugged in response. 'I don't know, you just seem in this whole other realm from everyone else here.'

But I *was* in a whole other realm. I was in it for the money and the story, and in every way I viewed myself as the detached observer, thinking I could integrate into a foreign culture and learn all about it without getting too involved. As a model I'd been accustomed to decadence and absurdity under the privileged umbrella of fashion – everything for free, earning extravagant money for virtually nothing but a smile – so it might be fair to say that I felt myself slightly untouchable. I had seen it all before – the wealth, the power players. I had received the superficial adulation. But apart from that, I wasn't on the market, and I wouldn't be falling under any spells, because I was already married with exuberant happiness to a man I adored. Matt is my best friend, and marriage is just the sprinkles on our ice cream.

Besides, this job was like acting; I was starring in my own three-month Broadway show, and I wanted to make it as interesting as possible. I could deal with a few Japanese men. I could deal with a warped reality. It might be puzzling, but that was all it was. I was in control. I could stay in control.

And so I answered: 'I'm fine, thanks. Everything is fine. Things are crazy here, but I'm happy. I have a lot of peace in my life right now. Things are good.'

Christopher contemplated my face. He looked around. People were falling off stools, shouting and slamming back tequila. A grown man sat in a trance, studying the songbook. Girls of all nationalities were singing along to highlighted lyrics and shrieking with laughter. Nowhere was there calm. Slowly Christopher turned back to me. 'I can see that. But you know . . . three months in this place is a *long* time. You're going to need to drink to be on the same frequency as them.' He waved a hand across the drunken riot around us. 'Otherwise you won't survive.'

BOTTLED

'Hey, Abie, what's that sign on the change-room door about being fired?' It was nearly 11.00 pm and as the two newest additions to the fleet, we still hadn't been seated with anyone. It was only my second night, and Abie had been at Greengrass for a little over two weeks. She gave me a blank look. 'C'mon then,' I pulled at her forearm, 'I'll show you.'

'Oh, *shit*! When did they put that there?' Abie gasped. The paper on the change-room door was yellowed, with dog-eared corners. I guessed it had been some time ago.

'They're not letting us take customers to the American? That's bullshit. Where are we supposed to go? I'm not drinking with the fuckers for free,' she spat resentfully. *Hmmm*. The thing with little Israeli Abie was that while she looked docile as a mouse, she often expelled artillery, hard and bitter, at a pace more rapid than the machine gun from her days in mandatory service. 'Whatever,' she sighed, 'we can still catch them on the street.'

Confusion must have shown all over my face. '*Ohhh*, you don't know about bottling yet, *do you?* Well . . .'

Bottling /ˈbat(e)ling/ v. to identify and approach a man of apparent wealth – usually indicated by his watch (Rolex, Cartier, TAG Heuer) and shoes (shiny, new and expensive) – to entice/ask/demand him to buy you a drink (in this case $200 wine, $600 Moët, or $850 Dom Perignon, by the bottle) and reap 40 per cent commission on every bottle until he stops paying, the bar closes, or you get too tired or drunk to see straight and have to go home. Game over.

According to Abie, bottling may not be the most *honest* way to make a quick buck, but the only reason anyone came to Roppongi was for the money anyway, right? It wasn't an exchange program, and it was hardly Mecca for young women looking for a good time. It was a dirty, filthy, bloodsucking hole, full of men with disposable cash for the taking.

'I mean, at least with bottling you can afford to buy a goddamn apple. Who gets off charging $5.80 for *one fucking apple*? Crazy Japanese. I don't care if it's perfect, it's still just a stupid apple, and those rich motherfuckers can buy as many goddamn apples as they want. They might as well pay for me to buy a few, whether they know it or not.'

Holy smokes. Abie really *was* a very charming girl.

—

My cheeks hurt. My gums hurt. Even my teeth hurt. I'd been smiling like an overzealous Miss Universe contender for so long now I was afraid that my face might actually get stuck, just like my mother had warned my five-year-old self when I'd occasionally stick fingers up my nose, bulging my eyes out in delight.

I felt a strong urge to pull my best out of the archives right now. I needed to know I wasn't dreaming. This was mental exhaustion, brain-drain of the first degree. For two hours and counting I'd been actively engaging in a conversation with the staff of General Electric, and I was about to S.C.R.E.A.M. They were like the machines that assembled their products. Monotonous. Repetitive. Overworked. They were aged specimens of the Japanese post-World War II school of thought, where leisure and play were simply synonyms for work with your colleagues *outside* the office.

I wanted to be interested; if they'd only talk about GE's renewable energy program in Aomori Prefecture, but no such luck. They were drier than the Atacama Desert. My eyes kept closing. Maybe I *was* dreaming, endlessly mixing drinks and lighting cigarettes in a karaoke twilight zone. The men had already incinerated three packs between them. I had reason to wonder how long the fluid in my lighter would last. Or how long my lung tissue would.

When were they going to leave? The only clock I had was on the phone in my purse, and I wasn't going to look. I'd get another cut-throat sign from Soh, who was watching me like a hawk. Soh was Tehara's subordinate, and he was from Burma. Only the fact that he refused to call it Myanmar allowed me to overlook his transgressions – which happened to involve picking on me, the new girl, silently scolding me when ashtrays accrued more than two butts, for drinking pineapple juice too fast or for letting a customer's drink fall too low. Then again, some customers weren't much better. I poured too much whisky and too little water. There was too much ice. There was not enough ice. *Well perhaps you should mix your own f%#@ing drink then, kind sir.* I wanted to say that. I probably could have said anything so long as I smiled.

When they asked me to guess their ages, I nailed it like a one-minute multiplication drill. After I correctly stated the fourth man's age, they were astounded. Did I have psychic abilities? Nope. Was it keen observation? No way. To this man there was only one obvious explanation. 'Have you spoken to my wife?' Hilarious.

It was 1.00 am by the time we bowed the men off into the elevator, red eyed, waving and giggling. I was slowly becoming accustomed to seeing Japanese men giggle. It helped remind me of what a different social realm I was in. *Tee-hee-hee.* That was my signal, Toto. I've a feeling we're not in Kansas any more.

Back inside, Tehara threw his arms across his chest into a big X to signal that work was over. The Big X and I were already acquainted; we'd been introduced in a store when the phone that I'd wanted was unavailable. It was an ingenious sign, and extremely effective in getting one's point across. I loved it, and had already started plotting how I could use it when I left Japan. '*Hello, how are you today? Do you have a minute for Greenpeace?*' The Big X flies up.

—

Abie and I circled Roppongi, sizing up anyone who passed. The streets were congested with taxis. People in an advanced state of intoxication crowded the sidewalks, but they were mostly young party animals on a budget looking to get laid, and not prime candidates for bottling. We'd be lucky to get a bottle of Moët out of any one of them; it was Saturday night and the men with bank accounts for that were at home with their families. Abie didn't protest when I finally said *maybe next time*. I'd lasted ten minutes. I needed to escape to the empty backstreets of Moto-Azabu and try to make it home without getting blisters.

Roppongi was overwhelmingly claustrophobic. I needed fresh air, but where could I find that in a city of twelve million? That was a stratosphere away. I'd had enough cigarette smoke blown directly into my face to slap on a nicotine patch and start the ten-week program. I hadn't eaten in five hours, except for all six of the rice snacks and Hershey's Kisses meant for the customers I'd been sitting with, who hadn't noticed because they'd been too busy repeating themselves.

I wondered where Matt was among all this insanity. I had so much to tell him, but it was doubtful he'd be back at our apartment. We'd found the modern, space-efficient techno box that we now called home only the day after our arrival, and we counted ourselves lucky. Nestled in the serene, affluent streets of Hiroo, it was a sanctuary, albeit at $1500 a month. When faced with a choice between going out and staying in with a television with no English channels and eighteen square metres of space for company, though, I knew what Matt would have picked. The man was a lion: you couldn't cage him, and I had no idea where he might be.

Since we'd arrived, he'd worked one night as a bartender to keep himself amused, but quit after the twelve-hour shift earned him less than a hundred bucks. It seemed every temporary job for a white male was slave labour, so instead he'd spent the last two nights at Lexington Queen, getting smashed for free on account of being a model. I wanted to see my husband, but I was uninterested in going to a nightclub to hang out with the praying-mantis crowd. He'd be home sooner or later. I was tired, I was hungry and I was going home.

At least that was my plan . . .

'Excuse me!' A widespread hand thrust itself haltingly into my face. 'But which country do you come from? Are you from England, New Zealand, Australia or America?'

'None. I'm from Canada.' I gently lowered the hand from my face to reveal an unusually tall and robust Japanese man in his early thirties. 'From British Columbia.'

'Even better! You can be my English teacher. I will pay you thirty dollars per hour.'

'He wants you to be his girlfriend. He thinks you're sexy,' piped up a shorter, younger version of my new student, who was promptly smacked on the back of the head.

'Don't listen to him. He is an idiot. I am Taka. I need to practise my English. How long will you stay in Japan?' *Was this the standard method of finding a teacher?*

'He wants to know if you'll marry him.' Another, harder smack. I held back a laugh.

'I'll probably stay three months, I think, but your English is already very good. Why do you need a teacher?'

'He needs someone to teach him how to fuck.' *Wham!* Taka's briefcase collided with the other man's head and both of them, clearly intoxicated, stumbled from the impact.

'I apologise for my brother. He is very drunk, and before that he is already a very foolish man. I need to practise my conversation skills. They are very poor. I will give you my card.'

I reached to accept, but Taka snapped it back, darting a look of suspicion from head to toe. 'For *what* reason are you in Tokyo? What is your profession?' he demanded.

'I'm a model. A fashion model.' It didn't seem like the time to say 'hostess'.

'Okay. You will find my name, email and phone number on this card. Please contact me when you are available. I am sorry we cannot stay, but we must go home. We have drunk too much.' *How disappointing.* With a handshake and a bow, Taka staggered to the waiting throng of taxis, pulling and shoving his foolish brother all the way. As I watched them head off into a traffic jam, I thought I'd be free to continue home, but no.

First a dishevelled old man accosted me outside a noodle shop, firing familiar questions from some kind of *Standard Japanese First Acquaintance Manual*. When he engaged me in an awkward pedestrian waltz and refused to let me pass, I studied the glowing Coca-Cola slogan of a vending machine just beyond his head, and then the thirty or so beverages inside, including a dubious, murky electrolyte drink called Pocari Sweat. Where else could you find such a refreshing concoction . . . but on every street corner in Japan?

As in no other country, the humble vending machine is an iconic, ubiquitous necessity providing the masses with affordable convenience in an urban jungle of skyrocketing prices. For the serially time-deprived, they even stand guard outside convenience stores, waiting to dispense beer, cigarettes and sundries at the drop of a coin. The Japan Vending Machine Manufacturers Association claims there is one for every twenty people in Japan – that's over six million nationwide – and looking down the street I could believe it. It was aglow with them.

When my amusement with the badgering old man fizzled out, I forcefully crossed my fingers and gave him a miniature X. 'Please stop! I do NOT want to drink any wine, okay? No wine!' Taking advantage of his surprise, I gently pushed around him but threw in a quick parting bow just for the hell of it. I'd hardly moved on when yet *another* man closed in.

'Would you like to drink?' he asked. *Oh my God!* What was happening? Since when did strangers line up to ask you for a drink at 3.00 am?

I felt like running away, but the salaryman shyly swooped his bangs aside with a heavily Rolexed wrist. He waited patiently for my answer, clutching his briefcase, white knuckled. The Rolex reminded me of Abie, diligently circling the streets in search of customers. Everything she'd told me crowded into my brain. Were her claims of an easy hundred bucks gospel?

I decided to see what happened. This *was* Roppongi, entertainment district of Tokyo, and drinking with men for money *was* my current job description. What difference did it make where or how we met? We'd still be in public, and funnily enough I found myself feeling strangely compassionate towards this man, with his overt loneliness. His was a harmless request, and one that would be mutually beneficial: he needed company and I needed to stock up on yen, because cash could run perilously low in Tokyo, the world's most expensive city.

'Okay, sure,' I agreed with a genuine smile, and the stranger's face lit up. 'Do you know the American Bar? It's not far from here.'

PAYING FOR IT

A waiter appeared instantly to usher us past the pool table to a dimly lit booth in the back. Whisking away its brass *Reserved* plate, he swiftly presented a wine list that began at roughly $160 and ended in an extravagant $850 for Dom Perignon. *Ouch*. I waited for my new companion's unpleasant reaction, but it never came. When the waiter came back for the order, he responded without hesitation. *White wine. This one.* As somewhat of an afterthought, he asked if that would be all right with me. Sure. I hated the stuff, but why not.

We sat in silence. Him slouched. Me upright. Since introducing himself along the way, we'd hardly said a word. *I am Kazuki. My English is very poor.* That was it. Kazuki had no questions and, contrary to protocol, didn't tell me his age or his profession. What he had been doing out so late among the crowds on a Saturday night was anyone's guess.

When the waiter came back, Kazuki started at his voice. '*Kurijetto-cardo mata wa cash-o desu ka.*' The waiter required payment first, like a gas station in downtown LA.

'*Cash-o*,' Kazuki replied as he pulled out an envelope thick with $100 *ichiman* notes. Skimming two off the top, he asked for a receipt. Evidently this was going to be a tax-deductible expenditure, right out of the manual *Accounting for the Wealthy*. I could just imagine page 47, paragraph 2: *Equations for the Uninitiated: hundred-dollar bills an inch thick = something to be tossed casually into your briefcase in a manila envelope.*

With a sheepish grin, Kazuki raised his glass in *kampai* (cheers) and turned his attention to a bloody, big-screen K-1 fight across the room. K-1 is a brutal combat tournament fanatically revered in Japan, which pits international fighters from mixed martial arts against each other, gladiator-style, to determine who can sufficiently bash the other to a pulp or knock them out cold. At the moment it was a Japanese sumo wrestler v. a Caucasian kick-boxer, and it held Kazuki's attention better than mine.

I noticed the bar was empty except for a few loners and a crowd of cool, unaffected foreign men packing the booth next to us, a steady cloud of smoke rising to a communal halo before being sucked into the ventilators. Looking from one face to the next, I found my gaze met by another. I smiled, and he nodded ever so slightly, dragging on a cigarette.

Kazuki tapped on my arm. He'd extracted a crisp business card, held lightly in both hands. I noticed his empty glass and he smiled shyly. *TANAKA KAZUKI, PRODUCER.* One glass of social lubricant later, I learnt that he produced variety shows, the eclectic nonsense that filled prime-time television in hourly segments. He'd been at a meeting with one of the networks before he'd hopped into a taxi straight to Roppongi and coincidentally 'met' me on the street. Quick calculations scanned through my brain. I knew the time now. I knew the time then. Kazuki couldn't have been drunk, but he'd just blurted it out: 'Would you like to drink?' In another city, I would have been surprised, but this was exemplary of how Japanese businessmen often approached foreign women in the entertainment district.

It wasn't long before we were discussing which movie stars we liked and what movies he loved. Kazuki mentioned that he played golf, twice. He asked my name three times, and eventually I wrote it down. I was relieved when he ordered two glasses of water, but the moment they arrived he ordered a second bottle of wine. I didn't know whether to be happy or not. My head was beginning to spin. I must have drunk more than I'd intended, but I couldn't gauge how much. The circling waiters subtly kept our glasses full.

When Kazuki abruptly excused himself and went to the toilet, a grey-suited manager moved in. 'Hello. What is your name?' *Chelsea.* 'And where do you work?' *Greengrass.* He jotted both down swiftly, shook my hand and thanked me. I realised that he was identifying me as the recipient of the 40 per cent commission that would be calculated from Kazuki's bill. I'd been wondering what to do about that.

I sunk back into the seat, amused to be banking coin by drinking expensive wine, but there was only one problem. It had been a year since I'd last drunk, and after such a long hiatus I was getting dizzy just looking at the second bottle, perspiring in a melting bucket of ice. Everything had adjusted to soft-focus.

'What's your name?' The voice sounded fuzzy when it came. It was my neighbour from the next booth. 'I'm Luc. I saw you the other night at One Eyed Jack. Are you gonna be working there?' I told him how I thought they'd given me the runaround, and when they'd said to call on Monday I'd decided to start working at Greengrass instead. I didn't have time to waste.

'But Nathan actually is gone until Monday,' he said. 'You should call back for sure.'

The conversation was cut short when Kazuki came back. Then the bar flooded with people, the music climbed to a cranking bass and dialogue became impossible. It was 3.02 am, the neighbouring clubs had just closed, and apart from being a place where you could bottle Japanese men, the American Bar was the place where the foreign hostesses, bartenders and strippers came to sip, snort and smoke any residue of the last six professional hours away. At least for a while, you could transport yourself right out of Japan.

Surrounded by foreigners, Kazuki tapped along to Missy Elliott on my shoulder. He watched the plethora of flesh writhing to the music. Every so often he stole a quick kiss on my cheek. And then he left abruptly, scooping up his briefcase, just as he seemed to be enjoying himself most. No deep bows. No *see you laters*. No handshake. With nothing more than a simple *excuse me*, I was abandoned like the bottle of $200 wine sitting half-full on the table. Had I missed something? Abie had said it was that simple, but when I actually found myself in the situation, it left me more than a little dumbfounded.

As I sat wondering what to do with my drunken self, Luc turned around, looking to the empty seat beside me. 'You finished now? Why don't you come join us?'

Everyone shifted as I shimmied past to the back of the booth. Luc and the boys were their own United Nations. They came from Australia, France, Russia, Japan and Mexico, and all of them were waiters at One Eyed Jack, or Jack's as they affectionately called it. Two high-cheekboned girls in their midst were Jack's hostesses, one of them the current runner-up in the Miss Canada beauty pageant. Marc – the skinny Frenchie – offered the remainder of his avocado salad and I suddenly remembered being starving before Kazuki came up to me on the street. Maybe that explained the remarkable high I'd got off just a couple glasses of wine. At least you couldn't call me a cheap drunk. Not at the prices of those bottles.

'*Qu'est ce que tu bois?*' Marc asked.

'*Rien, merci. J'ai bu trop.* Really, I don't need anything.'

A waiter walked past. 'Excuse me! Can we have a gin and tonic for the lady please?'

When the drink came, every guy there pulled out a ¥1000 note, but Luc's hand stretched further than the rest. 'I've got it.'

Right. Having already sold my sobriety for a hundred and forty bucks, I drank it without hesitation.

—

At 5.00 am the lights came up, their incandescent ugliness making our eyes smart, nagging us to leave. We spilt out into the darkness of the street, where the sun had yet to rise, and trooped along the neon Roppongi strip en masse to another bar that would stay open well into the afternoon. It was far too early to go home.

—

A Kama Sutra mural carved into stone played out along one wall of the den-like Bar Shisha. I sank onto a long lounge next to Amy, one of the high-cheekboned girls from Jack's. She was Polish, lived in the UK and had come to hostess to save money for school. She ordered a banana milkshake. I ordered an orange juice. I was saturated in alcohol. With my sparkling clean liver, I'd probably be drunk until Tuesday.

The elevator doors opened and a group of girls in dark shades spilt out, orbiting an alpha male like a bunch of electrons. They shimmied around the dance floor as he hurriedly sniffed his way to the toilet, thumbing a lump in the deepest corner of his pocket. I made the mistake of making eye contact with one of them, and a cute, dark-haired girl with perfect teeth scooted down the lounge to introduce herself. Nathalie. Her pupils were so dilated she hardly had an iris. A Russian-Israeli, she talked incessantly in a clipped, hard-edged English.

'I have to tell you that you really are so beautiful,' she gushed. 'Vhy are you hostess? You are vasteing your time! Vhy don't you be stripper? It is good money. It is much better money.' I just smiled and said I didn't want to.

'You are pretty. You should do it!' Nathalie gestured wildly, spilling half her cocktail. 'Just do it, *come on*. Last time I come here, I vaste three months of my life as fucking hostess. It is shit, hostess. Stripping in Japan, it is same job. It is easy. Nobody told me about this vhen I vas hostess. Second time I come, I make in *one veek* vhat I make in three months as hostess. *Fuck!* You can make big money, princess. How old are you?'

It took me a second to think. God, I was drunk. 'Twenty.'

'Twenty! *Fuck!* So young! You have so much future, you can do so well. I am twenty-six. I am not stupid girl. I am not cheap girl. I have university degree. In Israel I am interior designer, but in Israel there is no money. How can I survive this shit? I do vhat I love, but I must come here to pay for it. Listen to me.' Nathalie paused to point an impassioned finger into the air, a late-night evangelical intensity to her sharp voice. 'You have customer villing to pay seven-thousand yen for three minutes private dance. You know vhat it is, private dance, right? You have customer villing to pay five-thousand yen, *ONE FUCK!* I mean, *c'mon*!' The remnants of Nathalie's cocktail spattered across my knee as she preached the good news.

I stared at her. On the glossy surface of her huge black pupils I could see a tiny portrait of myself, eyes wide in a face stilled by shock, but she was soon yanked away by another electron girl and I *vasted* no time in moving close to someone more familiar, who happened to be Luc. He was slouched down on the couch, both hands on a beer, staring at the mural. All that was left of Amy was the film of a banana milkshake coating a glass on the table. She had gone home.

Luc looked at me. I rolled my eyes. 'Crazy Russians,' I said.

He smiled back. '*Fuckin'* crazy Russians.'

—

It wasn't until 11.00 am that I left the bar. It was humid and hot. My skirt clung to my thighs. My heels were killing me. My mouth was parched and I hadn't had a meal in sixteen hours. There was only one solution. I needed ice cream.

By the time I'd navigated the unfamiliar streets back to our apartment, I was satiated on green-tea Häagen-Dazs. As I started to search for the door pass, my purse began to vibrate. *Ahhh*, the phone! I'd forgotten that one of the waiters had silenced it to 'manner mode' at the club. Manner mode. That was hilarious. *Bzt! Bzt!* Oh, crap. 'Who is this?' I demanded.

'It's me. Where are you? I've been trying to call you all morning!'

'I'm right outside the door. No, I mean the apartment. Building. Downstairs. Outside. *Downstairs, outside, on the street where you live,*' I sang. I was fucking everything up. Matt started laughing. I couldn't stop. I was cleanly smashed. God, that sunlight was bright.

'I'm coming down to get you.'

When Matt came through the automatic doors of the lobby, I was sitting on the steps, stuffing an ice-cream sandwich into my mouth as morning joggers ascended the hill behind me. 'You want some?' I must have looked like an intoxicated monkey, offering up a banana found somewhere deep in the jungle. I was sure he was glad to see me home in one piece.

'Give me that,' Matt chided playfully, shoving the last corner into his mouth before helping me up. 'You've had a bit of a big night I think, hmmm? Grab your purse. Let's get you upstairs.'

—

My drunken, wandering thoughts short-circuited as I winced under a spray of water, reaching blindly for the tap that would bring it to a more familiar temperature. *Ahhh!* Cold. The water was too cold, like all those times my mother scooted me into the shower after an afternoon playing in the backyard. Only I wasn't five years old, covered in mud, and it wasn't my mom standing next to the tub; it was my husband, trying to get me clean after a night out in obscurity, drinking with other men and absorbing their second-hand smoke like a sea sponge. Not that I didn't know the water was coming, but that was beside the point. Cold. The water was too cold.

As I focused enough to get the temperature just how I liked it, Matt reached up to reposition the standard-Japanese-height showerhead. I was almost too tall for it, but the water fell over my face as I closed my eyes and opened my mouth. I heard Matt squirt shampoo onto his palm. It smelt like lemon. *Oh, goddd. THIS is bullshit.* I sank to the porcelain floor. He massaged the shampoo into my scalp. Head between my knees, I watched the soapsuds slip into the drain. He scrubbed behind my ears and complained of the stench that had permeated everything. My hair. My eyelashes. The pile of clothes that he'd peeled me out of, now discarded on the floor of our micro, one-piece, capsule bathroom.

'So how did you go? How was your second night?' Matt put my cocktail dress on a hanger. It was dry-clean only.

'I think I'm gonna die of cigarette smoke.'

'So how did you go?' he asked again. 'Here, wash your face.'

I lathered up. 'Good, I guess. The girls are really nice. Mostly Israelis.'

'And what were the "customers" like?' he laughed. 'Oooh, that sounds dodgy.'

'Freakin' crazy.' I mentioned the General Electric zombies. I told him about bottling Kazuki at the American Bar. I told him about Luc, our fellow Australian, and Nathalie and her $5000 ONE FUCK! He laughed and laughed, and I just kept going, until it was time to get out.

'C'mon, don't slip over.'

We clasped hands as I climbed precariously out onto the bath mat, and Matt towelled me down.

NINE FOR ME,
ONE FOR THE YAKUZA

My left heel felt completely devoid of skin, the membranes masticated to a pulp as I ran the narrow sidewalks to work in my heels. It was Tuesday, and after drinking with another stranger who'd approached me on the street the night before, I'd met up with Matt and we'd stayed out with Luc and the Jack's waiters until the sun rose. I'd overslept. If I didn't make it to Greengrass in five minutes, I was going to get a fine equal to an hour's pay.

There were beads of perspiration on my face when I flopped onto the couch next to Abie, gulping back my third glass of water from an absurdly small, regulation hostess-sized glass. It looked like it should be for kindergartners, but the much bigger, adult-sized glasses were strictly for customers.

'Hey, Chels, I saw you at the American last night with that old Japanese guy. How many bottles did you get?'

Abie was brushing the knots out of her hair. She'd woken up thirty minutes ago too, but unlike me she wasn't hot and sweaty. She lived in a *gaijin* house only five minutes away. (*Gaijin*, literally 'foreign devil', is the term – more neutral than it sounds – used for non-Japanese.) *Gaijin* houses are like dingy, crowded and overpriced hostels, usually run by a punitively strict and unrelenting middle-aged *mama-san* but still the only affordable option for a foreign hostess living on her own in Tokyo.

'It was just one bottle, but I didn't drink any of it. The guy didn't even speak English.'

'Awesome. I love it when they don't speak English. I hate talking to them. *No, I do not have any hobbies. No, I do not want a Japanese boyfriend. Because why? Did you say because their dicks are too small? Is that true? I have no idea. No, I don't not like Japanese boyfriends because their penises are too small. No, I will not be your girlfriend then. Just keep handing over your credit card, you crazy Jap weirdo.* God I hate this place.'

'Oh come on, it's not that bad. You should hear yourself. I don't know why you get all the crazies. I think they're just lonely. You know, after I left you on Saturday night, someone just came up and asked me to drink with him too. It was really weird.'

'You took him to the American Bar, didn't you?'

'Well, yeah. That was my first time. He was a television producer, and he bought two bottles of wine. I made a hundred and forty bucks. Or at least, I *should* have. When I went to pick up my cash last night, 10 per cent was missing from the envelope.'

'Yeah, that's just Yakuza tax, those bastards. Two bottles on Saturday: what a score! And then another one last night, on a Monday! Well done. We almost never catch customers on a Monday. Usually we have to drag them, and then sometimes they won't even buy a single bottle, the cheapskates. You should take them into the VIP room to sing karaoke, then you can . . .'

'What? Hang on, what the *hell* is Yakuza tax?' I knew about organised crime, but c'mon, that organised? Gangsters were gangsters, not accountants.

'Yakuza tax. They run the joint. What did you think — these clubs don't have to pay protection money? Ten per cent of everything. Otherwise they'll show up, smash everything and close the place down. Haven't you noticed that most of the bars around here were only established in the last few years? The old ones didn't go broke. They didn't *pay up.*

'I think the owner here must pay them well, because she never has any trouble. I heard Nishi say that they've never been raided. She only comes in once in a while. Nobody knows her name because she asks us to still call her *Mama-san*, even though technically that's Nishi's job.

'But anyway, right before I got here the Yakuza apparently gave the go-ahead for the immigration police to raid one of the dodgier strip clubs, and every girl who didn't have a proper visa was arrested. They can hold you for thirty days without release! I'm not kidding. If the clubs and the restaurants have to pay, then why not you? It's not like any of this goes through the books. You make cash in Roppongi, you pay the tax.'

Was I getting medical benefits with that?

—

One hour later Abie and I were sitting with a group of corporate customers drinking juice concentrate – a filth worse than cigarette smoke. With a taste like petroleum, its fructose-bound molecules silted down the back of your throat on their way to all those places you need them most. Your butt. Your thighs. Your cheeks. It ought to be illegal, but because Greengrass customers didn't pay the club for hostess drinks, we had limited options for refreshment: cheap 'fruit' juice or cheap headache-inducing house wine. I was doomed, I thought, until Tehara brought Jamie along to the table and, in between banter with the customers, she introduced us to oolong tea.

Tasty hot or cold, oolong tea is chock-full of antioxidants and flavonoids, nearly empty of calories and 100 per cent allowable as a hostess drink. I preferred it iced, except for when sitting at the table situated directly under the air conditioner and its polar gusts of air. *Polar gusts of air?* Uh huh. Nearly every customer who came into Greengrass wore a suit. Every single hostess had to wear a sleeveless dress. Even the temperature in a hostess club is biased, just like the drinking glasses.

—

He reined me in with one forceful yank. My wrist cracked, I lost balance, and the Korean's human vice tightened until I couldn't move, not even an inch. From the corner of the eye that wasn't intimate with his armpit, I could see two other men, minding their own space *and* the space of their hostesses. Everyone was sitting nicely, making conversation. Everyone, that was, except for us. This was not how people meet each other.

'*Release me, you crazy bastard!*' I wanted to yell, but there wasn't enough air in my lungs. I was enveloped in his arms, and someone had licked the seal closed. Right when I might have passed out, he slackened just enough for me to wrench out of his iron grip. I quickly picked up my tea and held it as a barricade between us. The steaming oolong was my only defence.

The Korean leant in casually to utter his first words. 'Let's fuck.'

'*WHAT?*' The mouthful of tea I'd inhaled in shock scalded the roof of my mouth.

He snatched my tea away, spilling hot liquid everywhere, and in an instant I was back in his gorilla grip.

'Let's fuck. *Dohan?*' he screeched.

'Excuse me?'

'You want to go on *dohan* tomorrow? If you fuck me, I will go on *dohan*, so you can make points.' He squeezed tighter still.

What? Was he crazy? A *dohan* did not entail anything other than a nice meal and pleasant conversation.

'I am NOT a prostitute,' I wriggled desperately, and the Korean frowned.

'You are strange girl.'

'Why? Because I won't fuck you? I am not a prostitute!'

He released me. 'Okay, let's sing. Cyndi Lauper.' A heavy karaoke book was dropped onto my lap with a thud. Just like that. Fucking, or Cyndi Lauper. It was a logical second choice. I moved as far away as I could without sitting on the next table's customer and started flipping through the pages, looking for 'Girls Just Wanna Have Fun'. I found it and frantically waved the little white request slip at Tehara so he'd come and collect it.

'I want. To moooove. He is *scary*,' I mouthed. Tehara nodded but motioned for me to stay seated until he found somewhere else to put me. By the time Cyndi Lauper came on, I was sitting at another table, far, far away, and carnal-iron-grip-gorilla was squeezing the life out of my replacement. What was worse, she had to sing.

FRIDAY NIGHT

'During Edo period, *shogun* forbid going outside Japan to Japanese people. If disobey occur, traitor is coming back and *shogun* make beheading, like this.' *Whoooosh!* With one swoop of an imaginary sword my history *sensei* collapsed into a violent heap, clutching desperately at his throat. I waited for the rebound, and it came abruptly, one leathery finger erected high in the air.

'No country making trade with Japan at this time. Only Chinese people and Dutch people, coming only one place, Nagasaki. Then, *shogun* making ban on Western book and Western idea that is corrupting Japanese way of . . .'

'Chelsea-san,' Nishi interrupted sternly. 'Prease move now. Request.' With hardly an apology, Nishi scooped up my drink. I followed, wondering how it could be that *I* had a request. I hadn't been at Greengrass a week yet. I had zero customers. Who could have . . .?

And then it all made sense.

I could feel him from ten feet away. Half-hidden in the shadows, he interrupted the airwaves around him. He was handsome, in the way of Japan's ancient war generals – powerful and distinguished – and many other things you couldn't possibly be all at once. Arrogant and charming. Smooth and razor-sharp. A groomed, polished, virile specimen, he was egotistical to the point of narcissism, yet he oozed an invisible nectar that made him irresistibly attractive. And that was just my first impression.

Nishi let me seat myself. Without making an introduction, he simply bowed deeply to the customer and vanished. I smiled at Erma, the Swiss hostess sitting next to him, smoking a lean cigarette and looking bored. I extended my hand across the table. He didn't move.

'I like your hairstyle,' he cooed, 'but I only shake hands with those I intend to do business with. Sorry.' Unimpressed, I snapped back my hand, and Erma leant forward.

'He doesn't shake hands,' she clarified, rolling her eyes.

'What is your name?' I asked politely, and an insolent smile spread across his face as he pitched forward to make supremely confident eye contact. He paused while his eyes, small and precise, creased into perfect linear slits. I gauged him to be about 40.

'*Superman.*' The word slid off his tongue. Then he reconsidered. 'No . . . Mr X.'

'That's quite the name,' I said coolly. 'It doesn't sound very Japanese.'

'Nice bag,' he replied haughtily. 'You have good taste.' In the dim light my Takashi Murakami bag, à la Bangkok, looked completely genuine. I was surprised he'd taken notice.

'Evidently, so do you.'

'Excuse me.' Mr X slammed down his drink and disappeared to the men's restroom. Nishi started to clear the table.

'What's the matter, is he leaving?'

'No, no, Chelsea-san. Moving. Over there. Come.' Across the room, Nishi placed Erma's glass next to the customer's and hesitated before leaving us to wait for the return of Mr X. 'Very good customer, this man. Very rich man. Prease, Chelsea-san, be nice.'

'I'm always nice.' A doubtful amusement surfaced in Nishi's weary eyes. I'd been foolish enough to think that no one ever paid attention.

The moment we started to wonder if he really was coming back, Mr X came striding across the room like a peacock, silver buckles gleaming on his Gucci shoes. I stood to offer a steaming *oshibori* and he wiped his face and every one of his ten digits systematically. 'I'm glad you found us,' I smiled sweetly.

He laughed indignantly and shook a cigarette loose to place between his lips. I leant forward with my lighter. *Click. Whooosh. Inhaaaale.* He prolonged the ritual a second longer than he should have. It was strangely sexual, and I snapped the lighter closed as he forced a channel of smoke up into the air.

'That's better. See,' he addressed Erma, '*she* is a professional hostess. I know this is your second day, don't worry. She is your senior, that's why she knows how to do things properly.' Erma's eyes rolled. My professional seniority amounted to five days, but I didn't mention it. I might have embarrassed him. He seemed to like his presumptions.

'So, what type of music do you like?' I baited.

'Music? You're asking what kind of music I like?' He puffed on his cigarette in aggravation.

I smiled innocently.

'That depends. At the disco? Driving? Fucking? All different. Which you wanna know?' His wrist flicked up so we could look at the $4500 Rolex adorning it. Erma rolled her eyes again and Tehara came to take her away. I was moved next to him.

'It's about fucking time, I thought they'd never take her away.' Mr X squashed his cigarette into the ashtray, grinning devilishly at me. 'This is much better.' I suddenly felt pressured, in the way an ant must underneath a magnifying glass, sweating from the heat.

'So what really is your name, then?'

'My name? I told you already. Did you forget?'

'No you didn't, Mr X. I doubt your mother calls you that.' His spine straightened at the mention of his mother. 'What's your name?' I repeated.

'Yoshi. My name is Yoshi. What's yours?'

'I told you already.'

'I don't remember, tell me again.'

I told him, and that was the beginning.

~

I can recall Yoshi's next question distinctly, because I didn't understand it, and because it came out of nowhere. 'So do you like Charlie?' *Who?* Then he said something. Something else. *Something.* Exasperated by my blank stares, he lowered his voice. 'Coke. You like it?' He inhaled sharply, right next to my ear, one knuckle pressed gently into the side of his nose.

'Cocaine?' I said, louder than I probably should have.

'Yes, *cocaine.*'

'I've never done cocaine. I don't know.'

'You've never tried Charlie?' He grabbed my hand instantly and pulled. 'Oh my God. C'mon, let's go. *Now.*'

'I'm working.'

'So what? Who cares? Are you Miss Drug Free, Goodie Two Shoes? I don't *think* so.' He pinched me on the cheek. 'How about sex? Do you like it?'

'What kind of a question is that?'

'Nothing. No question. Just making sure that you are perfect. Do you like fishing?'

'I don't usually fish. Do you?'

'Of course, I *luuhv* it! Trawling, on my boat, off the coast of Hawaii. And California. Big ones, like this.' He held his arms out. 'I love it, but there's something I love more.'

'What's that?'

'Fishing for women.' Yoshi grinned, sly as a fox. 'I saw you from over there, across the room, and I requested you straight away. Nishi made me wait, you were busy, but he said to me *I know, your type.* So I had to wait for you. I don't wait for anybody.' There was a fierce glint in his eye. 'But for you, I change my mind. Not only beauty, but grace. So sexy. Everything so sexy.'

He pinched my butt, and I smacked his hand away.

'Sorry, just checking. I am devil.' He winked. 'Where do you live? Guesthouse? Apartment? Alone? Where?'

'Alone,' I lied, 'in Hiroo.'

'Wow, nice place. I am living with my parents, but soon I am moving. Next month.' *With his parents?* I was surprised, but as I later found out, Yoshi was the *chonan* – the eldest son – which meant that even in a family as wealthy as his, he'd been born with a filial duty to provide for his parents and live with them in the same house.

'Wow, what does your wife have to say about that?'

He looked at me in revolt.

'Wife? What wife? I don't need a wife. I am never getting married. Are you crazy?' His biceps bulged out of a luxurious black shirt.

I humoured him. 'Do you work out?'

'Yeah, of course. I have to. This week I am very busy, but usually I am going to the lousy gym all the time. I have a Western mind, but still this fucking gook body. Whatta can I do?'

He made me laugh out loud. He was hard bodied. Tanned. Lean and sinewy, with perfect, luminescent skin, framed by thick lustrous hair along a receding hairline.

'I am a devil, but I tell the truth.' He bit my ear, kissed my cheek.

I pushed him away. 'Don't bite me.' There was nothing playful in my tone.

'I am going to LA and Chicago later this month on business. I don't wanna, but I have to. Before then, I wanna see you. Can I call you?' He'd already entered my phone number into his phone. He'd also tried to kiss my lips, but all he got was the back of my hand.

'I don't think so.'

'You know why I like you? You have attitude. Like . . . like this.' Yoshi stuck his nose up in the air. 'A snob. I *luhvv* it,' he purred.

'I don't put up with bullshit, Yoshi, so don't try any of it.' Two seconds later, he called for Tehara's attention.

'Excuse me! Cheque please!' He made a show of letting the light bounce off a black American Express card he slowly extracted from his wallet. Platinum and gold I'd seen. But never black. As he signed with a flourish, he looked sideways, assessing me, weighing me up. 'What is my name?' he demanded.

'Yoshi.'

'You are so lucky,' he cooed.

—

Shortly after Yoshi left, Soh, the Burmese waiter, pulled me aside. 'Chelsea,' he said. 'Very fucking rich man, Yoshi. You see his credit card?' He'd placed his fingers into a rectangle. 'It's black, right?'

'Yeah, it was black. So what's that supposed to mean?'

Soh looked at me in disbelief, and I looked back at him, unimpressed. 'A *black* Amex? Black means rich.' He paused for effect. 'Very fucking rich.'

THE FOLLOW-UP CALL

I'd met all six of them earlier in the week, a Monday or Tuesday, I couldn't be sure. Every night at Greengrass was as random as the last; the days and names all seemed to mesh together into a singular mass of memory without labels.

I had been sober, everyone else drunk beyond dignity. Especially Jodie. *Get drunk, sing as much as you can and say whatever the fuck you want.* That was her motto. She was a Billy Joel, Stevie Wonder kind of girl, and in my opinion the exclusive reason that Nishi had said 'some girls sing too much'.

The customers were part of a consortium of seventeen companies under the direction of a single man, and their visits were part of the corporate schedule. I'd joined them late in the night, and to mark my arrival I'd been forced to sing. Until now, most customers were disappointed whenever I'd refuse, but tonight I felt an inescapable sense of duty to the karaoke collective. Ask me why I picked 'Somewhere Over the Rainbow' and I couldn't tell you. I guess I was just nervous, it was my first time, and I was *forced*. When I finished, there was silence, and finally a polite round of applause. I was mortified.

Until now I had been hopeless at remembering Japanese names, but tonight I remembered Taizo. He wasn't easy to forget, particularly because his name had become the group's war cry before every round of Kamikazes.

He also took the brunt of the group's jokes, distinguished as he was by a high forehead, wide eyes and sweeping cheekbones. The others said he was from Hokkaido, which was what was wrong with him. Taizo laughed heartily at this. He was always laughing, when he wasn't singing, inserting my name into a whole catalogue of songs. My favourite was 'Only Chelsea'. Apparently, only I could make his world seem right, but I didn't mind, because Taizo wasn't mediocre. Taizo wasn't good. Taizo was brilliant. He could belt out 'Bohemian Rhapsody' with more feeling than Freddy Mercury, but tonight he insisted we sing together. While he projected with acoustic perfection, I silently mouthed backup vocals with as much animation as I could. After my humiliating debut, I liked to think I was progressing.

Another vocal knack of Taizo's was his use of original compliments: 'Chelsea of the little forehead. So little! And so big eyes. I love your contrast! I love the lineality of your nose. So straight!' He pushed in his own nose forcefully. 'Japanese nose so round, pig nose! But Chelsea is so great. I love you!'

'I love you too, Taizo,' I laughed, and we downed our first Kamikaze of the night.

—

I jolted awake to hear my phone ringing: it was 2.00 pm.

I looked down at Matt, sleeping peacefully on his makeshift swag on the floor. We'd tried sharing the single bed that unfolded from the wall, but one sharp elbow in the ribs is one too many. Tomorrow I would be joining him down there, on the double blow-up mattress we were going to buy, but for now he had volunteered to be the one in discomfort. His broad shoulders barely moved as he breathed in and out.

As soon as he'd heard about it, Matt had secured the most coveted position for a young foreign male in all of Roppongi: the job of scout. It was a single man's dream, and a constant joke between us. Essentially, Matt was paid to chat up chicks. His job was to make sure that One Eyed Jack and Private Eyes were stocked with the best strippers and hostesses in all of Tokyo. And there were potential fringe benefits. Free alcohol. Access all areas. An atlas of girls.

These new recruits were his bread and butter – $500 for a hostess, a grand for a stripper – but Matt also took good care of the girls. He tried to ease their culture shock by giving them a tour of the neighbourhood, showing them the best grocery stores and where to check their email. In a little under a week, the entire multinational community of hostesses loved 'Handsome Matt'.

It was, however, still a full-time job, and by the time we met up at 3.00 am to walk home together, the glory had all but gone. Matt was often as exhausted as me.

—

'Hello, my Chelsea, how are you?' cooed an unfamiliar voice.

'I'm fine, who is this?'

'What do you mean who is this? You forget me already? I never forget you. Yoshi! This is Yoshi!'

'Oh, Yoshi,' I laughed. *How could I forget?* 'Of course I haven't forgotten you. We only met last night. What are you doing?'

'I am talking to you. Hey, can I see you next week?'

'What day?' I asked playfully.

'How do I know what day? It's only Saturday. I'll call you Monday. Before I go to Chicago, I wanna have dinner, okay? Where you wanna go?'

'I don't know anywhere, Yoshi. I've only been here a week.'

'Okay, okay. I know some good places. This weekend I am busy but I'll call you later, and you tell me where you want me to pick you up, okay? I always have time for you. We go to dinner. Then we party.'

'I work during the week, Yoshi.'

'All right, all right. Dinner first. That's all, but if you change your mind, call me okay? I am open twenty-four hours, just for you. Ring me any time,' he chuckled. 'Booty call.'

'Hah! Good luck. Bye-bye.'

'*Hai*-bye.'

—

The moment I'd told Matt about Yoshi, he was not keen. 'I'd be careful of him,' Matt said. 'Seriously. He sounds like he can get you into a whole lot more drama than he's worth. I'd phase him out if I was you. Just trust me on this. Cocaine plus a black Amex equals big mouth, which can turn any situation into a whole lot more shit than I want you involved in. Saying that, though, I don't know the guy, and he might be an interesting character. It's hard to say. Just tread carefully. All right?'

ISN'T ZAT FUCKED UP?

'Zo, did you find your boyfriend zee uzzer night?'

There are some things you'd think would be obvious to anyone.
Such as:

1) A hostess does not have a boyfriend.
2) A hostess does not talk about the boyfriend whom the hostess does
   not have (and by default, the boyfriends whom other hostesses do
   not have).
3) The possession of a boyfriend is unthinkable.
4) The possession of a husband is *impossible*.

Which means that, as a hostess, you should be the consummate,
unattached young woman. From your castle in the sky, you will never
render services of the sexual kind, but neither will you be expressly out
of reach. 'Available but unobtainable', that's the hostess motto, and the
clear distinction that distinguishes you from an escort or a prostitute. To
maintain this delicate pretence it is permissible to lie, play dumb, naive
or innocent, but under no circumstances should you ever be less than
100 per cent single. At least within earshot of customers, which is what
Colette, the new Swiss-German hostess, had failed to realise. I thought
about saying as much, but instead I just looked to Jodie.

Whenever there is explaining to do, Jodie is the one to do it. Almost
a permanent hostess, Jodie had come from England numerous times to
work in Roppongi, currently lived with a Japanese boyfriend (who had
nothing to do with hostess clubs), and was full of loads of wonderful,
detached and perverse insights – the girl did like to watch porn while
eating her breakfast cereal – that somehow helped us all cope with the
inexplicable.

'This is just a game,' she explained. 'They know it, and you'd be best to know it too. They know we're not single and not in love with them. They'd shit their pants if they thought we actually wanted to marry them. They'd be horrified. They *want* to pretend. These are men who have no social lives, no intimacy with their wives. They are paying to create an illusion, and we are here to humour them.'

'Yes, but may-bee zey are serious, you don't think?'

'There are the odd ones who come in here looking for wives, and I can tell you, it's pretty hilarious. They really believe that one of these girls would consider it, and that every word coming out of her mouth isn't total bullshit. I mean, okay, maybe they're not complete whackos, because it does happen. Look at the Russians. It could be worse for them, right? They don't *want* to go back to Russia. But for us it's just a job, and all it takes is one stupid girl to fuck it up by actually sleeping with a customer because she thinks she falls in love with him, or whatever. Then they think they have a shot because it happened to one guy once in a million bloody years.

'But it's all bullshit. None of this really exists. They know what happens when we all leave. We go home and fuck our boyfriends, and they go home to their wives and families for two seconds before they have to get up and go to work again. That's just the way it is. See it for what it is and don't get caught up. Get smashed every night and you'll have a blast.'

I had one problem. It's awfully hard to see something for what it is when you couldn't even understand what it was in the first place. Colette, the Swiss-German, said it best: 'Wow. Zat is pretty fucked up.' But no, apparently *that* wasn't fucked up. That was only the beginning, the structure of the thing. What was fucked up was this:

'This total whack job of a guy, right? I'm not going to tell you his name, but he's really strange looking. He comes every couple of months. He's really, really smart, but he's got this thing about everyone making up rumours and lies about him. One of my friends went on this trip to the States with him. He paid for it and gave her money just to go along, with separate rooms and everything. They stopped over in Hawaii because she wanted to go scuba diving, but then you know what he did? He came into her room with his dick out, *jerking off*, but *that's* not the worst of it. All he had on was a scuba mask, and fucking flippers! She rang hotel security, and when they came he tried to say that she was beating him up, but they just laughed at him. I mean the guy is standing there butt naked in a scuba mask! So my friend flew back to Tokyo, and he kept calling *me* to find out if she came back. I said she flew back home, but then *he* came back *here* and found her still working here. He got her fired from the club and tried to get her deported. He is such a bastard.'

'Isn't zat dangerous?' Colette asked, gobsmacked. I thought it was hilarious.

'Nah, he's just a freak. I wouldn't say he's dangerous. Hostessing isn't dangerous. Dangerous is working at a gas station in some shitty part of town where the last dude got shot. Just don't be stupid and use your judgement, because otherwise yeah, you could get into trouble. But how is that different from anything else? I mean, you don't *have* to go anywhere with them, and working at the club is nothing to be concerned about. It's not normal, but the worst it gets is the odd weirdo. And anyway, it makes things more interesting. I mean really, what do you think is normal, wasting your life away in an office for minimum wage? I'll take the weirdos any day.'

—

'I really love you, baby, but I dislike them. Really, all of the-em!' Taizo hiccupped as his hand swept despairingly over the room. His tall frame slouched into the low sofa as he glared across at a hyperactive sexagenarian wreaking havoc on an Elvis Presley classic and bouncing up and down like a gleeful schoolboy.

'Oh no! I dislike *him*. He should not sing. No! No! No!' Taizo pointed a stern finger at Elvis and crossed his arms triumphantly. Taizo had been regressing since he first sat down, and I'd been mixing more water into his whisky as the night wore on. Every one of his colleagues was in a pleasant mood. But not Taizo. He let out a sigh of frustration and I offered him a golden Hershey's Kiss. He swallowed it before I could point out that the little white strip was still hanging on.

'Mmmm, good!' Taizo beamed at me. 'I love your short hair, your white forehead. Your big eyes. I love the . . . em . . . you.' He threw his hands up.

'Did you have a bad day, Taizo? Why are you so glum?'

'Because of now is such bad situation. My company is having so big project, so many problem. Next week is the having of the big meeting where every boss will come, and that is bad, bad sitch-ew-ation,' he hic-cupped. 'I want to sing: 1234-04.' He knew the karaoke-program code for 'Only You' off by heart.

As the words began, Taizo closed his eyes and we swayed along together, back and forth, shoulder to shoulder. 'Ohw, ohw-whoa, only Chelseee, I love you-ooo-ooo, your face, your forehead, it is so cute! Oh-oh-oh onleeee Chel-seeeeeee . . .'

For some reason, it made me inexplicably sad.

~

The indentations of a perfect top bite severed a fluffy slice of cake suffocating beneath thick icing. Half-detonated popcorn kernels lay saturated in grease, and plumes of cigarette smoke hung stagnant while the ink of prestigious vineyard names bled minutely under the sweat of liquids equalising temperatures via a hundred cubes of ice. Around the crowded table there was only one spot, and Nishi pointed to it. Straight away there was a problem. The rotund man spilling into my space didn't blink. Or speak. He only stared while I sat uncomfortably under his gaze. Finally Nishi tapped me on the shoulder.

'Sorry, Chelsea-san, he is no Engrish.' Nishi seemed to think it was funny enough to laugh silently to himself and transferred me two spots to the right to make conversation with the back of a customer's head. I waited. And waited. When the man finally turned around, I was shocked.

'*Jimi!* I tried to call you yesterday. How are you?'

Jimi was a short, balding multimillionaire who flew his own jet around the world as a hobby. He'd taken Jodie for a joyride in it during her first week as a hostess in Japan. It was an expensive adventure, but so too was dining out with foreign young women. Last Tuesday he'd taken two Israeli girls and me on my first *dohan*, to the exorbitant Maxim's de Paris in Ginza, where he'd spent close to $2000 for us to eat like queens.

'I did not get a phone call from you today,' Jimi clipped disapprov-
ingly. 'I had Chinese tonight. Peking duck. These are my friends, very
famous chefs from my favourite sushi bar in Azabu-Juban. When I
didn't get your call, I invited them instead. Now I can't have the same
thing two nights in a row. Tomorrow I can eat Italian, or perhaps sushi,'
he specified, which I took to be him indirectly opening an invitation.

'Jimi, you told me to call you on *Sunday*, but you didn't answer.
I tried several times, so I thought you'd call me back.'

Jimi looked at me curtly. '*You* have to call *me*,' he lectured indignantly. 'I will gladly take out the ladies who call to me, but please, I will
never call to them.'

I started to protest but thought better of it. 'Okay, I understand. I'm
sorry. How was the surf on Sunday? Did you end up flying your friend
to the beach in your jet?'

'No, there was some mechanical problems. My plane is still being
fixed. I was very busy with other things, so my phone was not contactable. But today I was not busy and my phone was available to
receive calls.' He smiled rigidly, but I ignored his juvenile stabs.

'So how was the Chinese food? Delicious?' At Maxim's last week,
Jimi had made plans to take me for Chinese on my birthday to force
me to eat Peking duck.

'Of course. Maybe you would like some cake? It is my friend's
birthday. That is why we went to dinner, and now I am treating them
here. Your birthday is what day this week?'

'Tomorrow.' Of course Jimi already knew that.

'Then perhaps we cannot go to dinner. You must want to spend it
with your friends.'

'No, I don't mind. I've never been to a real sushi bar. I'd love to go.'

'Okay, so where do you want to go tomorrow?' he asked. 'Italian?'

'No, *sushi*, please.' I knew not to fail this latest trick question. It was
best to allow Jimi to reinstate his upper hand after such a superbly
indirect effort to reproach me.

'Okay. If tomorrow when you wake up you decide you still want to
go, you must call to me and I will book. The restaurant is very busy, all
the time. Otherwise, not possible.'

'Okay then, I'll decide now. Let's go.'

Satisfied at last, Jimi spoke to one of the 'famous chefs'. Without responding, the chef carefully positioned his palms on his thighs and performed three deep-seated bows to Jimi. To me he gave a fat thumbs up, and it seemed our reservation was confirmed.

'Okay, I have booked a table for three,' Jimi beamed. 'Please bring along a friend. I never invite only one lady. I do not want to be uncomfortable, do you understand?'

'Completely.' But who was I to ask at such short notice?

⌒

Abie sucked on her cigarette like a resuscitated patient at oxygen. She'd agreed to come on my birthday *dohan* with Jimi under one condition: she, under no circumstance, would have to eat meat.

'So, what else are you doing for your birthday? Is this it? Sushi with an old Japanese guy? You and Matt should come out with us after work. The poor guy. I can't believe that you two didn't even go out to dinner. Doesn't he care?'

'Nah, we bought ice-cream sandwiches from the convenience store instead. They were cheap, one buck each. Besides, I need the *dohan* points. You know what I mean.'

'I don't understand you,' Abie complained. 'But I love your husband.'

I wanted to explain to her that normally I wouldn't be abandoning Matt in favour of a Japanese millionaire, but what could I say? I didn't want to blow my cover. She seemed to expect a better answer, but luckily I spotted a taxi bellowing across the intersection towards us at precisely ten to seven, carrying a shiny bald head attached to two frantically waving arms.

'C'mon, that's him.'

The door flew open, we hopped in and I was on the way to spend my twenty-first-birthday dinner with an old Japanese millionaire and a vegetarian Israeli to eat a meal that would cost more than I'd make in a week. What a bizarre little world.

CAN'T STOP THE FUNK

I arrived at Shibuya Crossing just as the sun began to fall behind a forest of buildings and explode through the few cracks that fissured up between them. Its searing rays fragmented into blinding splinters, piercing through the neon and incandescent glow of the square to cause a thousand squints, obliterating my vision. The air was full of an electric energy. There were so many people. Like a swarming nest of ants, the single intersection that serviced sixteen lanes of traffic swelled to the brink as pedestrians spilt off aching sidewalks, each racing for the other side in a sea of indistinguishable suits.

Shibuya is madness. As the arterial connection for the commuters of a city whose population has breached twelve million, it is a maze of hyper-organised, super-efficient complication, train and subway lines converging with overpasses, escalators, department stores, buses, cars, pedestrians and an odd cyclist. With more than two million consumers passing through each day, the advertising space in Shibuya Crossing is one of *the* most expensive in the world, and it is never more spectacular than at night.

From sky-high, old-school billboards Shibuya touts international cosmetics while bright neon outposts flash the logos of Japan's electronic giants. A huge HMV sign pours its pink mega-wattage into the high-voltage airspace. Far below, double-sided billboards circle the block on the sides of trucks, selling everything from ice cream to holidays. From a two-tiered fortress, a frenetic, one-size-only Starbucks dispenses relief to an overworked, caffeine-dependent population, right below a CGI brachiosaurus lumbering across ten storeys of television screen.

And then there is the soundtrack: pop videos, commercials and news updates, an audio fun house of shrieking, shouting, laughing, singing and every wonderfully weird and whacky noise adored by the Japanese, assaulting from every direction. It all hits you in less than a second. One should be blindfolded at the airport and brought to this place.

—

I was abruptly broken from a trance when a packet of tissues was thrust into my hand. Emblazoned with advertising, it came from atop a stack piled up to the chin of a white-gloved girl standing strategically in the middle of the sidewalk. As the tidal wave of passing throngs split around her, she tried to force the colourful packets into hands that mechanically brushed them away. Apart from me, her success rate was miserably low.

I shoved the tissues into my bag along with the street map I'd been following since I'd left Hiroo and quickened my pace along Meiji-dori Avenue to Shinjuku. I had a train to catch, to a last-minute ballroom-dancing rehearsal for a crackpot J-Pop TV show, and I probably shouldn't be late.

—

I was ballroom dancing for a variety show called *SMAPxSMAP*, brought to you by Fuji Television every Monday at 10.00 pm. Roger, an ageing British chap, and I had been paired off as the couple with the most height. Apparently a troupe of *actual* ballroom dancers had been previously hired and then fired, which was when my talent agency stepped in to save the day. That certainly explained the weird telephone call for the casting: 'Can you dance? I mean good? Really, *really* good?' Somehow, I didn't think we were fooling anyone.

Sports Music Assemble People. That's what they were called.

'It means nothing, darling! Like this dance, and this stupidly ridiculous song. It's just a nonsensical name for an utter load of nonsense,' Roger explained as he spun me around. I popped the name off my lips. SMAP-*PUH*! What an acronym. It was catchy, but inevitably it morphed in my mind into PAP, as in smear.

It's hard to describe the phenomenon that is SMAP, the enigma incomparable to anything else that ever was, but it could surely exist only in the cultural landscape that is Japan. SMAP produce hit singles called 'Celery' and 'Raion HAATO' (Lionheart). They are what the Japanese call *bishounen* – beautiful boys who double as actors, dancers and singers – and they have become *the* undisputed kings of the bewildering world of J-Pop ever since being discovered as skateboarding backup dancers in 1991. That's right, *skateboarding* backup dancers. I have no idea either.

SMAPxSMAP is their weekly variety show, and in it they are mediocre masters of et cetera. It is one of the most popular shows in Japan and opens with the segment Bistro SMAP, in which the boys compete to prepare unrecognisable dishes for a guest celebrity based around their favourite food. Think putting curry into custard to achieve more flavour. That embodies SMAP perfectly. I loved it, they were crazy, and now I would get to be part of the great legacy.

While the SMAPsters were off doing other multi-talented things, we moved to a huge chessboard soundstage with potted palms and a four-poled stage at the back. After our first run-through, the director called a huddle around a white X on centre stage. A shy, skinny fellow, he spoke only Japanese. One of the Russian girls volunteered to be his mouthpiece.

'He say that SMAP vill be seating on the stools there in front of sexy dancers. After second time singing verse, uh, after second verse, you vill move to outside and they vill come valking inside the middle. Then, please shut back together. After that point, you going . . . if you vant . . . it's okay to . . . I . . . I hav no idea vhat he is say now.'

The director clutched his papers and tried again, slower and louder. We all leant in to try to understand. 'I think the chap's trying to say that we should be staying put over there!' Roger shouted, and the director nodded enthusiastically to point at another X situated behind a line in the square tiles. Then he pointed where he stood, jumped, shook his head, stomped and held up the Big X with his arms. We *all* got that point. Next, he took one giant step over the line toward the other X and miraculously just came out with it.

'Okay, prease,' he spread his arms wide to indicate the area. 'Uhh, rel-come space.' Then he stepped back over to the stomping spot, 'And *not.*'

Luckily the director found himself as amusing as we did. Those in the production crew who understood English burst into fits of laughter, doing their own imitations of the 'welcome space' until the director threw up his hands in good humour. 'NO ENGRISH!' he pleaded, and retreated to his post off camera.

~

SMAP still hadn't appeared to replace their stand-ins as the first rehearsal shot rolled in an overkill of cameras. It wasn't until the director shouted 'Cut-to!' that they did, and I found myself suddenly underwhelmed in the presence of greatness.

'Who's that one, right there?'

'That's Katori Shingo, but don't look at him. You're not supposed to look at the talent. Those are the rules . . . these guys are megastars.' They were dressed like crazy men, as you'd expect Japanese pop artists to be, and not as cute as expected. When they started to sing, they sounded terrible. All of them looked bored.

As Roger spun us back upstage, I felt what millions of Japanese women all over the country would kill for. Katori Shingo was staring me straight in the eye.

'Oh my God, he just looked right at me!'

'Who?'

'Katori Shingo, who do you *think*? There! He did it again!' Marketed as the baby of the group, Katori Shingo wore the most outlandish outfits and had the most outrageously dyed hair. He was most famous for his comedic cross-dressing television characters, including the notable 'Mama-Shingo'. Little birds *say* he might be gay.

When they returned, five aides carrying personalised water bottles shadowed their every move. Katori had changed into an interesting ensemble: terry cloth with gold costume jewellery and a white mesh singlet cropped beneath his nipples. For some reason, it didn't stop him from confidently seeking out eye contact. I don't know why. *Tweet tweet?*

—

I woke up just enough to realise that my phone was ringing before quickly returning to a heavy-headed sleep. When it rang again some time later, I made the effort to look. It was Yoshi calling. Great. I'd totally forgotten about him and the dinner I'd been putting off since Monday. The dinner I'd been promising to go on.

Monday, Yoshi had said, 'How about dinner tomorrow?' but I already had plans, so he said he'd call again on Wednesday, in a disappointed but understanding tone. Wednesday, he'd said, 'How about tonight?' but there was the last-minute SMAP rehearsal, so, sounding somewhat annoyed, Yoshi had said he'd call Thursday. Today was Thursday. Had I agreed to dinner tonight? I couldn't remember, but he sure was persistent.

'Hello?' I croaked, trying unconvincingly to sound awake.

I *had* told Yoshi that I would go to dinner tonight, but I couldn't. I was too tired. In fact, I was exhausted, and I had to work. Who knew whether I'd be able to get to Greengrass on time? At any rate, I'd be showing up alone, because Yoshi didn't want to take me on a *dohan*. He'd made that perfectly clear – 'I am not your sugar daddy' – and I didn't want to just go to dinner with him. If our time together wasn't connected directly to the club, I'd be treading on dangerous ground. But apart from that I could barely string my words together. I tried to explain earnestly, but Yoshi cut me off abruptly. 'Okay. Maybe some other time,' he said. '*Hai*-bye.'

This time Yoshi's tone was one of finality, but maybe it was for the best. I set down the phone and snuggled back under the covers, pressing up against Matt to sleep for a few more hours until the sun began to go down.

THE MUSICAL FRUIT OF 'NOWHERE PRACE'

I closed my eyes and melted into the back of the couch, hoping that no customers would materialise through the door. There was a rule that expressly stated 'NO SLEEPING AT THE CLUB', but at this point, after two hectic days and only thirty minutes' sleep, I'd gladly pay whatever fine they wanted to slap me with.

'Chelsea-san! Chelsea-san!' I opened my eyes to Tehara attempting a strenuous look of menace, but his poorly disguised amusement was obvious even as I blinked sheepishly and rubbed my eyes. 'Come, Chelsea-san,' he repeated. 'Is customer.'

~

'Beans. I am guy of beans!'

Beans? O-fuckin'-kay. I felt my face morph into the expression that Matt always uses when he's keeping comical expletives inside his head. 'What kind of beans?' I asked politely. 'Green ones?'

'Some green, but of many kinds. Do you know Japanese name, *a-zoo-key* bean? From Hokkaido is berry famous, but you must be careful. Only certain company of highest reputation are honestly selling 100 per cent *azuki* bean, because berry expensive. Usually mixing 10 per cent *azuki* with 90 per cent kidney because smaller, but same taste. Nobody is knowing this berry big secret of Japanese bean industry.'

'Really? I saw *azuki*-flavoured Häagen-Dazs at the convenience store yesterday.'

'Yes! Berry popular for Japanese people,' he laughed, 'but maybe strange for foreigner. However, not most strange flavour. Japanese ice-cream producers also making the fish ice cream, noodle ice cream, fried eggplant ice cream, cactus ice cream . . .'

'Have *you* eaten those?'

'No, I cannot say I have ate those. I am not sweet person. I am savoury, rike beans. What is your favourite Japanese food? Sushi?'

'No, I like sushi, but my favourite so far is *o-kono miyake*.'

'Japanese pizza! You know *o-kono miyake*? I so impressed. Then you should also try *daifuku mochi* if you are fan of the *o-kono miyake*.'

'Die foo what? Could you write that down?'

'*Daifuku mochi*, sticky rice ball. Berry famous Japanese desert of festival time. I think maybe you can buy at grocery store, but best in Japan is Kyoto. Have you been?'

'No, I'd love to go, but it's just so expensive, and far away . . .'

'Expensive yes, but not so far. You take *shinkansen*, bullet train, maybe three hour. I recommend you go many prace outside Tokyo. Nikko, Hakone, Nara, all berry beautiful. Tokyo is not Japan. Every Japanese person coming one reason only. Money! Tokyo is only money city. I rike more countryside place, such as Kyoto and Nikko.'

The Guy of Beans stopped to survey his guest, a deeply tanned man engaged in uncomfortable conversation with Bianca the Romanian.

'He is from Brazil. I think hostess crub is *weird* for foreigners. There is no such crub for conversation in their country. Always foreigners are squirming, when they should relax and enjoy. As Japanese custom it is my duty to bring customers to such prace, but always I am the one having better time.'

'I think he's all right. Every country has customs that are peculiar to others.'

'Yes, I think you are right, and so I will recite to you a funny story. In December many years ago I travelled to Mongolia on business trip, to *so* small country town with no roads, only small airport. However, it is so cold that airplane cannot fly, so I must take train from China *two days* to reach this middle of nowhere. When I arrive, I discover one hotel only in whole town, but no hot water! I could not take shower for two weeks!

'I was first Japanese visitor, everyone coming to welcome my arrival, including town mayor! Everything *so* strange, and all Mongolian food look same, I could recognise only lamb. Many strange things, rike eyeball in my soup. As special guest, I was committed to eat such strange things, I could not refuse. Never had I eaten so terrible things, or so very strong alcohol. I was drunk every day! When I return to Japan, my wife, first thing she say to me is, "You stink. Take a shower." It was my most strange business trip.'

'What on earth were you doing in Mongolia?' I asked, and the Guy of Beans looked at me as though I'd asked what colour the sky was.

'For beans of course, to make the important contract for my company. Always we are testing many praces for growing beans most profitably. It is not of our control that one most difficult bean decided to grow best in nowhere prace Mongolia.'

ALONG CAME NORI

What if someone were to give you a beautiful acoustic guitar, a digital SLR camera and crisp five-digit yen notes? What if they spoilt you with lavish dinners and the invitation to accompany them on a business trip to Kyoto, staying in separate rooms of course, so that you could see part of real Japan? What if they tried to persuade you to return to university and give up the notion of *wasting time travelling to dirty India* by offering to give you the $15,000 it would cost for tuition and living expenses? What if they said *Do you want cash, or bank transfer?* Would you be satisfied?

Abie wasn't. She wanted a laptop computer.

I felt sorry for the man Abie so affectionately referred to as 'Grandpa'. Like many of his generation, Grandpa was short in stature – no doubt thanks to a lack of certain nutrients from McDonald's-o during his post-World War II hormonal years – but he made up for it with his exuberant and singular generosity towards Abie. In his eyes she was a meek little creature who needed taking care of. In anyone else's she was strong-willed and opinionated, but the lonely heart of a lonely life tends to cater only to its own whims, and it wasn't hard to see that while the man was a wealthy and accomplished businessman, Grandpa was deluded.

With Abie's every detail of her upcoming Kyoto itinerary I sank further into a capsule of gloominess. Where was *my* crazy patron of goodwill and indeterminate wealth? I didn't even have contenders for the title. Jimi had all but disappeared and Yoshi was in Chicago, although I was certain he wouldn't be calling again, much less whisking me off to Kyoto. *Maybe some other time*, he'd said. His motives weren't exactly what you'd call philanthropic anyway.

I tried not to pout while Nicole, another returning Israeli hostess with golden curls, sparkling blue eyes and a contagious smile, offered seasoned advice on what to do when Grandpa took Abie shopping. To Nicole it was simple. Hostessing was like a quick trip to the ATM; you just try to make as big a withdrawal as you can. That was easily said, but there happened to be a few restrictions on my account, and I wasn't earning any bonus airmiles. Not this month. With my two-*dohan* quota behind me, I would just be scraping in enough points to get the hourly pay rise if I managed a few more requests, or so I thought, until I saw the weekly scoreboard on the change-room door and discovered that I was somehow sadly lacking. It read: *Mae: dohan (4), request (5), points (28). Abbii: dohan (1), request (3), points (14)*, and so on until, *Cherishi: dohan (½), request (2), points (2)*.

What? Half of a *dohan?* How was that possible? I'd gone to dinner with Jimi twice, and two does not one half make. Even all of Sesame Street knew that. Nishi had some rather complicated explaining to do, and the explanation was not a good one. Dinner at Maxim's hadn't counted. It equalled zero. Three girls was one too many according to the unwritten rules of *dohan*, so I'd been the one mysteriously axed from receiving any dividends. That was bullshit, but there was nothing I could do about it. Credit for my birthday dinner was split clean in half between Abie and me, but with Jimi refusing to take me alone, how was that fair? It became clear only when Nishi reluctantly disclosed that like every customer who took a hostess on *dohan*, Jimi had to pay the club over $200 for doing so. No wonder only a handful of men threw *dohan* invitations around freely. Still, you'd think that from such an unscrupulously large fee the club could afford to pay both of us the $25 bonus instead of making us split it, but no. 'That is not crub system, Chelsea-san. Prease, I cannot change.'

Great. So no points. No bonus. No customers. Nothing but a minimum hostess wage and the need to go on another 1.5 *dohans*. I slumped down to stew in splayed-leg frustration. *Come on!* Where was the sweet old man who'd take pity on me and soothe my loneliness with material things? *This is absolute shit. I hate this job and I feel like crap.* I was worn out, overtired and pissed off that such an exuberant show of wealth and money was not including me. Not one yen of it.

To be honest, there were a number of key indicators that should have shed light on what I viewed as an unfair situation. No one was taking pity on me because I didn't act lonely. I wasn't. I hadn't once asked a customer for a business card or a *dohan*, and I never called anyone who hadn't asked me to. Maybe I had to change my strategy, or rewire my brain. My skills desperately needed drill practice, because I was having a really difficult time following the advice of how to be a successful hostess.

What couldn't I get my head around? Let me make a list.

1) Viewing men as nouns. A customer as a thing to be acquired. *A man is not a resource to be mined.*

2) The use of the phrase 'my customer'. *Awkward. It conjured up all sorts of social stigmas (that ironically don't exist). But still Awkward.*

3) Asking customers to take you to dinner and buy you things. Fringe benefits. *Shouldn't it be their choice? They'd paid to come, paid to drink, paid to relax. Had they paid to be besieged for material goods as well?*

4) Calling customers at their office during the day. Calling customers at their homes in the evening. *Wasn't that a bit presumptuous? You know, busy with meetings, busy with family dinner, busy choosing not to be at the club?*

5) The treacherous use of tricks, schemes and lies to dishonestly manipulate poor, lonely souls. *I just couldn't.*

I didn't want to change, but goddammit I wanted that bonus, I needed those dinners and, to be fair, the odd pair of Manolo Blahniks wouldn't hurt either.

—

Soh's chin doubled in shock as I seethingly asked for white wine. I'd been drinking oolong tea like a good girl for a week, but sitting next to yet another anonymous customer, I was feeling dejected and miserable, so why the hell not be *drunk*, dejected and miserable? I couldn't tolerate another sober night of this crazy make-believe. Oolong was over. Everything was just too absurd. Without a chemical buffer, the nights were piling up on me in one unfathomable heap.

If a man could spend hundreds and thousands in a single night on simply the company of a hostess, why did he consider that a luxury? Was it not just a little bit crazy? Was it not crazier still if, like Guy Tuesday, he refused *to speak* but sang willingly, or like spasmodic Guy Thursday – who called himself Johnny Depp – he never stopped trying to grope my breasts? What caused such behaviour? Why were these men out cavorting past midnight with young Western girls while their families were home sleeping? Worse yet, why did they show us photos of those families and tell us their names, ages and how they were a *good wife*, or *so cute-o*? If most were chivalrous gentlemen, why did some behave like pubescent children? Why did some leave with dignity while others had to be carried out, incapable even of saying their own name? Why did *men* want to discuss politics, historical unrest and the environment, while *males* wanted to know whether you were a virgin, how much it would cost to bang you, or how big your boyfriend's cock was? Did they really believe any of the stupid answers we gave to any of the stupid questions they asked? Could anyone believe any of this?

I wondered if the peculiar man sitting next to me did. Maybe he was contemplating the exact same things. Like an uncanny personification of Cogsworth the Clock from Disney's *Beauty and the Beast*, his hair was a bouffant that flowed into a flippant upturn just above the ears, his stomach a slight paunch, and he sat precariously, as though he would topple at any moment. We'd managed polite snippets. Stock answers to stock questions. Bland. Boring. His family name was Ito. I was from Canada. He lived in Yokohama, where he ran his own practice. I'd been in Tokyo eighteen days. He liked to work seven days a week. I was a model. He was a surgeon of gastroenterology. We sat in uncomfortable silence. He stared at the ceiling. I stared at my cuticles. Until.

'Did you come to Tokyo alone?' he blurted suddenly, and only my eyes moved towards him. *What did it matter?* I was so disenchanted with our predictable charade that I answered him like a robot.

YES. I CAME. ALONE.

'Do you have a boyfriend?' he asked.

NO. I DON'T. HAVE A BOYFRIEND. This caused him to smile and ask if I lived with other hostesses.

NO. BY MYSELF. IN. AN APARTMENT.

'By yourself?' he frowned. 'You must be very lonely.' A deep sympathy engulfed his face, and somehow, something about his tone triggered in me an unusual response. It blew a tiny fuse of patience.

'Yes, I am *soo* lonely, I just don't. Know what. *To do.*' My monotonous sarcasm must somehow have managed to resemble loneliness, because Ito's sympathy underwent a remarkable metamorphosis. It became sheer delight.

'Lonely? Oh I see. Do you have any Japanese friends?' I shook my head no. 'And, uh, what about other hostesses, they are not . . . friendly?'

My mouth fell open slightly, but I caught myself.

'Yes, but it's not the same,' I lamented with false pretence. 'I don't really know anyone and, well, we don't have anything in common. I have trouble talking to them.' I was laying it on nice and thick, like raspberry jam on freshly toasted bread.

'Hmm, I see. Don't worry. I also am lonely. I told you that my name is Ito, but you can call me Nori. I will be your new Japanese friend.'

That obviously meant an immediate check-up on my health. First, both of my forearms were tourniqueted in his hands, and then all ten fingernails pinched until the blood stopped flowing. Then my palms were scrutinised, and finally, when more pressure points than I ever knew existed had been painfully activated, Nori had adequately analysed my energy force to conclude that I had no gastroenterological problems. The relief was incalculable.

Unexpectedly, I actually started to enjoy myself. Nori was intelligent, and his frequent karaoke gave me space to breathe, even if he did make John Denver, the Beatles *and* the Bee Gees sound exactly the same. It was past midnight when Nori decided to leave. Yokohama was still a one-hour taxi ride away, and he had to work at 6.00 am.

'What plans do you have for this Monday?' he asked. 'It is a Japanese holiday, and maybe I can take you to Kamakura, the old samurai capital. Sunday will be impossible for me. I must conduct some important surgeries in Yokohama. However, if you are free . . . I will call you.'

Sure, I agreed, but I doubted he actually would.

When Tehara brought the bill, Nori handed over a small envelope. Tehara shook out the bills to count in full view: one, two, three . . . nine, ten. *Crikey.* It had cost Nori *$1000* for him and two friends to sing karaoke, drink cheap Scotch and have meaningless chit-chat with foreign girls. I was still slightly shocked when I felt a tap on my leg and something scrunched into my palm. '*Shhhh*, secret,' Nori whispered, and I pushed it into my purse as he patted my knee and stood to leave.

The moment the elevator doors made contact, I started to look. Lighter, phone, a few coins. There it was, wedged between two name cards. It was larger than I expected. Nori had slipped me an *ichiman* note. One hundred bucks. Maybe he would be calling after all.

SATURDAY-NIGHT SUSHI

'They might as well just let us go home now.'

There hadn't been a single customer since Greengrass opened two hours ago, and apart from the subdued background music, there were only murmurs about the usual things: food, customers and Israel, because, majority-wise, Greengrass was practically a Jewish sorority. A large percentage of customers even knew how to say cheers in Hebrew, with perfect pronunciation· *l'chaim*.

'Why don't you ring the guy who gave you the *ichiman* tip, the surgeon?' Nicole suggested. 'You have his number, right, so call him. Ask him to come in.'

I scrunched up my face.

'What? I think he could be a good customer for you. He likes you, I can tell. If he comes, you can make request points, and then maybe you can get a *dohan*.'

'It's eleven o'clock at night! What am I gonna say?'

'So what? Wake him up. He'll be happy. He's probably awake anyway. Every one of these crazies is awake. I am telling you, they never sleep. Just do like this.' She held up an imaginary phone. '*Hello, surgeon, this is Chelsea, how are you? Thank you for last night, it was really nice to meet you. I had such a good time. What are you doing tonight? I would love to see you again. Can you come to the club?* That's all. He will come. All you have to do is ask. That's what they're waiting for. Now go on! Do it!'

The idea of making up so much bullshit made me feel queasy, but I buckled like an obedient child and reached for my mobile. 'No, no, no, what are you doing? Put that away, come on! You use Nishi's phone, don't waste your own money. Are you crazy?'

'But I thought we weren't . . .'

'No! *Of course* you are allowed. It's to call a fucking customer, of course. Tell Nishi you want to ring the surgeon and he will throw the phone at you, because look, there is nobody here in this place. Now go call him,' she cried. 'Go!'

—

Nori had shown up an hour after I'd called, and Nicole had congratulated me when she saw him pad through the door. He'd brought his best friend Fumio, who was top brass in the Yokohama police department. That was why Fumio had to come to Tokyo to play, because he was too well known in Yokohama to be seen out with girls two feet taller than him, dancing like a maniac and generally acting the fool. Every time we made eye contact, he'd flutter his sausage fingers high in the air, like a sea anemone. It was hard to imagine him in uniform, imposing fear and commanding respect. An hour later it hadn't got any easier.

'Are you hungry?' Nori asked. *Was I hungry?* My stomach rumbled at the question. Payday was twenty-one days away. Matt and I were surviving on French toast, free coffee at the internet cafe and ¥100-ice-cream sandwiches bought with tips and the money I'd made bottling after work. This sounded like my first chance for a free after-work meal.

'Um, yeah,' I agreed tentatively. 'I'm a little hungry, yes.'

'Good! We are going now to have sushi, very near to here. We can walk, don't worry,' Nori laughed. 'Then maybe, if you want, we can go karaoke at Deep Blue. We can walk also. It's very close. I will check with Nishi if you are free to leave and we can go.'

—

The pulsation was intangible, but it was there. In the background. You could feel it. The collective vibration of a thousand footsteps had turned the sidewalk into a conduit of live current. *Pulsing.*

It was a Saturday night and Roppongi was at its hedonistic best. Packs of American marines, walking straight and sober only hours before, stumbled down the pavement, slurring, shouting and leering. Japanese women in heels half their height teetered along, clutching hands and giggling as the shouts of Nigerian street hecklers fell on deaf ears. Israelis shifted intensely from foot to foot as they hawked DVDs from China on plastic tables next to muscle-bound Iranians selling kebabs out of mobile stands pulled up along the sidewalk. More than one salaryman had passed out on his briefcase, sprawled along the step of some day spa or flower shop.

All around us inebriation had reached saturation point. Waiting outside a packed sushi bar for a free table with Nori and Fumio, I looked around for Matt. He was never far from Roppongi Crossing and I wanted him to see what Nori looked like, but his gaze was nowhere to be met. Instead there were five pairs of inquisitive eyes fixed on me in unison.

The men were charming, like robots functioning from a centralised operator interface. I had to smirk. Did marines do anything out of formation? Even in my Pumas and blue jeans, they'd be mistaking me for a prostitute. I couldn't fault them for the assumption. There were a number of glassy-eyed prostitutes, mostly Russian, accompanying old Japanese men on the streets of Roppongi. How were these corn-fed boys supposed to know that I was simply out for a non-salacious meal? The majority of them probably didn't even know what a hostess was, because hostesses don't often have a reason to talk to marines. Prostitutes do.

As a table became free and Nori moved inside, I met their stares and beamed an insouciant message back through my smile. *Free sushi. Oooh rah.*

YOKOHAMA

Cement and blue sky. Solid steel and feathered cloud. Kilometres and kilometres of spotless factories and vast oil tanks plastered with international logos ran seamlessly alongside a shiny Mercedes-Benz, each smokestack billowing plumes that formed pleasant, unthreatening shapes. The industrial workhorse of Tokyo Bay was so pristine that it looked like a magnified model of itself as I peered out at the drivers of cars zooming past. Were they heading to Yokohama too, or somewhere further, speeding along bitumen arteries so efficiently and unobstructed?

I glanced over at Nori in his plush leather seat, placidly driving with both hands on the wheel. After I'd recounted every detail about him to Matt, we'd agreed that it was safe for me to spend my Sunday with him.

I'd promised to call Matt every hour, but I wasn't worried. Matt only ever needed a trivial snapshot of someone to pin the tail on the donkey, and I trusted his judgement completely. He had said Nori was harmless, and I was fine.

—

There was a low buzzing in the car as I realigned my seat, every angle adjustable from a control on the door panel. With a fan and a heater, it was almost of Japanese public-toilet calibre. *Bzzzzzz.* Nori looked over at me. 'You like that seat I think. Do you want one?'

'Sure,' I replied, 'I can put it in my living room.' He chuckled in a pained sort of way, and I suspected he'd been somewhat serious.

—

Brilliant sunlight bounced off the elegant arc of Rainbow Bridge and streaked across the bay, turning the mottled reflection of Yokohama city into a shimmering, undulating carpet of concrete greys, blues and greens. In the near distance I could see the seaside docks lying dormant in the afternoon sun, the towering orange cranes speaking more of progress and the future than of their city's difficult past.

The city of Yokohama dates back to the eleventh century, but it wasn't until its port opened in 1859 that it became an integral part of the nation's industrial economy. During the Edo period, although Japan still upheld an isolationist policy, forays were made into international trade. However, to separate the Japanese districts from those of the *gaijin*, a foreign-resident zone was established.

When the Great Kanto earthquake of 1923 devastated the city, the previously thriving infrastructure was reconstructed in just six years, only to be destroyed by heavy air raids during World War II. Nearly half the city was reduced to ashes before Yokohama was rebuilt yet again into what is now one of Japan's foremost international ports of trade.

Nori pointed at a building jutting from the skyline across the bay. 'Yokohama's most tallest building. It is office building, but very top floors are one famous hotel. When you come to live in Yokohama, I will pay for you to stay there, in a suite on the top floor where the view is most beautiful.' His presumption sounded so innocent, but it made my skin prickle.

'Why would you do that?' I demanded. 'When am I coming to live here?'

He laughed uncomfortably. 'You should not stay in Tokyo. Tokyo is very bad place and, uh, Yokohama is much more cheaper and way of life is better. Also it is not so small a place. It is Japan's second-largest city! People are nicer. It is more beautiful. It is my home. I will show you my city, and you will decide that you must come to live in Yokohama.'

I said nothing and turned to watch the light sparkle outside the window.

—

'You don't want to have pizza?' Nori shrugged, but I shook my head. 'What are you going to drink? Some wine maybe?' he asked. I chose blood-orange juice. I wasn't going to drink if I didn't have to. We'd driven around until sunset on a tour of Yokohama that included Nori's boyhood neighbourhood, Chinatown, the New Grand Hotel, where MacArthur had stayed when he came to Japan in 1945 to sign the peace treaty, and a school where a hostess Nori met in Tokyo now taught English because she *came to realise that Yokohama is best place for living*. It wasn't dissimilar to spending the day with a real-estate agent. I was the prospect interested in the free lunch and sightseeing, and Nori was the guy with the desperate one-liner to close the deal: 'I can do everything for you.'

It was slightly disturbing.

Even apart from every fact that didn't need to be stated, we *had* just met yesterday. I was a passing person among millions, but Nori was convinced I'd return on a working-holiday visa and he'd sponsor me for a job until I decided what business I wanted him to fund.

'I will help you with everything. Don't worry. You will need to study Japanese, but I can send you to a good school. Then you can find much opportunity for a good life. Hostess is not a good life. Very difficult, always make-believe, sleeping during daytime. I know. I have many hostess friends for many years, and besides, Nishi is very bad man.'

'What do you mean, Nishi is a bad man?'

'He is great liar! For Nishi I am very important customer, because I have great amounts of money. Always he is overcharging me, making some lie to tell so that he can take more money. I do not like Green-grass! But, now that you are there, it is my favourite club.'

That was bloody fantastic. I smiled and gulped down another spoonful of soup.

—

Nori pulled his Benz up my narrow one-way street, slowed to a stop and sat staring straight ahead. 'Do you want to go home now, or some-place else? Maybe you want a drink?'

'No, it's okay. I'll go home now. You have to work in the morning, don't you?' It was late and Nori had given me an option out, but his reaction was still one of surprise.

'Home? You want to go home?'

'Well, no, whatever. You want to go somewhere *in particular* for a drink? Where?'

'I know one place, one very good small bar not far from here, but if you are tired . . .'

'No I'm not tired, I only woke up five hours ago. It's my holiday, remember? I told you, it's all right, whatever, we can go to your small bar. That's fine.'

Nori's eyebrows danced with glee as he pulled away from the curb. So close, but yet . . .

Nothing was open. Akasaka, home of Nori's One Small Bar, was eerily silent.

'Oh well, I guess nothing is open on a Sunday night. You can just take me home.'

'No, no, there must be some place. We will find it,' he insisted, and I trailed along behind him. Just as he resolved to return to the car, Nori spotted a light shining up from a darkened staircase, illuminating a small chalkboard sign. *Wine bar. Open to Late.*

Well, that was just great.

'Oh! Very good!' he exclaimed as his eyebrows shot up. 'We can go to there.'

'We can go *there*,' I corrected, trying hard to veil my dismay.

—

The first thing I accomplished in the empty bar was to accidentally spill a martini in a raspberry-hued splatter across Nori's crotch. But he didn't mind. He bought another one. He even slipped me an *ichiman* note, after I'd somewhat embellished how hard it was to save money in Tokyo. It was about time too, because apart from wanting to see Yokohama and escape the confines of Tokyo, Nori's tips were a prime motivational factor in spending time with him instead of with my husband on my one day off. I would have gone home long ago if I hadn't been, how shall I say it, *tipped off* by the always-resourceful Jodie.

'Jackpot! Looks like the surgeon likes you,' she'd said last night after he'd left. 'He's a really good customer, kinda creepy, but incredibly rich. Did you get a hundred-dollar tip? He'll probably come all the time now. He was my friend's customer last year until he went totally nuts and wanted her to marry him. He's all right though. Just try to drag it out as long as possible before he loops out. That's all you ever gotta do, really, because 90 per cent of the time, the ones that come alone, that's what they're eventually gonna do. You'll see. *Whack-o.*'

But tonight it was Nori who fed me with cautionary tales. 'You must be careful of some customer. Not every customer is so nice, like me. Sometimes they are very bad, and you should not trust them. Especially if they have a mysterious or terrible face.'

'A mysterious face?'

'Yes, but more often terrible. Sometimes a customer is very vague, or not telling to you the last name, or what job. What reason does he have for secrets? It is not typical. Do you know the story of Sagawa?' Nori's eyebrows furrowed deeply.

'No, should I?'

'Humph. Sagawa is very famous customer of Roppongi hostess clubs. He was at the university, in France, when he met one very young, very beautiful woman. She had blonde hair. Sagawa invited her to his home for dinner. He was very much in love with her, but she wanted only to be friends. Sagawa wanted to do some things with her, but she refused and so he shot her, like this.' Nori shot me with an imaginary shotgun. 'Pow! And he shot her, and she fell onto the floor. Then he thought if he ate her, she would belong to him forever and . . .'

'What? He *ate* her?'

'Yes, Sagawa cut her body into small pieces and then he cooked the pieces so that he could eat them, but some he tried to eat raw, like sashimi.'

'*Oh God*, gross! Stop it! When did this happen? How do you know all of this?'

'It is very famous story in Japan, but don't worry, maybe he ate her twenty years ago. Now he is old. Everybody is knowing the story of

Sagawa. He has made one CD of songs, and drawn one *manga* of how he ate the girl. You could see him, at one time, on a morning cooking show. Also, he has written one book about how he enjoyed to eat the meat of such a very beautiful girl. I have read it,' Nori proclaimed, seeming strangely pleased with himself.

I was utterly revolted. My palms were sweaty. 'Did they execute him? What happened?'

'No, the French judge thought Sagawa was insane, so he was put in mental hospital. However, I think because the father of Sagawa is one very rich and very powerful businessman, Sagawa was able to be sent back to Japan. Here he also was put in mental hospital, but after fifteen months his powerful father was able to use his influence and so Sagawa did not go to prison. Thanks to Japan, Sagawa could be set free.'

SHOPPING HARAJUKU

'I'm too tall for this store, Nori, forget it. I don't need any pants. I don't want to try on any more, so let's just go get a coffee.' For the fourth consecutive day, I was spending my free time with Nori, and he was standing in the middle of Harajuku Gap, arms overflowing with boot-cut and ultra-low-rise women's jeans. A meticulously helpful salesgirl stood beaming next to him. They looked ridiculous, and I felt like a moron.

'Okay, but first I know one place that might be better. It is very popular for Western ladies, and maybe you can find some pants.'

I didn't want to find pants. Mine were just fine, and it was weird shopping with a man who'd been a total stranger four days ago. But still, it was hard to argue, and we traipsed across the main intersection and into a glass-box store.

'How about this one?' Nori held up a bomber jacket in fire-engine red.

'*Umm*, I like black. Maybe I should look over there instead.' I started to flick through the monochrome section until I found what I hadn't even been looking for: a silk-lined velvet waistcoat with a Chinese collar. 'This one is gorgeous. What do you think?'

'Okay, very nice. And something else? Pants maybe?'

'No, I don't need pants, Nori. I don't think that . . . oh my God, look at this shirt!'

'You should choose it,' he nodded enthusiastically. 'And something else?'

I looked at the price tags. Holy shit. *Umm* . . .

'What? Are you crazy? Don't you think this is enough? I mean really, you don't have to buy me *anything*.'

Nori seemed disappointed that I didn't want to keep spending his money, but as he dumped the change from the cashier into his satchel, he caught me stroking a tailored fur in a luxurious deep chocolate and scooped it off the rack with lightning speed. 'Do you want to have this one?' he asked excitedly.

I gulped at the price. It was tempting, but I already felt dishonest enough. I knew it was normal for him to be buying such gifts, but the tenets of my own culture still took precedence over my emotions about it. I struggled to remind myself that I was in Japan in order to accept his generosity without feeling too guilty (or, more importantly, like a kept woman). The fur was just too much. 'Umm, no, that's okay. I like the black one. Let's just go get coffee.'

Nori frowned. 'Maybe so much coffee is not good . . . for health,' he advised. 'We will go to a Mexican restaurant, near here, instead. And I think you will like it.'

Right. I probably shouldn't argue. The man *was* a gastroenterologist.

—

Less than twenty-four hours after he'd supplied me with a new wardrobe, filled my stomach with quesadilla and unknowingly sent my husband a baked citrus salmon that I'd purposely not eaten, Nori was calling me again. But before I could answer, I had to fling open the door to our capsule bathroom. Matt was whistling in the shower. A heavy fog of steam blanketed my face.

'Hey, bubs! Shhhhhh! It's Nori. Be quiet for a minute!' The whistling stopped and I shut the door. 'Hello, Nori. How are you?'

'Uh, hello, Chelsea. I am now working. How are you?' He sounded fidgety. 'Uh, I want to see you. Now I am at my hospital, but tonight I will come to Greengrass to see you.'

'Oh, okay. Sounds good. I'll see you tonight then. Drive safe.'

'Okay, uh, you too,' he stammered. 'Um, okay, bye-bye.'

I'd found that it was best to cut Nori off early. Our conversations were always the same. I could play a recording of myself and he would still think we had spoken. His repetitive calls seemed a product of habit, to check up on me, to make sure we were still 'friends'. I probably should have talked to him longer, but I wanted to go for a walk before work, and I still had my muesli to eat – a dietary upgrade from French toast. Muesli was far more nutritious. It had raisins.

—

In the end Nori didn't turn up that night. I tried calling him from the club, but there was no answer. Not even his long-winded message; it just rang until a woman's voice announced, '*Denwa bango wa something-or-other desu.*'

I was hoping he'd show up. His frequent generosity was more than appreciated. It was my lifeline. Even with self-imposed frugality Tokyo was just so damned expensive that Matt and I only had ¥3000 left and fifteen days until payday. Who knew how the other girls managed? Many of them came to Tokyo on a last-minute whim with very little money, but I suppose they took up far more opportunities than me. The Israelis were out bottling every single night, but I didn't want to bottle for cash any more. It made me feel like a cockroach. An alcoholic cock-roach. Thankfully Abie and Nicole had lent me a couple of hundred bucks to carry us over, but Nicole didn't think I'd be having a money shortage for long. Not if I listened to her advice.

'So what, the surgeon didn't come? Spend the day with him tomorrow and you can ask for some money. And not just a little bit, Chelsea. Ask him to pay next month's rent. Don't worry, trust me on this. He will. He's got more money than he knows what to do with, so just call him! I want to see you on Monday with a hundred-thousand yen. That's one-thousand bucks, *American*. You'll see I was right!'

Of course Nicole was right. Nori had already offered to pay my rent, without prompting, but there was no way I was going to take up the offer. That would be just a bit *too* rich.

—

Matt and I sat side by side on concrete steps under the yellow glow of the twenty-four-hour grocery store's cow sign, devouring a fresh pack of ¥100 *mochi* – rice cakes. It was four in the morning. Parked in front of us along the sidewalk was a red Ferrari Testarossa 512TR.

'I met the most interesting guy at the club tonight. He was really odd, but good odd. Shin. That was his name. Shin.'

'What, like your leg?' Matt was staring at the Ferrari.

'Yeah, like your leg. Looking at him I don't know how he could afford to get in, but he said he'd been there before. He told me all about his last hostess friend, Karolina from Poland, who's now in Thailand with her friend. He was wearing pilled sweatpants and he looked like a bum, but he was really smart. Really, really smart. Oh, and he drank *orange juice*. In a big glass. Which is weird. Japanese drink like maniacs.'

'Ha, what a funny bugger. How old is he?'

'Don't know, forty-something, like the rest of them. He invited me to go to some place called Hakone, where they have these natural hot springs. I was like, yeah, *sure*. Let's go. Oh, and remind me, I've got something to show you: these Mensa puzzles with matchsticks that Shin . . .'

'What's Mensa?' Matt interrupted, and I stared at him.

'It's that club for geniuses. You know. You've gotta have an IQ off the Richter scale to be in it. Anyway, he arranged these sixteen matches on the table, which you're supposed to make five boxes out of by only moving three. I got the first one, and he was sort of impressed, and I almost got the second, except the cheeky bugger went and spoilt it for me. I like him. He's awesome.'

'I bet you he's rich as a mofo and drives around in a Ferrari Testarossa.'

'I doubt it. *Ugh*. I can't eat any more. Do you want the rest?' Matt reached over and I got up to put the container in the garbage. 'I told you that Nori called me again, didn't I?'

'Yeah,' Matt had his mouth full. 'You told me on the phone.' I wiped the soy sauce from the side of his face. 'What did he want this time?'

'Just to say that he was coming to the club, but he never showed up. He's calling me every single day, even if it's just to ask *how are you, what are you doing?* I don't know why the club has a rule that you've got to ring customers. They ring *me*.'

'Yeah, but that's cool. Doesn't he help you with your points or whatever crazy shit you've gotta do there? Nori's just an old boy. He's harmless.'

'I know, he's just so mundane. Did you find any new hostesses tonight?'

'Yeah, I picked up two, so we'll get an extra grand next pay, and there's this stripper who's probably gonna come in for an audition later this week.'

'Good one. Had enough to eat yet? We should probably go for a run. C'mon, let's go.'

I had to wait for Matt to do one last lap of the Ferrari, surveying its rear end, before we walked the half-block home.

—

Back at the apartment I tried out Shin's Mensa puzzles on Matt. The paper-folding challenge. The matchstick formations. He got them all, one after another, like he'd invented the goddamned things himself. 'What's Mensa?' I don't know, you tell me. Smartass.

TOWER RECORDS

Whump. I stared at the ceiling, shifted again. I couldn't sleep at all. There had to be a position that held the magic combination that would send me off into a deep slumber, but I had yet to find it. In four hours I'd had eighty-six failures. I was wide awake. The phone rang suddenly, and I found myself smiling even before I answered. 'Hello, Shin.'

'Hello. How are you? What are you doing? Are you sleeping?' he asked. Over the phone Shin's voice sounded even more monotone than in person, maintaining a single pitch from beginning to end. Definitely not from lack of intelligence; his speech patterns just seemed to be a product of his calm, placid nature.

'No, I'm not sleeping. *Any more.*'

Shin laughed and then, to my surprise, recounted the highlights of last night's conversation with remarkable detail. I didn't think anyone paid that much attention. His recollection of my word groupings was exact. 'What will you do now?' he asked.

'I will have some breakfast,' I answered. I liked Shin's version of English, each word spaced microscopically from the next by a playful pause, and found myself unconsciously bootlegging his unique use of grammar.

'Uh, I am wondering. Do you have any Japanese study books?'

'Yeah, I have a language set, with tapes.'

'No, not tapes. *Books.* History books. Last night you said to me that you are interested in the history of Japan and Japanese culture. I will go Shibuya at four o'clock this afternoon to buy you some books to learn about Japan.'

'You don't have to do that . . .'

'It is important! You can meet me there if you are not busy, at *Chu-ken Hachiko*. Dog statue. Do you know it?'

Chu-ken Hachiko is undoubtedly the most famous canine in all of Japan. Born in Akita in 1923, he was adopted by Professor Eizaburo Ueno of the Imperial University and soon accompanied him to Shibuya station every morning. When Professor Ueno returned each evening, Hachiko would be waiting, until one day in 1925 the professor died of a heart attack at work. Hachiko waited all night in vain, but when his master never showed up, he continued to come and wait every evening until dusk. Colleagues of the professor took pity on Hachiko and brought him home, but he only escaped. In March 1935 Hachiko was found dead of natural causes on the exact spot where he had so diligently waited for his master to return for so many years.

Hachiko's unshakeable fidelity inspired locals to erect a bronze statue in his honour, but it was melted down during World War II by the Imperial Army. He'd become such an icon, however, that after the war the Society for Recreating the Hachiko Statue commissioned the son of the original sculptor to erect a new statue, and now every year on the anniversary of Hachiko's death the *Chu-ken Hachiko Matsuri* – the Hachiko festival – celebrates the memory of the faithful dog in front of the landmark. Of course, if you happen to miss out, you can always visit the stuffed body of Hachiko himself, on display in the National Science Museum.

'Yes, I know the story of Hachiko. You pat his head for good luck, right?'

'Yes! How do you know? We will meet at dog statue, and then I will take you for a Japanese dinner, so now, maybe don't eat too much. Only a small French toast, this is better.'

'Okay, only coffee,' I countered. 'All right, so what time do you want to meet?'

~

I was in the food hall underneath Shibuya station, passing the time before meeting Shin, when Goro called. Goro was in the business of high fashion – he was the general manager of a company that imported all of the major collections from Europe. I'd met him at the club last night, and he'd asked if he had a chance to be my boyfriend, if he was nice enough. I might have led him on a little, but fair play. That's what he was looking for.

'What are you doing?' he asked.

'I'm in Shibuya, looking at six-hundred-and-eighty-yen apples.' Uniformly sized, individually wrapped apples to be exact, each gleaming like the clone of an unblemished, perfect specimen kept hidden in a lab somewhere. 'Where are you?'

'At work. I am working. Chelsea,' he began in a serious tone, 'I know you are busy, so I have only one question. Please tell to me what size is your shoe.'

'A European 40. Why? What are you up to?'

'Nothing. It is secret. Okay, so thank you very much. I must go.'

'Hey, wait . . . when am I going to see you at the club?'

'Friday. I will come Friday,' and Goro hung up.

Out of context our brief conversation was incredibly strange, but by now I hardly thought anything of it. I mean, I could see a perfectly hued cantaloupe that looked like a clay model of itself staring back at me from the shelf. It was ¥5800. Almost sixty freakin' bucks. To me, *that's* more odd than a man I'd just met calling me up to size me for some Blahniks.

Relativity. It's all about relativity.

—

I found Shin eating poppy-seed cake and drinking coffee on the second floor of Starbucks, after I'd arrived at the dog statue and hadn't found him there. The cafe was at full capacity and then some, but Shin immediately offered his seat and asked what I was drinking. I could see the markered scribble on the side of his cup – a large C, for cappuccino. 'I *thought* you said coffee was bad for your health?'

'But tastes so good! Sometimes is okay, but not every day.' I could see the smirk on his face as he headed off to get me a coffee. The cheeky bugger.

Outside the window a continuous tide of people piled up on the corners of Shibuya Crossing, condensed, and then spilt over, and over, and over. The changing traffic light was the long wooden branch that stoked the anthill, an anthill full of ants obeying the rules. Red was for regrouping. Green was for go. It was organised madness.

At the seat next to me a young Japanese woman was capturing it all on a camera that tucked neatly into her doll-like hands, but suddenly all I could see was the green apron of a Starbucks girl.

'*SUMIMASEN!*' the barista screeched, and dozens of coffee drinkers turned as she launched into a high-pitched torrent of disapproving Japanese.

What had I done? All I could do was throw my hands up stupidly into the air. '*Wakarimasen!*' I pleaded. I don't understand!

Instantly, she jabbed accusingly at a sign pasted onto the window and pointed at me. I shook my head, and her face went from flustered rouge to a brilliantly embarrassed red. '*Sumimasen, gomen nasai,*' she gasped in apology, somehow still managing a deep bow in the one cubic foot of space between us. I expected her to disappear as quickly as she'd arrived, but instead she turned a quick hundred-and-eighty degrees to throw her tiny arms into an exaggerated Big X, squarely in the face of the disobedient Japanese filmmaker. With no hesitation she repeated her complaint as audibly as she could. 'NO CAMERAS PLEASE!' Only this time she spoke in perfect English – just another quirk of a Westernised Japan.

Shin soon returned with an iced latte and stood until the seat next to me was free. Dressed in a pressed white shirt, blue jeans and recently shined black Birkenstocks, he had exchanged last night's beanie for a neatly combed side part. I'd liked the sweatpants, but perhaps he reserved his street-bum look for nights out.

'I was born here, in Shibuya.' Shin poked me in the elbow to draw my attention outside, and to a memory of a place quite different from what now stood in its wake – a panoramic view of a cityscape on steroids. It was hard to imagine Shibuya as the quiet neighbourhood that Shin had once called home. His school, the house he'd grown up in and other childhood memories were now gone forever, replaced by a *pachinko* parlour full of slot machines, a love hotel or perhaps a tower block of tiny, efficiently standardised apartments. Somewhere beneath bustling streets and the world's busiest scatter crossing there was a river that he once fished in, long-since redirected below ground-level when it had simply got in the way of things. The inconvenient swimming of fish had been traded in for pollution – the quintessential paradox of progress.

It hadn't always been this way. According to Shin it had all begun the year that Tokyo hosted the 1964 Olympics. He had just turned five. 'Before and after, so much different,' he lamented. 'So much change.'

It was a milestone year for the Japanese, a chance to formally declare to the rest of the world that their recovery from the war was now complete (on the surface at least). They certainly had an awful lot to recover from. In August 1945 the innocent nicknames of 'Little Boy' and 'Fat Man' had belonged to nothing less than atomic bombs dropped from the Japanese sky, by none other than a country that was to immediately become their surrogate parent. The cities of Hiroshima and Nagasaki were largely destroyed, killing hundreds of thousands and injuring an entire country with the aftermath of an experimental annihilation.

After the devastation of the war Japan struggled to rebuild itself, not just physically but culturally as well. This was a nation that had witnessed an apocalypse, and it had a profound impact on the Japanese psyche. It's said that in Japan there are no perversions of the social norm; there are only compensations for what happened during the war.

No one thought Japan would ever thrive again, yet somehow, only twenty years later, it had pulled itself together, won an Olympic bid and presented a fresh-faced, well-disciplined, rule-abiding version of its former self to the world.

With a collective intensity post-war Japan wasn't out to just *catch up* with the rest of the world; it was on its way somewhere, and fast. The unveiling of the *shinkansen*, the bullet trains, in 1964 was only the beginning of a forty-year propulsion that has seen Japan become the most technologically advanced country on the planet. What is more, Japan has miraculously achieved the integration of ancient tradition and custom with its hyperactive, über-modern self. In the face of extreme adversity it has spawned a harmonious balance of seemingly opposing forces, and Shin was one of its generational offspring.

There was the Shin who favoured peace and reflection over noise and overpopulation, choosing to live a one-hour train ride away from Roppongi in what he called a 'lower class, countryside area' – although in reality it was probably just as crowded as any major city's outer suburbs. He liked it because there were no tall buildings and not so many people. In his 'countryside', there were birds and greenery, a sense of solitude.

Then there was the Shin who enjoyed people-watching on over-crowded trains, who was happy shopping among the masses for the latest techno-gadgets and entertained himself among millions in a city of inexhaustible possibilities. He loved Tokyo. Why? He couldn't explain it. It just had an energy. But I think I could understand.

As I sucked up the last of my drink, Shin caught me staring. His mood seemed much heavier than it had been before he'd begun his trip down memory lane. With a grin that was hard to decipher he told me off for slurping and stood, asking quietly, 'Shall we go?'

~

On the street below Tower Records traffic had come to a standstill. A jovial parade in traditional Shinto dress had taken over, led by a Toyota with a six-piece band in the back. Following behind was a brightly coloured hand-carved building mounted on long palanquin beams atop the shoulders of more than two dozen worshippers.

'*Mikoshi*,' Shin pointed. 'Small Japanese shrine.' He grabbed my elbow and guided me into the heart of the crowd. Men and women circled around me, smiling and singing, shouting and reaching up to clap joyously in my face. Shin tapped my elbow and pointed to the smooth-skinned buttocks of the men dancing around us with a humoured lift of his brow and I jabbed him in the ribs. Tall enough to see above everyone, I received unsolicited winks from several of them, much to the delight of the all-observant Shin.

'They are celebrating *matsuri*, summer festival,' Shin explained, pulling me out of the throng to the opposite sidewalk. 'Do you know why they are making the shrine bump up and down? It is for the god living inside. He *likes* it.'

I laughed at the notion of a Shinto spirit jostling about in a state of divine pleasure.

We ducked into the busy ground floor of Tower Records, filled with rows of youths plugged into music stations, rocking out in their own detached little worlds. Shin stopped to stare at a flamboyant Harajuku girl wearing a Little Bo Peep costume and sporting a neon-pink Mohawk before motioning to the left. 'This way. You know seventh floor?' he asked. I shook my head. 'Bookshop.'

Upstairs he cocked his head. 'Okay, many books. You are looking here, I am looking there. I will meet you this floor,' he said, and with that debriefing left me to browse picture books full of postcard images. By the time we left, Shin handed three books to me in a closed bag. 'For later,' he said. 'Have you been to Harajuku?'

—

The streets were busy as we ambled along on foot to the trendsetting fashion precinct of Harajuku, idly tossing questions between long, comfortable silences. Shin wanted to know all about Canadian weather, in genuine detail, and every country I'd travelled to since I left home.

'Everywhere, summer, summer, *summer*. You have no warm clothes! It will become cold soon . . . you need long-sleeved shirts. Do you like Gap?' he asked.

'Everything there is too short for me.'

'That is because *Japanese* sizes. You are tall *gaijin* girl, so maybe this place better,' and Shin opened the door to a familiar store. 'Okay, so you are watching here, I am watching there. Find some things that you like.' I started to eye a wispy, yellow summer dress. '*Warm* things,' he advised, and meandered off into the men's section. By the time he wandered back, I had a collection of *warm things that I liked*, such as a black sweater. Shin stared at my choices. 'Why no colour?'

'I'm a Buddhist,' I deadpanned.

'Only black? Hmmm, I like *pink*,' he said, in a pan that was deader than mine, and picked up the sweater to examine it.

When we passed by a rack of expensive black leather jackets, Shin stopped to point. 'Your colour,' he smirked, and he insisted I try on almost every single one, but despite thousand-dollar price tags none of them were a perfect fit. Almost as a joke I tried on a satin jacket that was *très* young Hollywood, and Shin let out a surprised, '*Whoa!*'

'What? You don't like it?'

'No! Is good, but . . . you sure you want this one? It is *brown*. You won't regret it?'

I shook my head, and the Whoa Jacket ended up as one small part of an extravagant sum total, for which Shin had paid cash. As we left, Shin held open the door and asked, 'What about pants?'

TWICE IN ONE NIGHT

'*IRASHAIMASE!*'

The door slid open to an echo of assault-rifle shouts as Shin turned to mirror my wide-eyed delight. A waiter in traditional indigo *yukata* was pitched horizontally before us, spreading the grin on our faces only wider as he barked a second shout of welcome, which reverberated deep within the belly of the restaurant, Inakaya.

Constructed almost completely in wood, the centrally staged eating platform transported us back in time. We sat at the edge of a raised display of vegetables on bamboo trays and ice buckets overflowing with fresh seafood and skewered meats. Two costumed chefs kneeled at the back, tending to sunken open fire grills with twisted *hachimaki* bands tied around their heads.

'They are *yakikata*,' Shin explained. 'Grill person. And there,' Shin said, pointing to a wooden plaque, 'is name tag.' The row of hand-written paper above the chefs was the menu, but the distinct lack of prices indicated something I now took for granted in any restaurant I attended with a Japanese customer. Inakaya was incredibly expensive.

As Shin selected an endless list of dishes, our server shouted each one to the next waiter, and on until the order reached the chef. Even though we were the only customers, the noise multiplied around the room. I could only imagine how loud it might be when the restaurant reached capacity.

Shin seemed to be intimately familiar with the restaurant, and I wondered how many times he had delighted young foreign women with this culinary gem. Regardless, he seemed to enjoy every ounce of the experience as much as I did. He nearly cried as he watched me obstinately insist on using chopsticks, laughing as gingko nuts fell repeatedly from my grasp, and gave in and offered advice only when a skewered red snapper appeared, looking as if it had been electrically shocked out of motion. 'It is looking at you,' Shin teased. 'Don't eat me, Chelsea, it says.' I tried to jab Shin with my chopsticks and he nearly fell off his stool in retreat, but soon I was being schooled in peeling apart the little orange body, and it was absolutely delicious.

Every morsel was stunning, delivered straight from the grill on a wooden paddle by a chef with Popeye forearms. Each dish was announced with a booming big shout. It was hilarious, taking your dinner off the paddle as everyone around you shouted out in Japanese, 'SHITAKE MUSHROOMS! THESE ARE SHITAKE MUSH-ROOMS!' When your teacup was refilled, the tea boy would shout, 'OCHA! OCHA DESU!' and so would six others. With Shin beside me explaining every detail and putting me in stitches, I was absolutely enthralled with the magic of the place.

'This restaurant very famous,' Shin revealed. 'Last time I saw Yoko Ono, sitting over there.' He sounded unimpressed. 'Do you know meaning of *inakaya*? It is "country house", but maybe, I think not. Is mistake. Japanese house not usually so big,' he smirked. 'Maybe name should be "country *mansion*", but maybe it is right size for you. You eat so much!'

'You ordered it! Gimme a break. I haven't eaten anything since I woke up. *You've* been dragging me around Harajuku all day. What do you expect?'

'Yes,' Shin agreed solemnly. 'But how eat so much? You are so skinny.' He leant over to check under the bench. 'Where everything go?'

❤

One block away from the restaurant Shin stopped abruptly to hand over the shopping bags and my arms fell slightly under the weight. 'How far to your house?'

'Ten minutes walking, maybe fifteen.'

'You are okay with bags?' Shin asked, and once I'd reassured him I could cope he took two steps backwards and casually raised his right hand. 'Okay, I go home now. By train. See you,' he said, shoving both hands into his pockets and turning to walk briskly up the street.

I was knocked speechless. *What?* Who did this? I'd met Shin less than twenty-four hours ago, and even though I already felt like we'd been pals forever, the way he just left me, so casually, after all of this was . . . what was it? Who knew? It wasn't even a work night and this hadn't even been a *dohan*, but it was completely unthreatening and devoid of any expectation. Shin definitely wasn't like any other customer I'd met at Greengrass. I couldn't even think of him in the same context. But he wasn't a friend. I couldn't place him. All I could do was splutter lamely after him, 'See you! And THANK YOU!'

Shin simply raised his right arm in reply without looking back.

—

I was walking in the door with my shopping when Nori called. He sounded terrible. 'My patient died in hospital, and I . . . could not save him. It is most difficult situation for me. What are you doing now? I want to come to Tokyo.'

I agreed to meet him outside the apartment building at eight o'clock.

—

Nori pulled the car into a parking lot just up from Greengrass at five past eight. It was Sunday and all the clubs were closed, so I wondered what we were doing in Roppongi.

'We will go to one restaurant that is, uh, peculiar, and it will be a surprise. It is Japanese, but not regular. It is very . . . odd.'

A knot sprung into my stomach. It couldn't be . . .

'What do you mean odd? Where is it?'

Nori seemed reluctant to say more. 'Very close to here. It is funny place and . . . very noisy place.'

'Why is it noisy?' I prodded as we continued towards Roppongi Crossing.

'Because everyone repeating your order, and shouting,' he laughed. 'It is very odd place, but very famous.'

Oooohh, *shit*. I could *not* return to the same restaurant with a different man. Shin and I had left Inakaya less than an hour ago.

'Umm, you know, I'm not really that hungry. Do you want to just go somewhere for coffee instead?' I suggested, and Nori stopped in his tracks. His face fell.

'Not hungry? But it is very entertaining! Maybe you can be hungry, when you see it.' I started to protest, but Nori took an unexpected turn. 'This is it,' he announced. 'Inakaya.'

It wasn't the same place I'd had dinner with Shin, but it was still Inakaya, just a second, smaller version of it. Impossible. I couldn't believe I was going to the same restaurant twice in the same night! As we were greeted by the ubiquitous '*Irashaimase!*' my stomach turned.

I did my best to pretend everything was new, but the hour we spent at Inakaya was barely tolerable. It wasn't the chefs. It wasn't the food, although I felt like I needed a vomitorium when we left. It was Nori. As we drove frustratingly around Ginza looking for a bar that he knew, it was apparent that Nori had begun to creep out of the sphere of interesting companion and into the outer realms of the delusional, pressing for impossible answers and scowling if I wasn't providing them. I was finding it harder not to laugh at his bizarre notions or ignore them altogether.

'How about this one bar, here?' Nori asked, and I sighed.

'Sure, let's go inside.'

—

'I have great interest in Adolf Hitler, because, uh . . . he wrote that book *Mein Kampf*, you know?' Somehow Nori felt it the appropriate time to bring up another of his unusual inspirational figures. Last time it had been Alain Delon, whose role as a sociopathic murderer in *Plein Soleil* had influenced him greatly. It was Nori's dream 'to become like him'. But Hitler? This just got better.

'*Mein Kampf*? Uh-huh. He wrote it in prison. Why do you think he's so great? He was a terrible, evil man who brought horrific death and suffering to millions of people. What, please tell me, is so great about that?'

'*Heh heh*, yes, I know, he was very bad man, but he had great . . . great . . . how do you say? Psychological *influence* over people. I want to learn that influence, from him.'

I looked over at him dubiously and his eyebrows shot up. 'He was bad, I know, but I . . . I can be good.'

'And what are you supposed to learn from such an evil maniac?'

'Well, for instance, he used to look at himself in the looking glass . . .'

'Mirror,' I corrected.

'Yes, in the mirror, and he would practise speaking powerfully, and to make the face expressions so that people would listen, and I also am doing the same. Because he made for himself a strong mind, Hitler could have power over people of weak mind and make them to listen to him. For me that is important, because I am a businessman, and now I want to own many more businesses so I can be rich and powerful, and I . . . I want people to listen to *me*.'

'What kind of businesses do you want to own?' I asked quickly. I wasn't really interested, but I'd rather not continue a discussion about the supposed merits of Adolf Hitler and his 'strong mind', and I didn't know whether *the driver of the car I was currently in* would get angry if I tried to criticise his backward way of thinking.

'Many kinds, because I am not only doctor, I am businessman. Most important for me is to build more old people's homes because, uh . . . well, it is not nice to say, but in Japan they are good business. Many citizens are now becoming old and it is making good prospects.'

Yes, maybe you could use your powerful mind technique over their weak, feeble old brains. I didn't reply, and Nori let the silence slip by until he looked over at me and laughed. 'I like you, because you are never looking at your watch,' he said admiringly.

'I don't have a watch,' I said flatly.

'I know,' he laughed, 'and . . . that is why I like you. You are clever I think. Other hostess are always looking at watch and asking to go home. I think they want only to go shopping, or thinking only of money. They cannot be successful, but you can have much success in

Japan. Why don't you open hostess club in Yokohama? You could be Mama-san.'

'Hah, I don't think so.' *Wouldn't Matt be thrilled?* Maybe he could be a waiter. I wondered what had led Nori to this point in his life, where he spent almost every night travelling to Tokyo from Yokohama in his imported Benz to spend hours in Roppongi's hostess clubs and grasp at the spider webs he pretended to see.

Nori wasn't a bad man, just a pitifully lonely one. He'd worked so hard to achieve so much, but his lack of happiness permeated every-thing. Nori claimed that his visits to hostess clubs were only innocent fun, but I was finding that hard to believe. He seemed to think if only he could find a hostess to love him, to move to Yokohama with him, everything would be spectacular.

Nori's belief in this idealised future was a sad skewing of reality, but what I found saddest of all was his predictability. He dropped me off outside my apartment just short of midnight, another crisp *ichiman* in my hand, and I left him to drive back to Yokohama alone, no doubt with crazy visions dancing in his head. We'd do it all again the next time he called. And later so would the next girl. And the next. And the next.

AN AVERAGE NIGHT

Some of the leaves outside our window have started to turn a rusty yellow. A few of them are red. A couple are orange. I rarely look outside during daylight any more. These days I'm rarely awake to look. But today I saw them. Changing.

In the early afternoon Nori called from his hospital to cancel our *dohan*. He wanted to see me, he said, but was too busy to make it. We'd have to reschedule for tomorrow, the last day of the month. He was cutting it close. I needed that *dohan* to meet my quota, and he knew that. But then, the fact that Nori's patient was likely to pass away during the night and required his presence did take precedence over a lousy dinner.

Leaving early for work to escape the claustrophobia of our tiny apartment, I dragged the soles of my shoes along the manicured road, stilettos jammed somewhere in the bag slung across my shoulder.

As twilight fell to be replaced by a familiar artificial glow, I tried to tune out the city's intrusions and think of happy things: blue-skied places, the smell of fresh mountain air, huge bowls of salad and cute puppies stacked high in glass compartments of a pet-shop window. Okay, scratch the last one. It was just one puppy, a hyperactive male chihuahua among an encyclopaedic array of miniature dogs, all depressed, lonely and bored, but loveable and *kawaii* – cute – nonetheless.

Maybe the chihuahua was happy to be worth $3000, or maybe he just hadn't been let in on the secret that everyone else seemed to know, the secret Abie had told me – that he'd be incinerated soon, if no one bought him. All puppies were. Too old? Too big? Burn 'em up, and bring in the cuter ones.

—

Back at work Greengrass was a circus of emotions. Colette was folded into Erma's arms, crying her eyes out. You couldn't blame the girls for being upset, completely lost and utterly bewildered. The culture shock was fairly severe. Hell, even if you *weren't* a Swiss-German who'd just been building schools in an impoverished Third World country, talking bullshit every night in a purple cocktail dress is hard to adjust to.

Nicole, on the other hand, resided at the opposite end of the emotional spectrum. Already a shiny happy person, tonight her lacquer was extra-double coated and freshly applied. She was the embodiment of a burgeoning restaurateur, her passion easily reignited by simple acts such as persuading her favourite customer to take her to Inakaya. It was a juggling act to console Colette while listening to Nicole wish for a generous, wealthy customer who'd want to invest in a Korean BBQ in Israel.

If only she'd been the one to tell Nori of her supposed loneliness, they could be drawing up the plans right now, deciding on the colour scheme so that the menus matched the tiling.

And then there was Abie. Her father had called in a blind rage over an email she'd sent saying that she was thinking of accepting $15,000 from the customer she called Grandpa. In my opinion, it's rarely advisable to mention those things to anyone who's contributed to the composition of your DNA, but maybe Abie was seeking guidance. She got it all right. Among the many things that Father Abie shouted via satellite from half a world away was one bit of ancient wisdom that every one of us here might do well to heed: '*There is no such thing as a free lunch!*'

—

'Chelsea!' Taizo shouted the second he caught sight of me. 'I love you, baby!'

It seemed that tonight the memory of who I was had come back to him. Last week he'd been so drunk I'd had to reintroduce myself.

'Today was day of shareholders meeting, and now finish, with success! Finally I am with no stress for first time in many months. I am so happy. I sing for you, okay?'

I started to crack the karaoke book open when he spouted, '1234-04. Don't worry, I know.' He belted out 'Only Chelsea' to lyrical perfection. Then came the compliments. 'I love your forehead, your big eyes and nose, but *most* your ears and accessories. Totally all of you, so beautiful. I love you. Prease sing Celine Dion.'

'That's not a good idea, Taizo.'

He flicked my earrings, making them sway back and forth. 'Great, great, great! I love you, Chelsea.'

'And I love you, Taizo.'

'God made us,' he sighed, 'Chelsea and Taizo. Let's sing Queen.' But before we could, Nishi arrived to take me away. Taizo shouted out in protest.

'Don't worry, Taizo. I'll be back. You'll be okay.'

I was surprised to find myself seated with three white *gaijin* unaccompanied by Japanese associates. Michelle, Charles and Norman were middle-aged CEO bankers in Tokyo who'd decided to 'do something Japanese for a laugh' and celebrate a company achievement at a hostess club. It was rare to have Westerners in the club, even more so a woman, and as we answered an onslaught of questions about the intricacies of hostessing, I could hear Taizo singing a customised version of 'Bohemian Rhapsody' in the background. I couldn't help but laugh. *Was* this the real life? Or was this just fantasy?

'Is he singing about you?' Charles asked, peering toward Taizo's corner.

'Yeah, we were supposed to sing it together, but I got moved to your table . . .'

'Oh geez, sorry. Gosh. Why don't you go and sing it with him? You can come back when you're done. We don't mind.'

'Uh, it doesn't really work like that. They'll get angry if I leave, but it's okay. I always sit with him. See that one guy, with the longish hair? That's Misaki, Taizo's boss. He owns seventeen companies, and they come here at least two or three times a week.'

'All right. Well then, let's pick a song to sing together. I feel bad for him, although he's got an amazing voice. Where's that karaoke book? Are you any good at Bon Jovi?'

'Are you kidding? Is anyone good at Bon Jovi?' Needless to say, 'It's

My Life' sounded terrible, but every Japanese man in the club applauded the efforts of the fearless *gaijin*. Next up was Michelle singing the Police, but she backed out at the last minute and 'Roxanne' somehow became my responsibility.

'But I don't even know this song!' I panicked.

'Just read from the prompter. That's it!' Norman encouraged. 'You sound just like P. J. Harvey!'

I thought I was aiming for Sting, but I found it somewhat awkward to be singing a song that so obviously reflected Michelle's patronising view of the young women around her. Even though she was experiencing a hostess club first-hand, it seemed she still didn't believe that all we did was have conversation. I think Michelle must have thought there was some perverse sex room out the back.

If she had only isolated the scene from her preconceived ideas, she would have seen that we looked like five normal people enjoying a drink in any bar in the world.

DANGER FACE

'*Denwa bango wa* something-or-other *desu.*' Beep. Beep. Beep. It was the last day of the month, and Nori wasn't picking up. He had promised to help me, so I called back, repeatedly listening to the apologetic tones of the voice that spoke when his voicemail was switched off. Tonight was my last chance for a *dohan* – tomorrow our monthly bonus points would be calculated – and now he was knowingly standing me up. Super.

Once the rain eased to a fine drizzle, I made my way to the tiny East Roppongi apartment that Nicole and Abie shared to show them some abdominal exercises. After weeks of occupational binge drinking and little movement, we were all growing concerned about our waistlines expanding; the girls had even started running up and down the stairwell of their decrepit apartment tower in an effort to exercise.

Two thin futons, a gift from a customer of Nicole's, took up most of the worn-out room, with shoes, luggage and Abie's guitar from Grandpa filling up the rest. A micro-bathroom and playhouse kitchen completed the $1200-a-month apartment. It had been bearable, until the recent arrival of Nicole's friend Stacy from New York, so that now, in a space so small you wouldn't house your dog in it, they were living like three sardines in their own brine. I fully realised just how lucky Matt and I were to have our clean, modern, little abode. At least the state of it somewhat resembled what we were accustomed to at home. Without it I'd have already gone insane.

During a plank demonstration for the *rectus abdominis*, my phone rang briefly and stopped. It was a missed call from Nori, so I called back and waited. *Ring, ring.* '*Denwa bango wa* . . .' The same apologetic tones.

How bizarre. He must have hung up and switched his phone off in less than a minute.

As a last-ditch effort to scrape together a *dohan* I tried Goro, the fashion guy, but he wasn't answering either. Great. I'd been excommunicated, failed to meet the club's two-*dohan* requirement and lost my hard-earned $500 bonus in the process. I wouldn't be happy when Nori decided to resurface.

Ring, ring! This time it was Shin calling to interrupt in the middle of a downward dog, beneficial for the *adductor magnus*. 'Hey, Shin, how are you? What are you doing?'

'I am now taking my cat to my wife's house. My cat cannot stay at home by herself. I go China on 7th, but only chance is today.'

Excuse me, what? Shin had a wife? Why did she have her own house? Was she his ex-wife? Were they separated? His casual indifference caught me completely off guard. It obviously was a non-issue, but I was still shocked. 'Oh, uh . . .' I didn't know what to say.

'What are you doing?' he asked suspiciously. 'Running?'

'No, yoga. I'm at Nicole's apartment. We're doing yoga so that we don't get fat.'

'No choice! It will happen . . . everyone coming to Roppongi is getting fat. Ask Karolina. She knows. Anyway, she is coming tomorrow, so I will see you tomorrow.'

And with that, Shin left me chuckling yet again as he smugly hung up.

—

The reapplication of smudged mascara to inner lashes is a delicate procedure, even when there isn't someone banging at the door of a change room too small to execute a jumping jack in. I narrowly missed an uncomfortable impact as Tehara knocked again, this time more swiftly. 'Chelsea-san,' he announced sternly, 'Ito-san.'

'*What* is he doing here?' I seethed, jerking open the door. 'It's not even nine-thirty!' Tehara shrugged and pushed up his glasses. 'Ooooh, I can't believe it, that lying little jerk!'

According to Nori, he'd forgotten to take his phone to work. It wasn't until 8.00 pm that he'd seen my missed calls and no message. As he explained it, 'I thought, maybe you need my help, and so I came straight here.'

'Why didn't you just call me? You knew that tonight was my last opportunity for a *dohan*. I could have asked someone else, but you promised! And how did you call me earlier, before eight o'clock, when you just hung up? I thought you said you left your phone at home.'

Nori laughed uncomfortably. 'Uh, when? When did I call you? I . . . I don't think so. I could not, my phone was at my home, and I was at my hospital, in Yokohama.'

'Your number came up on my phone, at around six o'clock,' I insisted.

'No, uh, I . . . I . . . uh, I don't think so.' He looked sweaty. Squirming. 'I don't know.' I was about to press further when Nishi interrupted to seat a new Israeli at our table. I didn't know who was more annoyed by her arrival, Nori or I. 'Is it all right that she is sitting with us?' Nori whispered after a particularly ignorant slew of comments from her about how Japanese men 'wasted their money in these places'.

'Of course,' I snapped. 'Why would I care? That's what happens in a hostess club. Girls sit with you.' Nori was visibly put out by my retort, but I didn't care. His lack of acknowledgement for the disservice he'd caused me got on my nerves. So did his singing, every familiar inflection more grating than the last. The only thing that was tolerable about Nori was that just like clockwork, right before he left, he pressed another ¥10,000 into my hand, adding to a slowly accruing stack from the Bank of Ito.

—

He was absolutely adorable. Decked out in black suit pants and a pink shirt, Kazuhiro Kobayashi had dressed for a night on the town. Plump and round right down to his bright, shiny eyeballs, his animated face was accentuated by chipper giggles and outright startling squeaks. Even a chipmunk couldn't have said 'Call me Kozy' any cuter. I wanted to squish him in a huge hug.

Almost immediately after arriving at Greengrass, Kozy had invited me to his apartment for a weekend lunch of *o-kono miyake*, his house speciality and, coincidentally, the only thing he could cook (for everything else, Kozy clarified, he ate out). A veteran bachelor, Kozy lived alone in the Setagaya ward of Tokyo, and although I declined his offer, I agreed to a thumb war to determine whether I'd go to a movie in Shibuya with him. If I lost, I had to go. If I won, I didn't. His thumb was so much fatter than mine. It was an unfair advantage.

'All right, but it has to be a Sunday, and I get to choose the movie.'

'You have some paper for me?'

I handed him a Post-it note from my purse. 'Pen?' I offered, and Kozy squirrelled both away to write furiously before handing back way too much information: his full name, phone numbers (including the area and country codes), three different emails, and his sex – *male*, in case I was wondering. On the flipside he'd written, '*Every Saturdays and Sundays is holiday.*'

'What sort of face do you like?' he asked suddenly, pushing his lips into a pout.

'What do you mean, what sort of face?'

'What . . . sort . . . of . . . face?' he repeated slowly, as if I couldn't understand English. '*Handsome* face,' he said, jutting out his chin and exaggerating the pout, 'or *wild* face?' As Kozy patiently held his features in a mask of 'wild' fury, I realised he was serious. 'What face?' he repeated. '*Danger* face?'

I burst out laughing. 'Danger face? *What on earth* is a danger face?'

'Like this,' he demonstrated, and the only change from '*wild* face' was that his eyes didn't look so crazed. 'Like Bond.'

It took everything I had to pull it together.

'YES! That's it! How did you know? *Most definitely*, a man with a danger face is what I like.'

Kozy puffed up in extreme satisfaction. He was, after all, a man proficient at a danger face. 'And what about body?' he asked. 'Short and round is okay?' I had to strain to hear what he was saying. Bon Jovi had just cut in on the karaoke system and an over-amplified bass line was muffling out Kozy's consonants. I raised my voice to be heard.

'UMM, WELL, NO. THEN I COULDN'T WEAR HEELS, SO I THINK I NEED TO HAVE SOMEBODY *TALL*.'

'*SMALL!*' Kozy shrieked, dropping both hands in a double-barrelled karate chop to rest either side of his masculinity. 'What *PART* small?'

I totally lost it. Kozy was just too much.

TYPHOON #20-SOMETHING

The dream was peaceful. In it I was weightless, suspended in one of those fuzzy, all-embracing states of whacked-out possibility when *RRRING!!!* Everything turned lucid. My eyelids became heavy. My body jerked awake. *Ahem.*

'Hello?' I had no idea what time it was, but a thin plane of sunlight seeping into the darkened room indicated that it was still the middle of my night.

'Hello,' came the familiar voice. 'Were you sleeping?' It was Nori.

'Sleeping? No, I'm not sleeping. I just woke up, but . . .' I slipped quietly into the hallway so that I wouldn't have to whisper. Matt was still asleep. 'Are you in Yokohama?'

'Now yes, I am in Yokohama. Uh, what are you doing tonight?'

'Nothing, I have no plans.' I yawned audibly.

'Okay, uh, that is good. Ummm . . . so I will come to Tokyo and we will go to have a nice dinner somewhere.'

Couldn't he ever leave me alone? I suppose I could say no. However, a free dinner and a guaranteed $100 were well worth a couple of hours of my time.

'Sure, I'm free from now. What time is it?'

'Now it is 3.30. How is 5.30?'

⁓

At 5.23 I was outside, waiting under an alcove to avoid the by-product of Typhoon #20-something as it blew west over the Kanto Plain. Over the course of a year there are so many typhoons that Japanese meteorologists don't bother with personalised names; they stick with sequenced numbers.

Even though this one was mild, it was peak season for cyclonic behaviour and the north-west Pacific was doing its best to pump the suckers out; there had already been three major cyclones since the night that Matt and I had first arrived, bringing torrential rain, pounding waves and ferocious winds to Japan's exposed coastline.

Due to their historical regularity and an average speed of only twenty kilometres per hour, Japanese *taifu* – great wind – are exhaustively documented events, their entire lifespan tracked by an enthusiastic media who issue advance warnings of wind speed, projected course and their impact on public transport. Reporters in bright raincoats stand next to whiplashed trees as waves thrash the shoreline, yelling into weatherproofed microphones while the network cuts to satellite images or a scene of unfortunate office workers caught at the moment their umbrellas are vacuumed inside out. It provides hours of high-drama viewing. You could only imagine the creative bullshit they'd have to spin just to stay on air for so long.

'...*And continuing with the typhoon coverage, it's now just in that Typhoon #18 has caused rain to fall from three directions today, forcing the shinkansen to close temporarily due to gusting winds up to speeds that will dehydrate your eyeballs and rip right through the black dinner coat that Nori bought you in Omotesando, the very one you're wearing right now as a feeble sign of your appreciation, waiting under an alcove . . .*'

I lifted my gaze skyward to watch the rain for precisely seven minutes until Nori pulled up in his glistening white Benz. Even in a typhoon, he was right on time.

'Do you like crab?' Nori grinned as I hurried into the front seat of his car. 'You told to me one time that you like crab, so we will go to Ginza, to one famous restaurant.'

I had *never* told Nori that I liked crab. I'd never *once* eaten it. I think Nori was beginning to confuse my details with those of someone who had already left him behind.

Sometimes, I feel like the exposed coastline.

'When I was a young boy,' Nori mused over a late-night beer, 'Japan was very poor. At that time, one famous writer wrote that Japan would become a great country, but I could not believe that. Not so many people could believe it to be possible. But slowly, when I became older, everything began to change and I came to think maybe . . . that he was right. Japan worked very hard to become successful. Don't you think so?'

'Well, Japan owns half of America and the entire state of Hawaii, doesn't it? So I guess so. Did you know that people call Hawaii the forty-eighth prefecture of Japan?'

'Hah, hah. I think so. And it is nice there, in Hawaii.'

'But how do the Japanese *really* feel about the Americans? Are they angry? Do you resent that they've been in your country ever since the war?'

Just down the street was the New Sanno, a military hotel classed as American soil, and Jodie had told me that when 9/11 happened, she'd been in a bar full of Japanese who'd cheered at the footage of the towers crashing to the ground, yelling, 'Down with America! We hate Bush!' There had to be at least an undercurrent for an entire room full of people to collectively yell such slogans, but if there was, Nori wasn't aware or, perhaps more accurately, he wasn't telling.

'I think if Japan had not attacked Pearl Harbor, we would not have suffered through the war, but at that time it was government decision only, of soldier and military. It was not the feeling of the people. They were very silly government, and I think most Japanese people are thinking this. It was mistake. Old people are not angry . . . I don't think so.'

'The Americans are. My dad used to fly the German, American and Japanese flags on his property, but he had to take down the Japanese one because so many Americans complained. They hated the Japanese – they came right out and said it. Their friends had died. Pilots had come crashing out of the sky. Why did the Japanese have kamikaze pilots?'

'I do not know the military strategy behind such a decision at that time, but I think kamikaze were not bad. It is important to know the meaning of kamikaze before you can understand them. For the Japanese, this word does not mean suicide pilot. We call them "*tokkoutai*" and kamikaze is "god-wind". This is from a famous story, when seven hundred years ago the famous Mongolian conqueror Khan came with a vast army across the sea to invade Japan. They came in so many ships with thousands of men, but as they approached, a great typhoon appeared. It swept them back out to sea and caused many damages, forcing the warrior Khan to return to his country. But the Mongols would not give up, and they came again with more ships, but again the great winds of the typhoon appeared to keep them away, and they too were destroyed, and they did not try again. It is Japanese belief that the divine wind was sent by the sun goddess and the storm god, and it was they who were protecting Japan, and the Mongols could not conquer the great Japan.

'It is my feeling that this is why kamikaze pilot were not so bad. They were military men who dedicated their lives to the emperor and their honour to their country, but inside their head, maybe they are thinking only of mothers and wives, and they sacrificed their own life to protect their family. Maybe this was true reason for them to commit the suicide, but . . .' Nori trailed off and smiled meekly. He sipped at the froth of his beer.

'Uh, this weekend, Fumio will come to Tokyo, and with his hostess friend we will go to special places in Asakusa. Then you can eat eel and we will go to Akihabara, because I remember that you told to me you want to buy a Japanese computer, and I will present you with one, if you want. Have you found out about your working-holiday visa?'

'Yeah, I looked it up on the internet. You have to apply from outside Japan, so maybe I'll apply when I get to Vancouver,' I fibbed. I really had no intention of coming back. 'It can take up to four weeks, and since I'm going home for Christmas anyway, the visa would be ready by the time I wanted to leave.'

'Okay, this is a good plan for you,' Nori smiled, raising his beer to toast an imaginary future. I started to raise my glass of water in cheers, but he quickly recoiled.

'No, no, no,' he hissed. 'You must never do *kampai* with water!'

'Why not?' I'd met with this same unexplained reaction at Green-grass before.

'This is one more thing I did not tell you about kamikaze. Because the pilots still had to fly many miles to their destination, they made a toast of *kampai* only with water to honour the success of their last flight. It is reserved only for people who make suicide pact.'

—

I'd never known a doctor to pre-emptively diagnose a patient and then pay them in cash to implement the corresponding medical advice, but as I grabbed my purse to prepare to run through the rain into the lobby of my building just short of midnight, Nori handed over two *ichiman* bills. 'It is my present to you. Earlier, you told to me that you do not want to get fat in Japan, so tomorrow you can go to gym,' he smiled. 'For good health.'

Matt and I decided that he should go to the gym instead. He was becoming listless with the predictability of his job but, more importantly, could fit a few workouts into his life. As long as he occasionally brought in a new girl, nothing much was expected of him. Matt was enjoying Tokyo. He didn't have multiple men talking nonsense in his ear night after night. He only had me, regurgitating each development in my ongoing saga.

By now Matt was almost as familiar with the regulars as I was. He'd laugh at the latest parables from Shin – whom he'd dubbed Tao Te Shin after one of China's most ancient texts – and pull faces at Nori's increasing desperations. He'd actively listen, throw back some male perspective and curl around me as we went to bed. Yet still I could never fall asleep right away. The ceiling was becoming much too familiar.

MELTDOWN

I cannot deal with this shit. Tomorrow I am leaving. Gone. I will tell Nishi that I'm quitting tonight, cut my losses and fly out on the next available plane. I cannot take it any longer. Why the *fuck* did I think it was okay to be here, that it was even a good idea? How could I possibly have thought that I could pretend normalcy in such an insane environment? No one should ever come to this place.

Last night I discovered that Greengrass is the very same club where Lucie Blackman was working when she disappeared only three years ago and, as if in a vacuum, I suddenly ceased to be Alice skipping through a metaphorical wonderland, whistling gaily in her powder-blue dress. No. I became a cold skeleton, raped and murdered and left in pieces.

Lucie had done nothing wrong. She had only done what I had done – got into the car of a slightly eccentric, middle-aged Japanese man, and she just happened to meet him where I now worked. It was the very same room. The very same karaoke books. The very same low tables around which she would have held the very same ridiculous conversations.

She'd met the man who'd killed her there, and no one had bothered to tell me. Greengrass was Casablanca rechristened, as if it were just that easy, like planting seed above a grave to grow something green and mask the fact that death had occurred, that murder lay below.

Nishi had known Lucie. Some of the current customers must have met her. They *must* have. And although all of them were wary of the situation, warning new hostesses of the dangers, the entire thing was just so ominous that out of necessity it had become trivialised.

I felt like one of those geeky storm chasers, caught smack bang in the middle of a fucking tornado, only by fault of their own over-excitement and miscalculation. Was I advocating the circumstances that had led to this poor girl's fate by working as a hostess myself? Or should I see it for what it was: an isolated tragedy that could occur anywhere, regardless of environment?

I didn't know what to think, and the only way I could cope was by switching it off completely. But that wasn't what bothered me most. It was the tiny things; the imperceptible scratches that had silently built up and suddenly turned to a deep, dark chasm.

I cried my eyes out before I left for work, sobbing for my total lack of comprehension, for everything that was so . . . unbalanced. The deception, the lies, the pervasive sexual innuendo, all held together under a thin veil of smoke.

Matt was sympathetic, but he didn't have to experience any of those things. He only saw the show-reel Roppongi. The bright lights. The good times. I had to deal with things that belonged in a seedy thriller, not the daily workings of my life.

I was worried – alarmingly worried – not so much at the ease with which the Japanese men accepted my make-believe, but the ease with which I slipped so languidly into it. Sometimes. Other times it was the hardest thing in the world, to maintain the illusion that you were . . . well, what the hell were you? I had no idea.

If I knew, it would be simple. Maybe then I could classify emotions into spectral lines to at least come up with a visible wavelength, but how *then* do you examine micro-elements in an experiment conducted entirely under pretence? There was no control group. There was just a never-ending procession of men who, without meaning to, sucked the life out of you, paid for it by the hour and then came back for more. But what happened when it was all gone? And where was it coming from in the first place? What exactly *were* you giving them? Where was the line between being a human being and being a rip-off artist? And at what point do you start to believe your own hype?

At some point when I wasn't looking, my mind had begun to change, and not to my liking. Surrounded by an ostentatious show of wealth in which hundreds and thousands of yen were thrown around like mere pennies, my concept of money had been hijacked. I was beginning to idolise it. I hadn't yet been manipulative in extracting it, but there was the possibility. It was too comfortable being handed things on a silver platter for no reason. I needed reasons, but everywhere I looked there were only more questions.

Nori Ito was a nutcase. He was a *surgeon*. The man owned a hospital. He was responsible for hundreds of staff and thousands of patients, yet his consuming priority was foreign hostesses. And it wasn't just me. I knew there'd been others before me, one after the other. How much thought had they given to how they impacted on the lonely lives around them? How much of a thought *should* be given to that? The flip side was that these men needed us, many of them, as much as we needed them.

Nori had told me that he knew the game, it didn't affect him, but he had already proved himself wrong. Nori's mind was stuck deep on the same old track, scratchily playing it over and over again, every three months or however long his latest hostess happened to last. He couldn't help it; the pattern was too deeply ingrained.

So what was this place? Transsexuals across the hall. Russians upstairs. Yakuza driving by in Phantoms while Nigerians hustled you on the street. Roppongi might have meant *six trees*, but for me it was better translated as *three vertical blocks of drugs and sex and money that sucked people in, chewed them up and spat them out.*

I'd thought I could walk right in, but my life was in polar reversal. Sleeping as the sun came up, rising when it fell. Breathing in absurdity. Drowning in a sense of meaninglessness. I was exhausted. Bottomed out. Game over. And I couldn't leave. If I'd been just another one of the girls, I would have bought the next plane ticket back to reality. But I needed to know. If this was a normal reaction, what happened on the other side?

Matt was completely supportive. If I thought I couldn't handle it any more, he said, we could leave.

'Maybe you should just take it easy for a while,' Matt said. 'Don't go out with them so often. Come home after work. You don't have to try to do so much. Enough happens at your club anyway. Don't you think?'

Maybe Matt was right. It was only conversation, hollow words dropped into empty wells. It should be easy. But it wasn't. I'd seen enough pictures of babies and wives, ferrets and toy dogs to make me sick. I wanted to vomit all over them. I'd grimaced through more karaoke than a person should ever be exposed to. And God, the alcohol. I didn't drink when I came here. I *wasn't* going to drink when I came here. But now I'm a working alcoholic. It's bloody fantastic.

THE REAPPEARANCE OF SUPERMAN

It's been nearly a week since I melted to a liquid pile on the floor. Things have improved, but I still struggle. Daily. It's not so easy to numb yourself enough to be able to smile convincingly when someone light-heartedly promises you the world and its moon every day of the week. At least Nori hadn't called in four days. That was ninety-six hours, and I was counting them with relief.

Everyone who came into Greengrass in that time was decent, intelligent and polite, even if their names refused to stick, like worn-out magnets falling from the refrigerator door. K. A. Missing letter. U. O . . . 'Thanks for coming!' But it didn't matter. I wouldn't see most of them again.

During the week Taizo came in twice with the big boss, Misaki, and we sang all our usuals. On account of no longer giving a shit, I increased in volume from backup singer to shared lead vocals on 'Bohemian Rhapsody', but Taizo still drowned me out.

I am always happy with Taizo. We have fun. He never tries to pinch me. I never have to slap him. To think about it, most days since I arrived have been full of Japanese men like Taizo – hard-working, committed individuals with a brain and a soul – but in my attempt to adjust to it all I'd been overwhelmed by the whacky ones.

Jodie reassured me that my reaction was natural: the one-month benchmark. At least for those who lasted that long.

I certainly had no inclination to adopt this maniacal way of life as my own. I had to remember that. This was just an experiment. If I had to attune myself to this existence for any longer than three months I'd implode, or self-destruct – I don't know which would happen first. I am still completely baffled that Japanese women cope with this as an extended vocation, but then, they'd grown up in this culture. They understood the dynamics. Not me. I had a hard time perpetuating lies, however white they were, night in and night out, face in and face out.

But yet, *something* had shifted, and I couldn't quite attribute it to any one thing. It had nothing to do with Matt. He was the E to my mc², the unfailing constant in my life. The only shift in Matt was that as I struggled to cope, he was taking on ever more dimensions: Foosball of Stress Relief; Stand-up Comedian; Anchor Scraping the Bottom of a Salty Sea of Tears.

Matt was instrumental to my sanity, but this recent, almost imperceptible change was entirely apart from him, as if a thirteenth light bulb had switched on in a small room of twelve, and I was the only one to notice. I don't know. I can't explain it. There's no reason why this faint 'something' had to come to be just at the point when I was ready to pack it in. There must have been a thousand triggers. But whatever had caused it, I started to feel a calm within the chaos, an acceptance of the dichotomy and a peace that remained a mystery.

After that, everything was okay. As okay as it could be.

~

Nishi had a little problem with the bottle. It wasn't his fault – perhaps the affliction was inextricably linked to his job – but every night as time progressed so too did Nishi's level of inebriation. And thus, it was probably inevitable that I was going to leave perplexed when I was called to sit with him one night at the powwow table.

'You have business to make,' Nishi began with a rasp. 'Chelsea is young girl, I know ... so young. Maybe you stay six months,' he mused, imploring me with his gently comical features, 'make more business.'

'Six months is way too long, Nishi. I'd never survive.'

Nishi's head bobbed up and down silently as he laughed. 'Yes, but prease remember, private life and business *separate*. Berry important. You have many Japanese friends,' he mumbled with a lopsided smile. 'Prease, you make more business.'

'Uh . . .' *Oh-kay. What did he mean by that?*

At a loss for words I simply shook Nishi's hand and rejoined the Israelis on the couch. Tonight we had a new addition to our hostess mafia. Sara, who was modest and demure, but golden and bright, had recently deserted a short-held post at a Roppongi strip club after workplace relations turned out to be much more than she expected. Prior to coming to Tokyo Sara had never stripped in her life, but when she'd arrived looking for a hostess job, she'd been enticed by the outrageous sums of money promised to her by a Nigerian selling the idea of 'only dancing in your G-string, like this,' which Sara demonstrated with a cute wiggle of the hips. However, our kind Nigerian friend failed to mention that not only is stripping in Japan a full-contact sport above the waist, but also apparently having shots poured over your breasts and sucked off your nipples by strange Japanese men is as commonplace as the gyrations to be overheard in the dark quarters where much more than private dances went on. Since it turned out that there was a time limit on how long one could get away with only wiggling one's hips in such an environment, Sara made the decision that she was *not* willing to go there.

Once Sara had purged her tales of sleaze, she felt at home at Greengrass; we were all friendly and clothed, and the club was free of the backstabbing and customer-stealing tactics that were rife in big clubs like Jack's, where cliques and conniving bitchiness were to be expected.

—

Karolina, Shin's favourite hostess, was back at Greengrass briefly, and we were talking about Shin's peculiarities when he walked through the door. Stopping to raise his right hand towards us, he smiled serenely and then sauntered after Tehara to his usual table by the wall until Karolina and I were brought to join him.

'So, today is last chance for me to see Karolina . . .' Shin began.

'Because I'm flying home in two days,' Karolina interrupted.

'Yes, I know!' Shin scowled at her, forcing breath out of his nostrils before turning to me and letting out a chuckle. 'She will cry, like baby, but I go China tomorrow, so now maybe is last chance. I should have stayed at home, and sleep, but then maybe she will be angry with me and call to wake me up and shout! She is so *noisy*!'

At some point Shin called for a goodbye song, and while he quivered with moist eyes through 'Sayonara Song' in Japanese, Karolina reciprocated as a sub-par Bono with 'With or Without You'. Then the earthquake hit. Suddenly.

Its first movement shunted the entire building left, *BANG*, and everyone looked with silly human instinct to see who could have pushed with such force. Then, *BANG*, the room slammed violently to the right and Shin grabbed my hand. After that the shaking started, shifting the tower of concrete and steel a foot in either direction. Back and forth. Back and forth. Faster and faster. I squeezed Shin's hand tightly. *Oh God, oh God, oh God.* I began to hyperventilate. I couldn't shut my eyes. Some people couldn't stop singing, or drinking or laughing, as if nothing out of the ordinary was happening, but I was frozen, waiting for the sky to fall, back and forth, back and forth, to the ground. Until it just stopped. Shin placed my palms together and closed his hands over mine. 'It's okay,' he said softly. 'It's okay.'

I could see Karolina laughing hysterically at the next table. She thought it was a riot, but I could feel tears threatening to overflow, and it didn't help when Shin said that this was the biggest quake he'd felt since he could remember.

'But it is okay. Not danger. This earthquake moving *side* way, it's okay. Not up and down one. Up and down one is dangerous. Maybe, this one level 4, but up and down, maybe you need only level 2, or level 3, then building fall down. But,' he added with a reassuring grin, 'not so common.'

—

Nishi came to move me without explanation. In the dark corner there was only an empty seat, an open pack of cigarettes and a tall glass of whisky. In isolation, none of these inanimate objects could have foreshadowed just who was to saunter out of the men's room, in slick suit, crisp shirt and Armani tie, but somehow I knew it would be him. My stomach fluttered when I saw him. It had been three weeks since we'd first met, three weeks full of new meetings with new faces, but somehow his magnets were all still intact. I could see them clearly. Blue letter Y, orange letter O, green S, yellow H, red letter I.

'Why are you here?' he barked. 'I didn't request you!'

'It's nice to see you again too, Yoshi.'

Yoshi sat. Then Yoshi fumed. He refused my hand, lit his own cigarette and pulled the pin on an explosion of heated complaints about my audacity for not meeting him for dinner all those weeks ago. I was bemused.

'I have been back from Chicago already two weeks, Tonight I was at a business party, with fifteen hundred people. I *hate*. Talking bullshit, yuuh, fuckin' this, fuckin' that. What do I care? "Go away!" I say. I don't care about them.'

It went on this way for two whiskies, until Yoshi's complaints curved unexpectedly into a hard-line pitch for my long-term affections.

'You will be my girlfriend. I am a sleazebag, I told you. At work I am all business: fuckin' *how are you?* Rah, rah, rah. I am professional bull-shitter. On my own time, I am bad boy. But for you,' he winked. 'I'll be good.'

Yoshi waved away my attempt to light another cigarette and continued in French. 'Oh my God, I love short hair. The first time I saw you, *wow*. Nishi said, "I know, your kind of girl." *S'il vous plaît, ma chérie.* Tell me. If I am a good boy, do I have a chance?'

'*On ne sait jamais,*' I answered ambiguously – you never know – and Yoshi took it how he wanted.

'Ahhh, okay,' he smiled, 'I am happy. We will go to small island, and then, at the membership hotel . . .' I leant over to straighten Yoshi's collar as he described the Italian restaurant on the marina, and he suddenly forgot how to speak. 'I forgot what I was saying.'

'You were talking about the small island,' I said softly.

'Oh yeah,' he grinned. 'Small island. Party time. Where else you wanna go? Europe? We'll go there. I'll take you to Côte d'Azur, Venice, we'll ride in a gondola, and then you'll have to fall in love with me. It will be impossible not to, and when you come back, you will see, you'll be my girlfriend. I'll try my best. So what you want for the small island? Ganga? Coke? Whatever you want, I can get it. What you want?'

'I want my own bed,' I said sternly. 'I'll go with you to your small island, okay, and we'll have a *civilised* time, but I won't sleep with you. It's not gonna happen. Got it?'

'Oh, I know,' Yoshi cooed. 'You are not an easy girl. I can get easy girls, but it's no fun. I just go to the bar. Ukrainian. Russian. Latvian. They're all fuckin' easy. But all they want is money. It's not my style. I am *not* your sugar daddy.'

'I know you're not. You didn't bring me diamonds.'

'*Pffff*. Diamonds. Am I just another fucking customer? A customer!' Yoshi huffed, and I deflected him by saying, 'You like jazz, right?' but it riled him even more.

'Of course! C'mon, last time we talked about fucking B. B. King, and you already fuckin' forgot! Fuck off.' Yoshi crossed his arms and the fuming recommenced.

'Okay, fine.' I sat back and peacefully waited for the steam to evaporate. Several minutes of silence passed until Yoshi looked sheepishly towards me. I stared back coldly and his look changed to defiance. '*What?*' he snapped.

'You went crazy.'

'I told you, I didn't request you. I went to the toilet and they just sat you here. Before, I don't want to fuckin' see you. *Ever*. Then I come back from the toilet and see you, sitting here, and I change my mind. I am looking for a woman like you. Luxurious, and with grace, but also, some of this.' Yoshi stuck his nose in the air. 'Like a snob. That's you. "*Oh, oh! I am sleeping,*"' he mocked. 'ONE time I ask. Never two times. Okay, fuck off. Two times! "*Tomorrow sleeping, oh I'm so busy.*" C'mon! Don't bullshit me. Someone does that to me I say no way, don't waste my time.'

'I'm sorry. It was the truth, Yoshi. It was my first week here and I was a wreck. You think this is easy to get used to?' Yoshi evaluated my eyes for an answer. It really was the truth.

He unfolded his arms. 'Can I call you tomorrow?'

'What time?' I asked coquettishly. I couldn't help but bait him.

'I DON'T KNOW! You're the one who's sleeping. One o'clock?'

'Better make it two,' I grinned.

'Okay, three. I will make reservations to go to the small island Sunday. Do you know Odaiba? We'll go from there, at ten o'clock. No, better make it nine. I'll check the weather. I'll check the marine charts. I'll take care of everything, no problem. I'll just tell my useless secretary what to fucking do.'

'You really are too much, Yoshi. You know that, don't you? You'll have to excuse me. I need to visit the ladies' room.' And with that I escaped.

Inside the change room the lights were brighter, and away from Yoshi I could breathe out long enough to clear my head. Had I just agreed to go overnight to a private membership island with him? Ridiculous. How much had I had to drink already? Was he serious? God, where was my eyeliner?

Just as I was rifling through my purse for the kohl black, Nori dialled from his home in Yokohama, anxious to know if I was all right after the recent earthquake.

'I was at my hospital when it happened,' he breathed heavily, 'and I thought that maybe you were afraid, but I could not call to you until now, and I am sorry. Are you sure you are okay? I think maybe not, so I will come to Tokyo now, to see you.'

Great. The last thing I needed was for Nori to get the idea that he was my protector or in any way responsible for my emotional well-being. That would be disastrous. I had to persuade him not to come – it would take too long to get here; it was way past midnight already – Nori was practically out the door before I finally dissuaded him. I shook my head and retraced the smudge along my outer eyelid.

By the time I finally returned to Yoshi, I was amused to see I'd been replaced by none other than Mama-san herself, during one of her sporadic visits. Usually cutting a stoic figure at the bar, at Yoshi's side she'd morphed into a girlish hostess. Thinking I was still unnoticed, I started to shimmy my way around the table when ... *WHAP!* I almost heard the noise before I felt the sting. Without even breaking conversation, Yoshi had slapped me hard across the ass. He didn't even look. Mama-san didn't flinch. But I did.

'Yoshi! What THE FUCK are you doing? Don't you dare think you can do that to me, do you understand? What did you do that for?' I was so incensed I didn't even bother to lower my voice. A Japanese customer whipped around to stare. Screw propriety.

'*Chelsea!*' Yoshi shrugged charmingly, looking surprised. 'Because I like you.'

'Fuck off. Then why did you slap me on the ass?'

'I thought you'd like it.'

'I *don't*. Do it one more time and I'll never speak to you again.'

Yoshi laughed indignantly, and I abruptly changed the subject. 'So, did you feel the earthquake earlier?'

'Nah, c'mon,' he drawled. 'What earthquake? Who fucking cares?' Then Mama-san giggled at something he said, and they both looked at me in expectation. '*Wakatta*, right?'

My Japanese wasn't that good, so I coolly answered, '*Wakarimasen*.' *I don't understand.* This got a delighted laugh out of Mama-san and a sharp huff out of Yoshi, who abruptly signalled her to leave by requesting she fetch me a new drink.

'So, Miss Chelsea, when did you break up with your last boyfriend?'

'Which one?' I played along. Matt had superseded the boyfriend title three years ago.

'The last one. I don't fuckin' know. When were you in Australia?'

'Two months ago. Can I try some of that?' I pointed to Yoshi's whisky and he slid his glass across. I took a sip and screwed up my face. He poured half into my water glass and suddenly that was what I was drinking.

'Humph. When I met you, I'd just broken up with my Australian girlfriend. We were together fifteen months. I never cheat. But the past is the past. I don't fuckin' care,' Yoshi grinned, taking a plentiful gulp of whisky. 'Only the present, and the future will come.' *What a romantic philosopher.* I rolled my eyes and Yoshi smoothed down a piece of my hair. 'Can I ask you a question? Do you like sex?'

'Yoshi,' I said flatly, 'you asked me that last time. Do I look like a nun to you? What kind of a question is that?' I unconsciously crossed my arms.

'Okay, okay. I wasn't sure if you were celibate or some shit.'

'No, I'm not celibate, but I'm not gonna sleep with you. Ever. That's an insult.'

Yoshi narrowed his eyes until they almost disappeared altogether. 'I know,' he retorted icily. 'I told you, I can get Russians.'

—

Six or seven whiskies and an indeterminate period of time later, Yoshi and I were still slinging each other hot potatoes when he finally decided to leave, but not before his black Amex made a casually eloquent appearance, slid from his wallet long enough for me to see it and then regloved in favour of a Visa. What was that old adage about a man of true wealth never *speaking* but always *showing* it? That was Yoshi. Soon he was lifting me in a drunken spin outside the elevator, and as I landed I told him to call me, although he was too fixated on three impeccably dressed Japanese women giggling their way into the lady-boys' club across the hall to notice. It was a relief when the elevator doors finally closed.

Dear God. What was I getting myself into? Preposterous trips to a small membership island. The Côte d'Azur. Venice. Dinner. Extravagant offers from customers were fairly standard, but Yoshi made them far more tangible than the usual make-believe.

Yoshi was too much to handle with indifference. Not only was he way too much fun, he was also gravitationally attractive, and oh, that other thing. You see, someone like Yoshi does not just invite you on his boat to a private island without a thought, but at the same time it's not really that big a deal to him. Not when he can buy a Lear jet with a black credit card that once only Michael Jackson was rumoured to have possessed before it became a commonplace, by-invitation-only acqui-sition of the gazillionaire's boys' club. Often this sort of accessory tends to change things. Fundamental things. Like judgement. Trust. The volume of a little red man who sits on your shoulder. But often they change nothing at all.

Oh, and Nishi confirmed it. Yoshi *had* requested me. Specifically. He'd paid $295 just to ask me out.

DOHAN WITH YOSHI

The next day I answered a call from Yoshi at ten to six, just as the molecular structure of my instant coffee was rearranging itself in the microwave. 'You were meant to call three hours ago,' I scolded gently.

'Hel-lo *ma chérie*! How are you? You were sleeping three hours ago, and I am nice boy, so I let you sleep. I made all the reservations – for small island. I even booked a special suite for you, since you need your own bed, right?'

'Right. But what about the typhoon that's coming?'

'Typhoon? Nah, don't worry about it. By Sunday it will pass. We can take my boat from Odaiba no problem, and you can have clear skies. Otherwise, if the ocean is still stormy we can drive one hour and take a ferry to the island instead, because you don't wanna die young, right? We'll see what happens. Where do you live?'

'Hiroo.'

'Okay, I'll pick you up outside Hiroo Citibank. You know it? Next to Meidi-ya supermarket. I'll call you on Sunday at 9.15, maybe nine o'clock. You better not be sleeping, or I'll fucking kill you. *Hello this is Yoshi* . . . WAKE UP!'

Matt threw a look sideways as I hung up in disbelief. This Sunday. That was three days away.

'What's happening?'

'Yoshi's actually serious about that trip to the small island. He wants to go this Sunday. We're going to take his boat from Odaiba. He's made the reservations today and booked a suite so I can have my own room and everything,' I laughed in shock. 'Can you believe it?'

'I don't think you should go,' Matt said immediately. 'The situation's out of your control. I don't want to have to say "*I told you so*". What good would that be? Then I'd have to kill a Jap . . .' he paused, 'and we'd have to leave Japan.'

'*Pffff*, *c'mon*.' I rolled my eyes and opened the microwave with a ding. 'It'll be good for the book. You haven't got anything to worry about.'

'It's not *you* I'm worried about,' Matt countered, and the conversation ended there.

Whatever. The small island was just a weekend trip, and Yoshi was just a big talker. It was hardly going to come to *that*.

—

Twenty-three hours later I heard the faint jingle of my phone above the constant battery of rain on my clear plastic umbrella. I picked up the call.

'Hello, how are you?' Yoshi cooed. 'I just finished at the office, and tonight I am free, so you wanna go for dinner? I'll pick you up, from anywhere you want.'

One hour later Yoshi pulled up outside the Grand Hyatt and I ran through a sheath of rain to sink into the passenger seat of a luxurious silver Benz. Yoshi flashed his Rolex at me. 'Sorry,' he shrugged in apology. 'The fucking traffic. The typhoon. Whatta can I do? *Vous êtes très belle ce soir*. So *ma chérie*, what you wanna eat?'

'Anything but Chinese. And not Japanese,' I quickly added.

Yoshi glanced at me and cracked up. 'Okay, maybe later. You are a funny woman, but I know, I know,' he patted me on the knee. 'Now just friends. How about Italian?'

'Sounds delicious.'

'I know a good place. A little place, but a good place. My favourite.'

—

Tonight, Yoshi was in Prada. Freshly shaven, he was smooth like a martini, his dark eyes sparkling, crisp like the Campari-grapefruit held between my fingers. *Cling!* 'To our first date.'

If that's what he wanted to call it. I was more inclined to call it a professional game of cat and mouse, but when the nuances were almost identical, why bother to protest? It was easy to remain elusive if you said little and revealed even less, and easier still if you just let Yoshi do the talking. The only hard part was trying to ignore the heat of his gaze. Even across a dinner table, *that* was far too personal.

Since Yoshi had first come to this little Italian restaurant twenty years ago with his father, he'd ordered the exact same thing. I'd been a one-year-old in nappies when the waiter had first described the entrées to him one by one. Yoshi would have been hard pressed to discuss Vivaldi and Chopin with me back then, or gush about how everyone was so jealous of him because I was so gorgeous, but he probably would have paid the same attention when I requested him to make a selection – *without* meat – for me: his first choice was *carpaccio*.

While Yoshi might be a little negligent towards others – endangering the lives of pedestrians with his U-turns, shouting at old women on crosswalks about whether they wanted to die young and parking with hazards only feet from the door – in the department of himself he was a perfectionist. Even his name meant '*the best*', '*number 1*' or '*the greatest*', all definitions that Yoshi had taken great care to typify in his forty-something years, cultivating an admirable cultural sheen and incredible intelligence. Behind this alluring facade, Yoshi was also an acute businessman. He was CEO of his family's international empire, or, as he liked to put it, 'the Boss', and along with the duties appointed to him as *chonan* he'd inherited the obligation to live in Tokyo and mastermind the millions while his younger brother had the leisure of living in Huntington Beach and running a subsidiary office to the sounds of a Pacific shore break.

It was hard not to fall for Yoshi's magnetic personality. I even found his negligence oddly charming, because it sprang from a need to put himself first when so much of his identity seemed to be for the benefit of others. It was that fracture that made you *like* Yoshi. He overflowed with charisma, but it couldn't mask a certain sadness. It made my heart go out to him.

As we sipped at Chianti Classico, he professed, '*Au futur*. I have found my star, *mon étoile*.' He pulled me in. He made me laugh. He treated me like a princess, and even though that was no different from the majority of my customers, Yoshi's intentions seemed authentic. There was too much weight in his words. He was too well travelled, too highly educated and too – dare I say it – un-Japanese to take lightly. With other men, it was their very *Japanese*-ness that kept the absurdity of the illusory hostess club alive. If Yoshi and I had been dining in New York, I might have been listening to his enticements very differently, but here in Tokyo I had to actively remind myself that he was just a customer, and that I was just his hostess.

By the time dessert arrived, it was 8.30 pm, and Yoshi had still given me no indication whether this was going to be a *dohan*.

'Have we got time for a drink somewhere?'

'I don't know, that depends. Are you coming to the club with me?'

'Of course, *ma chérie*,' he cooed, like it was the most natural thing to presume of him in the world. The *non*-sugar daddy. The non-customer.

'Then we have until 9.30. I have to call Nishi.'

—

Ring, ring! Ring, ring! 'Hello, Nishi? This is Chelsea. I'll be in at 9.30 tonight, okay? I'm on a *dohan*,' I explained, 'with Yoshi.'

Nishi gasped in surprise, '*Yoshi?*' but Yoshi interrupted, grabbing the phone away.

'He doesn't believe you. *Nishi-san! Hai, hai, Yoshi desu,*' and the two of them made small talk before the phone was tossed back into my lap. 'Hah! Mr Nishi cannot believe it. Never before *dohan* for me. You are so special, *ma chérie*. It is first time for you.'

Sure it was. Yoshi's marketing strategy was flawless. He knew every angle to play, exactly what to say and when to say it. It was maddening. How could you argue with a trip to a private island called the Grand XIV, Marine & Thalasso Resort? Yoshi had brought me the heavy-papered brochure – all sumptuous suites, fine dining and a beauty spa at which he'd already booked me in for a half-day treatment. The pictures showed views of Mt Fuji, wide-open ocean and small yachts leaving white brushstrokes in the jewel-blue water. Everything was perfect, but for some reason you just couldn't believe it.

—

Yoshi left his Benz parked in a fine drizzle and ran ahead to hold open the door to the Hobgoblin, a Roppongi pub brimming with an evening crowd that was almost exclusively *gaijin*. 'What you drinking, baby? Milk?' he teased, and I searched for a table under the lustful gaze of Englishmen who made Yoshi walk even prouder than before.

'Yeah actually, good idea, Yosh. Baileys and milk please.'

'*Humph*. You've got an answer for everything,' Yoshi puffed, and as he strode like a peacock to the bar, I checked my phone. There were two missed calls from Nori. *Shit*. I hadn't heard from him in a week and he had to pick tonight of all nights. It was already nine o'clock and he'd probably shown up to the club wondering where I was. I had to call him or he'd be angry, so once Yoshi returned with the drinks and disappeared to the men's room, I quickly dialled his number. *Please don't let Nori be at Greengrass*, I thought. Luckily he wasn't, but he did want to know why I wanted to know whether he was or not.

'Are you on *dohan*?' Nori inhaled sharply.

'Yes, I am, but . . .'

'Oh, I . . . uh, I see.' Nori sounded utterly betrayed. 'And that is why you are not at the club, because you are with another customer, on *dohan*. Where are you?' he demanded.

'Look, Nori, that doesn't matter. You know it's just part of my job. It doesn't mean anything. I have to go on *dohans* to make points, remember? I know that you know that, so please, don't be angry with me.' There was a long pause on Nori's end of the line.

'Okay,' he sighed heavily. 'Now maybe I will come into the club then, to see you.'

'Maybe? Umm, all right, but can you please come later, in an hour or so? I'll still be on *dohan*. He has to bring me into Greengrass and I don't want to – it might be difficult . . .'

'Okay, I will come.' Nori repeated. I could just imagine his sulking face and that silly bouffant hair.

'Yes, but later. Promise?'

'Uh, yes. I promise.' There was a strange tone in Nori's voice. 'Later, when you are free. I understand.' He hung up just as Yoshi returned.

'Hah, hah. Look, *ma chérie*. Everyone is looking at me because they wonder why I can have such a gorgeous girl. I never go on stupid *dohan*, but for you I don't mind. Anything for you. Everything for you. I don't want others, and I am not curious. Tomorrow, I will only be sleeping. Nothing else to do but see you. I am falling in love. This feeling for me I haven't had for so long. You have such grace,' he whispered softly.

See what I mean? Yoshi had practised his lines.

—

Twenty minutes later Nishi had barely seated me next to Yoshi at a table near the liquor cabinet when Nori came padding through the door clutching his doctor's satchel – decidedly earlier than promised. Nori's eyes darted menacingly across the room at Yoshi and lingered there unnoticed before he reluctantly allowed Nishi to seat him around the corner, out of view. But not for long. Soon Nori was up and dancing with Abie, something he rarely did, and not much later Soh, the Burmese waiter, was transferring me to his table. Nori was smug when I sat next to him. 'Is that your *dohan*?' he clipped.

'That's my friend, Nori, and none of your business. Why did you come so early?'

'Uh, I want to see you. I have the computer, in my car,' Nori smiled as he happily patted me on the knee. So this was blackmail. *What a tricky little toddler.* 'I am so happy to see you. This Sunday, Fumio will come with us to Asakusa, and then we will go to the eel restaurant, and you can see many places, in Tokyo . . .'

'Um, I'm not going to be able to go to Asakusa on Sunday, Nori. I've got other plans already. I'm sorry. I haven't heard from you all week, so I thought we weren't going.' The unexpected news dropped Nori's jaw. His chest deflated – in karaoke language you could say he was *shot through the heart* – but before I had to suffer the inevitable reaction, Soh was back to switch me to Yoshi. The next time I bounced back to Nori, he stiffly announced that he had to go, paid his $500 bill and glumly allowed me to escort him out with hardly a word.

Left alone in the corridor, I was suddenly struck with unexpected remorse for having just slain Nori's expectations. He was my regular, high-paying customer, and despite the dark idiosyncrasies that occasionally bubbled to the surface, we got along well. Plus, even though Nori hadn't given it to me tonight for obvious reasons, he had *actually* brought me the laptop computer I'd asked for, which wasn't exactly something I wanted but more of an exercise in whether he'd really do it, and I felt bad for that. Nori's shortcomings were juvenile, but he was an intelligent, generous man. Was I in the wrong, or was this abrupt interaction simply a misunderstanding? I had to question that, and I might have thought about it longer if I hadn't been blown away by what Yoshi did next.

The moment I re-entered Yoshi's orbit, he requested a karaoke song. I thought he was joking. Yoshi hardly struck me as one to partake in such ridiculous frivolity as karaoke. But then he bent to one knee. I told him to cut it out. He held the microphone in one hand and took mine in the other. I was still laughing when he started to sing, and then I was quiet.

For four and a half minutes Yoshi's gaze didn't leave my own. He held my hand and he serenaded me with every word of 'Right Here Waiting' as if they were his own. He was sexy, he was tender, and I was completely swept away. Yoshi put Richard Marx to shame.

'I will wait for you,' Yoshi continued once he sang out the last note. 'But not too long, okay? I am man, remember. Two years *maximum*, but maybe six months if I am good boy. When you go away to Canada, I can't take it, to be oceans apart. I'll go there. You ask your parents if it's okay if you have a gook boyfriend. I am serious, anything for you, but only one question. I booked the biggest suite so you can sleep on the other side of the room, but when we go to hotel, can I say you are my *chérie*?'

'Okay,' I laughed. 'All right, Yoshi. You can say it.' I could at least give him that.

'When you come back from Canada, I am so proud, I introduce you to all my friends. You are difficult, that's why I like you, but I know, in six months' time, you will be my girlfriend. I didn't request you when I came back,' he lied smoothly, 'but you were just sitting there. It's meant to be for me. Love is good. Even one-way love. When I went to Chicago, I was thinking only of you. I thought, wow, I really like her, but she doesn't like me. Tonight was expensive, three-hundred-and-eighty-dollar dinner, four-hundred and ninety-dollar Greengrass, but no problem. I am never going on stupid *dohan*. Nishi said to me, "Yoshi, are you okay?" Yes! I am so happy! Before I thought you could never like me, but now we are going to the small island. The hotel is very busy, because membership only, but the island is quiet. We can go for a walk . . .'

'Bring your digital camera,' I interrupted.

'I'll have to get one from the office.'

'I don't have one.'

'Okay, don't worry, babe. I'll present you one, of course. Everything for you.'

These words were awfully incriminating for someone who so vehemently denied being a sugar daddy. One whose mommy woke him up on weekends and did his laundry.

At 1.00 am I saw Yoshi to the door. After six hours together he claimed I'd worn him out and he needed to sleep, but it *was* a Friday night; maybe it was simply time for Yoshi to move on to the next club. At least it would make me feel better to think of him out chasing easy Russians, as opposed to his affections being true. My heart couldn't take it.

—

Back at the powwow table Karolina was wrestling with the fact that tomorrow she'd be flying back to finish her schooling in Poland. I was curious to know whether she knew Yoshi, and it took only three words to establish who we were talking about. *Filthy rich* and *Superman*. 'Oh my God, *Yoshi*, right? He wears little glasses and he's very stylish, all Gucci and everything. He's handsome, don't you think? And sexy. And *unbelievably* arrogant. He was here tonight? I didn't see him.'

'Yeah,' I ignored her questions. 'What do you know about him?'

'Yoshi was my friend Minka's customer before we went to Thailand, and he's totally addicted. To hostesses, I mean. We caught him in the elevator one night after he'd already been in to Greengrass to see Minka. He was going to Republik, that Russian club, but he pretended he'd just forgot something.' *Ah-hah*. Just like I'd thought.

—

You know that your life will never be the same when its most romantic moment happened in a Tokyo hostess club. I hated Yoshi for it. It was girlhood fantasy, Barbie dolls and princess dreams, and I *knew* that, but even though I couldn't believe in him, even though I wouldn't accept it as reality, when Yoshi sang that song for me, I'd fought back tears. Like a big, gullible baby. I might have been intoxicated by a vintage red wine and subjugated by the all-too-palatable propaganda of a master Casanova, but when Yoshi took my hand and kneeled on the floor in his Prada pants, his voice was so beautiful, *he* was so beautiful, that it felt like the world stopped around us. In a Hollywood movie, this moment would be when the impressionable young girl fell in love with the irresistibly flawed millionaire tycoon. But I knew myself better than that.

If my life could have been that fairy tale, at this moment I'd have taken it in a second. I'd have fallen over that cliff without looking twice. But that fairy tale didn't exist. The promise was not there.

The foundations of this peculiar cultural phenomenon were entirely smoke and mirrors — the 'relationship' built between hostess and customer was a fable of improbable possibility. We were enchanted notions building castles in the sky, never to be realised.

And you know what? Disappointment does not describe how it felt to know that nothing genuine could eventuate from circumstances such as these, but my faith in the human spirit's ability to give love was renewed by this moment. No matter how fucked up a life is, the human soul can love purely, if only for an isolated moment. This memory will save me, time and time again. It has caused such conflict — a feeling I don't want to own — but at the same time it has given me something I will cherish forever. Paradoxical existence is this life.

And every time I hear that song, my heart will cry.

That bastard.

—

When I finally made it home at 3.30 in the morning, wet, drunk and exhausted, Matt still wasn't there. He must have had to work late, but he wasn't answering his phone. Great. I really needed to see him. I needed him to stick a lightning rod back into me. I needed to set my eyes on him, to feel him, to hold what was *real*. Tonight had all been a bit too much.

I was about to retrace the route we usually walked home together to see if I could find him, but before I could find an umbrella, Nori called from Yokohama, sullen and angry.

'Now I am not good, and I have not good feelings, and I don't call to you,' he grumbled darkly. I took my shoes off and turned the TV on to the weather channel. A reporter was fighting high-velocity winds in a bright yellow raincoat, a map of Kyushu showing the path of a coming typhoon.

'Why? What's the matter?' I asked innocently. 'I don't understand.'

'You don't know?' Nori snapped. 'Sunday! I came to Tokyo to make plans with you for Sunday. That is all,' his voice dropped. 'I wanted to see you Sunday.'

'Look, Nori, you can't expect me to drop everything for you when you haven't called all week. I told you, I already made plans and I can't cancel them. I'm sorry.'

The reporter looked as exhausted as I felt. He kept shouting '*Tsunami desu yo!*' as accompanying wave charts displayed numbers over the Kanto coastline: 0.4–4 metres, 7–10 metres.

'Yes, but you can change them,' Nori insisted. 'For me.'

'No I can't. I have somewhere to go.' 5.4–7 metres.

'What?' Nori shouted angrily.

'I said I have plans, didn't you hear me?' Looking out the window I saw the wind had just begun. The red circle on the weather map was just off the coast.

'But . . .'

'No buts, Nori. I'm busy.' There was silence. The *shinkansen* were no longer running. Japan Airlines had delayed all flights. These were not good indications for a boat trip to a small island in thirty hours' time. 'Are you okay?' I asked.

'NO. *Not* okay!'

'Can't you take one of Fumio's friends with you?'

'No! Only *you*,' he continued desperately. 'Why can't you understand?'

139

There was nothing *to* understand. This behaviour was pathetic, and Nori above all should know that. I'd never said anything to foster his mountain of assumptions. I'd just been playing my part, fair and square. *He* was the one who'd gone and blown up the whole goddamned script.

KYOTO A GO-GO

It was a dreary, monotone morning when Yoshi pulled up late outside the Hiroo Citibank branch early on yet another Sunday. I jumped down off the planter box when I saw him, my stilettos tapping on the wet asphalt as he motioned for me to walk out into traffic to get into the front seat of his car. 'Good morning, *ma chérie*! How are you?' he beamed as I tossed my bag next to the Louis Vuitton luggage in the back seat of his impeccable Mercedes.

'Just take me to the spa,' I laughed. 'I've slept one hour, and I'm wrecked.' But Yoshi wasn't. He was alert in black Gucci and Prada. He turned up Norah Jones. He checked his watch. And then, just as we were speeding through the deserted streets of Roppongi, Yoshi nonchalantly put forth his disclosure. 'We have to make it to the train station by ten o'clock. The typhoon has destroyed small island, so we are going to Kyoto.'

'Shut *up*, Yoshi,' I protested blandly. 'We are *not* going to Kyoto,' but he grinned wildly and I bolted upright in my plush leather seat. '*WHAT*? Are you serious? No, you're not. Are you? Oh my God, Kyoto? Yoshi! You're kidding! How the hell did this trip go from a small island to Kyoto?'

Yoshi's smile widened. 'Because, late last night the hotel call me: "Small island is badly damaged so cancel all reservations." I called my friend in Kyoto and he arranged everything for me.'

'But it's a long-weekend holiday. Kyoto will be packed!'

'I know, but don't worry. You are lucky girl. My friend has ways of getting things – nice hotel, nice dinner – so sit back. Relax! You will *luuhv* it. Go to sleep, *ma chérie*, you look tired. I wake you up at station.'

141

At this point I realise that many would have demanded to get out of Yoshi's car, but I found the idea of fleeing to Kyoto on a whim terribly exciting. It was the city of Japanese dreams, the spiritual soul of the country, and what better way to experience it than with Yoshi? Hell yeah. How could I not?

The platonic sleepover with the millionaire was a totally acceptable part of the hostess/customer relationship. Abie had gone to Kyoto with Grandpa. Karolina had gone with Shin to Hakone and Chiba on several occasions, and I no longer had a problem with the idea. Four weeks ago the possibility of even stepping into a customer's car had scared the crap out of me, but since then something had changed. It was that thirteenth lightbulb. But there was something else. I trusted in Yoshi. He was familiar.

Like the man I loved deeply. Like Matt.

Not coincidentally I'd met Matt at a time in my life when my defences were down. I was seventeen, in a hedonistic spiral, experimenting liberally with drugs, drinking heavily, not sleeping for days. The ultimate party girl. Matt's hook sunk deep – because he was clearly the alpha male in my orbit, or at least that's what he showed me. Money. Notoriety. He lavished me with a pampering attentiveness that I hadn't experienced in small-town British Columbia, or even in Tokyo, Paris, Cascais or any of the places I'd carried myself to in a whirlwind of reckless abandon.

After that I stabilised and we grew together. I knew that because we had developed such a strong bond, going to Kyoto with Yoshi didn't compromise that. But at the same time here I was, although unwilling to acknowledge it, gravitating towards another reckless lifestyle, not dissimilar to the time when Matt had been forced to revert to sting-operation tactics to grab my materialistic attention. I thought I was over that, but the dark side can be awfully alluring when you're inundated afresh with its charms – or, perhaps, if you hadn't learnt the lesson completely the first time around.

In these past few weeks it could be said that I'd been holding on to a false sense of security. I'd chosen to mould myself back into the archetypal girl out on the town, at least within the confines of what a married woman could get away with, and I was gushed over, adored, desired and complimented six nights a week. At first I found it vile. Then it made me uncomfortable. Soon I was enjoying it, then revelling in it, and before long, like every other girl in a Tokyo hostess club, I was beginning to feel like I deserved it. Bingo! Guard dropped.

And then someone like Yoshi came along, lavishing me with attention when I was surrounded by men I couldn't relate to. Yoshi exuded the alpha-male pheromone; he stunk of it, and in my weakened state I picked up on the vibe. Anywhere else, at any other time, it would have been easy to dismiss him, but Yoshi was the real deal; the guy could walk into Jets-R-Us tomorrow and buy one, with custom rims. He had millions at his disposal, and here he was offering it all to me on a silver platter. And I mean *it all*, hypothetically or not. Because he freakin' knew what to say.

—

When you're speeding cross-country at 257 kilometres per hour on a first-class ticket to Kyoto, your eyeballs have to auto-correct with incredible speed just to keep the scenery in focus. Count to eleven and you've gone almost a kilometre. Count with enough patience and Yoshi is pointing out his precious small island on the distant horizon, then ordering you a coffee while he eats sandwiches. *One thousand eight hundred*, you gulp the strong coffee. *One thousand eight hundred and one*, he swallows the last of the crust . . . One hundred and thirty kilometres later, Yoshi is snoring loudly in your ear, his Gucci driving shoes exchanged for black suede loafers. You want to sleep, but this is too surreal to shut your eyes – you might wake up from this dream, and you definitely don't want to. Your eyelids might flutter briefly, but you'll be awake as the *shinkansen* gently descends the lush, green mountains into the Kyoto valley.

Outside the station it is a sunny thirty degrees. Birds sing. Sweat beads. A long line of taxis is queued up, but Yoshi pulls you by the hand until he reaches the front of the line, where a black Mercedes-Benz is waiting. The man doesn't even take normal taxis.

Here, you feel both rich and famous for the way people look at you when you're with him, and for the gallantry with which he treats you.

In the slow-moving traffic, Yoshi takes to pointing out various hotels: the most expensive, the one he'd stayed in last time, the one he'd wanted to stay in this time but it was full. He wanted to make a good impression – you are his *chérie*. Hypothetically.

Where is the count now? *Eight thousand one hundred, eight thousand one hundred and one.* He makes small talk with the driver in a language that is still foreign to you, and you look out the window at yet another concrete city drifting by.

~

I couldn't hide my smile when a bellhop hurried to open the taxi door and offer me a gloved hand in assistance. It grew even bigger when Yoshi took my arm and we strolled aristocratically into the lobby of the Hotel Nikko Princess Kyoto, sunglasses on and spines straight under a bevy of stares and whispers. While Yoshi undertook the task of paying dearly for a suite on the fifteenth floor, I lingered in the background, browsing through the gift shop and admiring the impeccably hospitable clerks behind reception. I maintained silence as we followed the bellhop into the elevator and down the hall, finally bursting into laughter when our hotel-room door was safely closed.

'Oh my God. This suite is huge! I thought you said this was a last-minute room?'

'Ugh, it's substandard,' Yoshi complained, throwing open the French doors from the lounge to the bedroom. 'Not my style, but whatta can I do? At least you have your own bed, *ma chérie*.'

I certainly did, and a bathroom larger than our tiny apartment in Hiroo – the one that Matt was asleep in right now, probably crushing my pillow beneath him. I'd have to call him soon. I had to tell him that I was in Kyoto instead of on an island, but I didn't want to wake him up. Matt needed his sleep, the big sook, and it was pointless to make him worry before he had to. He'd remained reluctant for me to go up to the last. He'd showered in silence that morning and lain in bed while I'd packed my overnight bag with a change of clothes and the essentials. It had been sad removing my toothbrush from next to his in the bathroom, but he probably wouldn't notice something so small.

I'd sat on the edge of the mattress and kissed him goodbye, and he'd penetrated me with those eyes. 'You be careful. I love you.'

I'd laughed and said, 'Don't worry. I'll call you from the island. I love you bubsteroo.' Now I'd be calling him from Kyoto, but not until five, when I knew he'd be up and walking to work in Roppongi.

'Chelsea . . . hey, Chel-seeeea.' I looked to Yoshi across the room. 'Just let me change into casual clothes and we'll go to Ogura, a beautiful hill with many shrines and temples in the north-west of Kyoto. The first of many places for you. You will *luuhv* it,' Yoshi purred, and as he closed the French doors behind him I sank onto the couch to watch NHK television until Yoshi the Tour Guide was ready.

—

It is said that in Japan, God is in the details. That's something I like immensely about the Japanese. Despite being the most fast-paced, technologically advanced nation on earth, they have retained a sensitivity to the spiritual forces of the natural world. They've managed to fuse daily twenty-first-century life with a reverence for divinity. It's a very poetic way to live.

Climbing up the stairs behind Yoshi to Nenbutsu-ji Temple, I could say, *God is in the sunlight that filters down to land on eight thousand stone Buddhas*, and I would be right. Or I could be more concrete and say *God is in the intricate simplicity of the Ghi-ohji Temple*, where we went next, and still I'd be right.

The thing about beauty is that you just absorb it. In some places on earth this is a little more difficult than others, but in Kyoto it is exceptionally easy. From the moment you enter its temples and shrines you feel a tranquillity ebbing and flowing through every beam and every rock until each step taken becomes a walking, breathing meditation.

Although Kyoto is now a fragment of its former self, it's easy to see why the Allied bombers chose to spare this beautiful city during World War II; even its enemies respected it.

And I had a new-found respect for Yoshi. It began as we wandered through the bamboo forest and along the banks of the Oi River. Whenever I looked at him, I was struck by some new light cast from his prism. Here amid the history of his ancestors, among the spirits of his gods and the regal beauty of his land, it was so easy to see: for once, Yoshi seemed at peace.

—

'Hey, bubs, it's me. Yeah, everything is fine. I'm in Kyoto. Don't swear. The small island was damaged by the typhoon yesterday so Yoshi changed his plans. We took the *shinkansen*. Uh-huh. Yes, I know. C'mon, I think I know what I'm doing. All right. Have you got a pen? We're staying at the Hotel Nikko Princess Kyoto in room 1015, and the phone number is 75-342-2111. Yes, I'll be careful. I know. Yes, I know that too. Okay, I love you too. Uh-huh. Okay, *moooooch*. I'll call you in the morning.'

—

'Oh God, I am *not* eating this. Is this sea urchin? It is, isn't it?'

'Give it to me, *ma chérie*, you spoilt brat. This is a delicacy in Japan,' Yoshi chastised me with a delicate glare at dinner as I slid the dish over to him. Well, he could eat it then. Fine by me. Sea urchin was positively disgusting, and I'd already had too many works of culinary art slide agreeably down my throat to ruin it with one small sea animal. The wine could have masked the slimy critter, but then I'd had too much of that as well. It was a concentrated effort just to make it to the top of the stairs in stilettos, where I gave myself a stern talking-to in the ladies' room mirror. *No more wine. Do you hear me? You can hardly walk, you bloody idiot.* But when I returned to our corner table, the waiter had already refilled my glass.

—

I was completely impressed with Yoshi. It wasn't all the extravagance — that was just pure opulent fun, and to him it meant nothing. It was the subtle effect of his gallantry. Not once did Yoshi press me for anything. Or insinuate or probe or demand. Not once did he step beyond the customer/hostess boundary. Not once did he even ask me anything direct. In fact, ever since we'd met, Yoshi had never really asked me anything personal, and I in turn hadn't bothered to ask him. We simply enjoyed each other's company, without knowing all the details that cemented a normal relationship. Maybe that was the key to being a hostess without being swallowed up by it. To be like the lights of urban Kyoto flashing by – beautiful but fuzzy, blurred by moving too fast through a dark expanse of night. Never entirely known.

'Fuck that was a beautiful dinner. I'm sorry, did I just swear? I don't like to swear.'

'Fuck it, do what you want,' said Yoshi. 'Do whatever you want. Oh *Godddd.*' He stopped to stare up at the sky outside the Princess Nikko. 'I am so drunk.'

So am I, I thought to myself, but said nothing.

We stood pleasantly on opposite sides of the elevator. I caught a glimpse of myself in the mirror. I looked happy. Satiated. And I didn't mean 'not hungry'.

Fifteen floors up, the doors opened. We sauntered down the plush hallway. I stopped to smell a bouquet of fresh flowers on a side table. Yoshi didn't look back. He turned the key ahead of me and quietly I shut the vault door behind us.

RETURN TO TOKYO

Behind two small slits I could see his dark eyes. Even under a glaring bulb they were matte on the surface. All surfaces were matte. The table between us. His shirt. My shirt. Even the air was dull.

I dropped my gaze onto a large plate of neglected sushi and then to a second, left by a waitress in stark *tabi* socks that played peek-a-boo with the broad hem of her kimono. *Scuffle scuffle* went her black wooden sandals. *Scuffle scuffle* went her white ninja toes. I never once lifted my gaze to her face. Not once did I offer a smile. My only concern was in keeping an *ocha* cup full, slowly sipping back the steaming green tea.

When we were alone in the cubicle, neither of us spoke. If we did, it was only to proclaim how sleepy we were. I stared into the *ocha*. I felt like there was no future, no past, just a gaunt void that made my teeth feel weightless.

Of course, there was a story for a morning that had just transpired, a morning that I was in and that he was in, but it was interwoven in a hazy reel of granulated panoramas, like a silent movie poorly cared for, shown far too many times.

Yoshi and I had risen early, after I had spent hours staring into the darkness, listening to him sleep in fits and thinking maybe he was dying, the small broken half of a white Valium untouched on my bedside table. I could have slept if I'd swallowed it, but I was afraid. Suddenly and childishly afraid of taking drugs from strangers.

I'd lain still under my covers, repeatedly bringing the vision of Matt's face to mind, meditating on what I'd known and loved intimately for three years, relying on it to keep me from spiralling into a hole whose depths I'd rather not know. My chest felt tight. I still couldn't breathe. Not normally anyway. I had no thoughts no feelings no fears no pains or senses save for one light that shone through the bottomless darkness slowly trying to drain my soul: I loved him. Matt. And it was greater than anything I'd ever felt. It was the only thing. The truth.

And then the kick-back started and I had to use everything I had to pull back to him, to the centre, to the beacon that kept me from being swept up and dashed against the rocks. And it was hard, it was so hard and so tempting to succumb to the weight of this dark swell that was upon me, to be pulled under and held down and drowned in its power. But I kept it at bay with love and I held it at bay with love, and in between there were the imprints of a chemical memory seared into my veins, still smouldering after the fire had suddenly gone out.

—

There had been a credit card. Not the black one, but a dusty credit card, which later he licked clean. There were two lines. A rolled up thousand-yen note. He took his. I took mine. It took my breath away. Shortened it and turned the oxygen into a controlled lifeline of which I could just barely get enough. It was unusual, he thought. My breathlessness. He got me something to drink. We emptied the mini bar. But that was my only problem. My *onleeee* problem. Holy fuck, did I ever have no problems.

Then there was a second swollen line, a larger collection of finite particles of $C_{17}H_{21}NO_4$, so mathematic in composition, so lucid in suspension, so very fuckin' good in your blood stream. *Cocaine.*

The extraction of another fun-sized ziplock. Then a third. Yoshi didn't believe it was my first time any more.

—

When the alarm sounded, I pretended I'd been asleep for all those hours when in fact I couldn't tell myself where I had been. I pretended to be refreshed, I pretended to be okay and to have dreamt of tranquil fields full of blooming diazepam flowers, but I was hollowed out. My eyeballs felt emaciated. So did my teeth, but I bared them in a new kind of smile while Yoshi whistled as he threw open the curtains.

Yoshi showered. Then I showered. He held open the door and as a last-minute thought went back to sweep the table clean. We had coffee in the lobby like zombies, and then took a taxi to Kiyomizudera, the centuries-old Clear Water Temple looming spectacular from its vantage point high in Kyoto's outlying hills.

When the crowds started to irritate us both, we disappeared into the emptiness of narrow backstreets and the shelter of small wooden buildings, Yoshi translating the discreet brushstrokes of hidden restaurants and inns as we passed.

There was something about the winding cobblestones, a soothing tranquillity born from a history of innumerable centuries before us. We could both feel it. Yoshi said I looked like I belonged in Japan, and I didn't question what he meant. I was suddenly in a movie again. Under the tall red *torii* of an old Shinto shrine, through a dressmaker's window and down every new alley, I found myself searching for geisha, for a woman more illusion than flesh and blood, but no matter where I looked she remained as elusive as her wares. Maybe all I had to do was catch a glimpse of my own reflection, gesturing with adopted mannerisms that hadn't been there two months before, content in the lee of a man I called Yoshi, sharing laughter and silence and looks that had vocabularies all to themselves.

—

'Where in Hiroo?' Yoshi asked as he led the way through the overwhelming maze of Tokyo station. *Where* in Hiroo? I'd been waiting for this question. Dreading it. I didn't want Yoshi to know where I lived – I'd already made that mistake with Nori. I could say the supermarket, and fumble an explanation of needing to pick up laundry soap before I got home and crashed out. It sounded stupid and contrived, and I knew that Yoshi would know it if I made anything up. But what was I going to say? He was driving me home; I had to be taken somewhere.

'You know the National . . .' I began, but Yoshi cut me off immediately.

'The National supermarket near Hiroo station, I know. Okay.' And that was it.

—

Passing through Roppongi I shut my eyes and covered my ears and Yoshi laughed heartily. *This place isn't me*, I wanted to say, but the words weren't necessary. This place wasn't Yoshi either. When he rested his hand on mine, I did nothing to remove it. It was just there. I was just there. And the rain fell softly against the windshield.

A few minutes later we were crawling alongside the wooded Arusigawa Park towards the National supermarket. 'Okay, where do you want to get out?' he asked.

'Anywhere is fine.' It was a red light and Yoshi had both hands on the wheel. I leant over to kiss him on the cheek and he closed his eyes again. 'Okay, see ya, Yosh. I'll call you.' I grabbed my bag and hopped out into the wrong side of traffic. Scissoring the rail to the sidewalk, I waved my arm as I turned to walk away, but Yoshi wasn't looking. His eyes were closed, with both hands still on the wheel. A gentleman, or a man dejected? I couldn't tell. The sad part was, it didn't really matter.

NO SLEEP TILL BROOKLYN

Hmmm. Fajita or tacos? I couldn't decide. I just wasn't hungry. Spanish music played in the background. Multilingual chatter floated among intoxicating smells. I should have been smiling in such an atmospheric setting, but instead cynicism had become the tone *du jour.* That's what happens when you haven't slept for two days straight and, instead of dreaming in bed, you are assembled around a table with three Israeli hostesses and one Japanese surgeon.

I had barely made it from Yoshi's Mercedes to the top of the hill past the supermarket when Nori rang with an invitation to the under-ground Mexican restaurant in Harajuku for dinner and oh, he mentioned ever-so-nonchalantly, 'I have your computer. Uh, what are you doing now? Are you busy?'

'No. I'm . . . just on my way home from the supermarket.' I stifled a yawn and made an effort to perk up my voice. *Why did Nori always have to call at the most crucially inopportune times?* Whatever. I'd have to make an effort to be bothered this time. 'When do you want to come pick me up?'

'Half an hour?' Nori had proposed eagerly.

'Oh. Okay.'

And so thirty minutes later I was back in the passenger seat of another imported Benz. But not, of course, before I had been home to see my husband.

—

I was slightly nervous walking up the corridor. Not that I had reason to be, but the slightly – okay, maybe *highly* – unusual circumstance of my absence lent my return an awkward tension, at least in my own mind. I suppose I could have rehearsed what I wanted to say, but I was so overtired you could hardly call any of my cognitive processes thinking. I was beyond that.

So what did I do? I normalised.

'Hi, bubs!' I called out. 'I'm back.' I dropped my overnight bag and let out an animated sigh of relief. The apartment smelt of freshly scrambled eggs.

'Hey!' Matt called back, appearing from behind the wall. He smiled at me without parting his lips.

I scuffed my feet along the carpet until I was within hugging range and collapsed into him. He smelt like freshly scrambled eggs.

'So how was it?' he asked, as if I'd just been to the museum or the fish market. He released me and sat down at the table to eat.

'Yeah, it was great, but I'm exhausted. We went to a crazy temple this morning above Kyoto, and when you look out over one side, you see all these stones far below. They were markers to commemorate all the people who'd jumped, who'd gone to the temple to commit suicide. It kind of did my head in. I hated being away from you.'

I stood over Matt as he looked down into his eggs and ran my hand over the bristles of his crew cut. 'Umm, what else? I saw the Golden Temple and a bazillion other shrines and stuff – I'll have pictures to show you, but Yoshi has to develop them. They're on his camera. Oh shoot, and Nori's going to come pick me up soon because he's bringing the laptop and he'll probably want to go for dinner. He called when I was walking home and I couldn't really say no. I should have – I'm fucked and I'm so bloody tired and the last thing I want to do is hang out with Nori – but he has no idea I even went to Kyoto; he thinks I was sleeping all day today. Maybe I should cancel. Do you think I should go?'

'Yeah, well, he's coming, isn't he? Why not?' Matt said.

I walked to the other side of the table and started to unpack my bag. I hung up a shirt I hadn't worn. Threw socks in the dirty pile of laundry. Then I looked over at Matt and he was looking straight back at me. He chewed his eggs. Once. Twice. Three times.

'We did coke, at the hotel,' I offered suddenly.

'Hmm,' he grunted. 'When?'

I watched him fork another bite into his mouth and felt the barometric pressure between us decrease, but only slightly. I *knew* that he knew something was up, and although it was something I could very well have chosen never to mention, I'd much rather clarify that it was merely *Erythroxylon coca* that I'd succumbed to, and not the home-wrecking, soap-opera prospect behind door number 2.

'After dinner. At the hotel. It's kind of overrated, I think.'

'I know.'

'It nearly gave me a heart attack. But you know . . . sometimes you gotta get it wrong to know what's right.' I hinted at a smile.

'Yeah,' he chuckled. 'I know.'

'Anyway, I thought you should know that. But I'm not going to stand here and spell out every little detail of the entire trip, because I really think it doesn't matter. Nothing has changed from two days ago.'

'Of course it hasn't.' Matt chewed, but he kept his eyes trained on me. I thought I caught a glimmer of patronising amusement beneath his surface, but so what? If it was actually there, fine. 'So when is Nori coming?'

I checked my phone. 'Fifteen minutes.'

'You'd better have a shower then, stinker.'

'Why?' I objected. 'I'm fine. I don't need a shower. I'll just change my shirt.'

Matt rolled his eyes and pointed the fork at me. Then he smiled, but with his teeth this time. He pointed the fork towards the shower door.

I got in the shower.

EXACTLY THE HALFWAY POINT

I could feel the liquid build-up under my left eye as the noise assembled into words, loud and fast. My mind was shocked into consciousness, the music mingling with the low buzz of an electric razor and the acute pounding in my cerebral cortex. Oh God. 50 Cent, shut up. I like you, but honestly, now is not the time. My body was stuck to the mattress like poured cement. Soon Matt was smooching my face, telling me I had to get up to finish shaving his head. 'C'mon, I gotta go to work soon.'

'Just a minute, please. *Chotto matte kudasai!*' Give me one second to scrape myself into something that resembled an actual living organism. So he turned up the volume and sat on the edge of the tub, talking about some custom rims on a something-or-other car he saw somewhere. I don't know. I wasn't really paying attention. All I could think of was getting back to sleep. I mean, fifteen hours? That wasn't enough.

As soon as the door closed, my eyes were shut.

—

I wonder what Yoshi is doing. It would have been compulsory for him to show up to the office this morning, all Valentino suit and Armani tie. I bet he'd felt terrible, and without a doubt he'd be on something, but he'd look impeccable. The crazy bastard. I wonder when he'll call again. He'd left massive latitude for variation over lunch in Kyoto. Something about a really busy week ahead. No, he'd said *incredibly* busy. An unprofitable golf course outside Barcelona was having major employee problems, and since he'd been there three months ago to try to iron things out, the situation had only got worse. Yoshi hated the whole thing, but as an obligation of his father's it meant that he, the dutiful son, had to sort it out. Of course he blamed the Spanish and their laziness for the golf course's problems, but he obliged his familial contract. Yoshi was a good boy, and he loved his mommy.

The phone rang. 'Hey, you awake?' It was Matt. 'What does Yoshi look like? I think he's sittin' right next to me. He wears Armani, right?'

'Yeah, sure, but so do a lot of Japanese. What kind of criterion is that?'

'I don't know. I've just got a sixth sense it's him. Small glasses?'

'Yeah, he has little eyes, small glasses, receding hairline but slick hair. His watch is a Rolex GMT Master II, the one with the red and blue bezel. Can you see it? What else? Let me think . . . perfect shoes? Does he have a tiny phone?'

'A what? Tiny phone? No, it's not tiny. Yeah, I think it's him. He's sittin' with a Japanese girl in Starbucks, but he's inside and I'm outside.'

'I don't think it would be him. I doubt Yoshi's interests lie in Japanese women, or that he'd take them to Starbucks. He's probably still at the office. He *is* Japanese.'

'Hmmm, he's tanned, like dark Japanese, with small, brown-rimmed glasses . . .'

'Yeah maybe. He's got a million different pairs . . .'

'And he's got an attitude. He's kind of arrogant, right?'

'Yeah. Well, that sounds like him. Maybe that's his secretary he's with. He did say he has an office somewhere in the area.'

'I don't know why, I just really have this feeling that it's him.'

'And he's not trying to kill you?'

'What? He's not trying to what?'

'Never mind. Okay, bye.'

I know it's impossible for any of the Japanese men I know to recognise Matt, but it still makes bells go off should one isolated player in the game recognise another. Maybe I should start walking home alone rather than meeting Matt after work. It would be safer. What if, by some obscure chance, Nori were to see us together and become 'very angry' like the irrational maniacs in his favoured stories of unrequited love? He might watch the apartment building. Who knew? The guy counted Hitler and various other sociopaths as heroes. But what was I talking about? Matt is my *husband*. No one even suspects his existence. Why would they? I shouldn't even be thinking about it. In fact, I shouldn't be thinking about a good stiff drink either, not when I just woke up thirty minutes ago.

Warped. Warped. Warped. This place is going to nail me to the wall.

—

Matt was sitting outside Food Magazine guzzling a one-litre carton of vegetable juice when I walked by on the way to the internet cafe before work. 'What's wrong with your eyes?' He squinted, as if to bring me into better focus. 'They look really puffy.'

'*Puffy?* I don't know. Why would they?' I stretched them open wide as I sat down.

Matt studied me closely. I wondered if he could see the microscopic shake that had started to invade my fingertips. I couldn't feel two of them when I woke up. I needed a coffee, but I was going to be late for work, so before Matt could analyse me further I drank a long gulp of his juice and smooched him goodbye.

Abie and Nicole were still at the internet cafe when I got there. 'You know we have to work in ten minutes,' Abie warned, squinting suspiciously as I signed in to Hotmail. What was it with my eyes? No wonder people wear sunglasses.

'I know, but I really have to check something. I'll be two minutes.'

I had two emails. One from my mom – something refreshingly normal yet simultaneously whacked about plush toy Popples selling on eBay for $20 – and this, from Matt:

Sent: Saturday, 9 October 2004 7:33:22 PM
Subject: I love you
I love you, love bird
that's what I know
I want the sun, the moon

the stars to show
my love is purest
at one with the way
through rain, hail, sunshine,
and even a typhoon today!

Our skin will age
but forever we will be young,
true love is all that's needed
for life to be fun.
The typhoon has passed
fallacies have shredded
true love has prevailed
our love has not ended

At your side forever dynamic souls
pushing our potentials together
we now lay a golden path through life
wuv birds
husband and wife

Oh no. It was beautiful. My first instinct was to cry. This was so unlike him. Matt didn't have a romantic bone in his body. He didn't write love poems. Even cute, crappy ones. Why start now, at this moment? Did he doubt me? That thought was so heavy. Did he *doubt* me?

Then I noticed the date. Matt had sent the email even before I'd left for Kyoto. It is my fault that he wrote me this love poem. It is my fault.

I like to be part of my 'we'. But now it's an unavoidable fact that here in Tokyo I tend to think singularly more often than not. Perhaps in this environment it is a survival mechanism, but for long periods each day I am moving through my life alone. Only when it's time to go home does he slot back into my life and 'I' becomes 'we' again, but somehow colder, and more distant. I know that he can feel me receding. *I* can feel me receding.

And now he is sending me love poems. What am I doing?

SLOWLY GOING CRAZY ...
CRAZY GOING SLOWLY

Yoshi called me the minute he knew I'd be at work. He'd let three days pass since we'd returned from Kyoto, but it was obvious that he'd been holding out on purpose.

'Hey! *Ma chérie*, how are you? Hah! Me, I am good, I am *soooo good*. Where are you?' He sounded a little on the crazed side, but still, I was glad that he'd finally called.

'I'm at work, Yoshi. There are people here already.'

'PEOPLE!' he shouted. 'What people?'

'Customers, what do you think?'

'Oh, okay then, enjoy,' he jeered haughtily. 'Have fun.'

'No, just a second.' I went into the change room and shut the door behind me. 'What are you doing now?'

'I just finished work. I am working until now! I don't have an easy life, *like you*,' he breathed in heavy mock accusation, fading into laughter.

'Why are you laughing?'

'*Because* I am talking to *YOU*!'

'Ohhh-kay. So are you going home now, or out with one of your girlfriends?'

'*What?* What did you say?'

'You heard me. I said, are you going out with your girlfriend now?'

'My girlfriend? No, she is working now.'

'Oh, is she?'

'Yes, she is. So I am going home. Alone.'

159

'Oh, that's too bad.'

'Yes, too bad. Okay, you go to work then. I'll see you. *Hai*-bye.'

—

For the rest of the night I couldn't concentrate. My mind was going around in crazy circles. I felt like I needed *something*, but what I didn't know. There was only the overwhelming feeling of a void that needed to be filled.

Abie asked me how I'd managed to get Nori to give me a laptop, but I couldn't remember. I might have told him writing would help overcome my abject loneliness. Then Dikla asked if I could get her birth-control pills from Nori. She didn't want to pay the mandatory $100 fee just to see a doctor, but how exactly was I to broach a subject like that? At least Jodie's request was simpler: 'Hey, when are you gonna see your doctor friend again? I really need some sleeping pills.'

'I hope never,' I grumbled, and that was her cue to notice. She summoned me over to the powwow table and demanded to know what was up.

'I want to leave, just take the money and go. I can't handle this any more.'

'Why, because of the surgeon? So what?'

'It's more complicated than that.'

'No, it isn't. You're just here for a job. The Japanese are crazy, every last one of them, and so is this hostess business. Of course you're gonna go crazy . . . *IF* you take it seriously. *They* don't, trust me. They come because they know they can never get it. You don't matter. You just happen to fill the part right now. If it wasn't you, it would be her, or her, or her. And when you leave, they'll just move on to somebody else. And they keep doing it, for twenty, thirty years.

'I can understand the old guys, they know the score, but not the young guys. My boyfriend has been to a hostess club twice, when his boss forced him to. He's Japanese, but he hates it. The second time I told him not to give his number to anyone, his name, nothing. He didn't understand. You know what he said to me? *But last time the girls really liked me.* Of course they did, you idiot! Don't be stupid! But they are stupid about this. They can't understand.'

'But I really think some of them are serious,' I protested. 'Nori, okay, he's a loony bin, but Yoshi, well, I think he actually means *some* of what he says. I think he's different. I believe in his reasons, even if I can't . . . I don't know how I'm going to see him any more without feeling like I'm totally betraying him by lying all the time. That's horrible!'

'Let me ask you a question. Did you meet Charlie this weekend?' Jodie looked at me intently and I nodded. 'And how was he?'

'He was fuckin' excellent.' I smiled in spite of myself.

'Okay, that tends to complicate things. But look, you're not betraying anyone. You just take it to the point until you can't put it off any more, and then eventually the ultimatum comes. They'll give it to *you*, don't worry. That's just what happens. They get sick of waiting. I had a guy who wanted to know whether he had a chance, so I said *we'll see, I have to get to know you.* That kind of shit. Then after three dinners he asked me to meet him in Shibuya and he ate really quickly, just vacuumed up his *soba*, and then took me by the hand to the love hotel across the street and said *now or never.* I said *never, see ya.* And he probably moved on to the next girl.

'They keep coming, saying the same things, talking about the same shit. Expecting and getting the same response. They have no lives. You and I, we have a life, we have friends. They don't. They're power players. All they have is work, and then the hostess club. That's their culture, and it's how they survive.'

'But they spend so much money I can't help feeling like I'm completely taking advantage of them. You know how much the trip to Kyoto with Yoshi cost? Even before I had to stop keeping tally, it must have been over seven-thousand bucks. *For thirty-six hours.*'

Jodie's expression remained unchanged. 'It's their choice, Chelsea. You don't force them to come here and spend hundreds of dollars. Do you tell them, *take me to dinner, buy me new clothes*? No, they do it because they want to, and they are *fucked up.* Listen to me. They love the thrill of the chase. I've been here a long time, and I see them just keep coming. They never stop. When I first came here, I thought what the fuck is this job? I spent the first night hugging the toilet in that shitty little loo because I drank so much. I cried, and then I laughed, and then I wanted to scream. And then you begin to understand that their minds don't work the same way as ours. Don't worry about it, just get drunk, laugh at them, and have a good time. Fuck them. They're crazy.'

Yet my mind kept going around in crazy circles.

—

I think about Yoshi a lot.

He is an enormous black hole into which I can't help but be vacuumed, suddenly, and at warp speed. It's as if I become an inflated version of myself simply by existing in his presence, and I should hate this – I know I should hate this – but for some reason I like it. I ought to avoid Yoshi like the plague, but there seems to be a problem: I know his coordinates, I've written them down, and I just can't help flying my little spaceship closer and closer. *Alpha Omega Six, we are approaching. We are fast approaching.* And then I am inside. All doors shut. All exits. But I am not trapped. I am not threatened. I am . . . *enchanted*. By a foreign galaxy roped off in velvet. Privy to a thousand stars. Each one lit just for me. At least that's the *feeling*. That's the *mood* of his galaxy.

But he is such a mystery, Yoshi. He is so closed in so many ways. And yet he is so open. Is it because of me? Am I the one to unlock him?

Sometimes I think about Yoshi right before I go to sleep. In the darkness, in the silence, I think about a million possibilities that should never enter my mind. I consider, ever so objectively, what it would be like to be with him in reality. What would an 'us' formulated with a 'someone' like Yoshi really be like? Dramatic, I think. But happy? Try *transparent*, as in how one would have to become just to attempt a solidification of what might always be a mirage to him. He would be forever anxious about what you loved: him, or just the lifestyle he'd given you. He would need explanation after explanation, reassurance after reassurance – your life as continual proof of purchase. I think about what it would be like to have to do that in a relationship. I think about *could that be me?*

I also think about Matt right before I go to sleep. After all, he's right there beside me. It would break his heart to see these tainted, whimsical thoughts recurring through my neural networks, slowly but surely hardwiring into patterns, strengthened by the invasiveness of new chemicals and the enticements of greed, power, lust.

These things are not me. I am certain of that. I look at Matt. I see his breath falling. I feel his skin. *He* is so certain. And so am I. I am so certain, but . . .

Therein lies the problem, spelt out in only three little letters:

B. U. T.

LAND OF THE RISING SUN

It's days like today that I really wonder what I'm doing in Japan. I hate to think that as I go to bed each morning, these men I know in the night-time are turning up to run corporations or direct hospitals. It pains me that ten hours later they will still be there, relentlessly pursuing excellence, while I wake to the daily musical broadcast that warns Minato-ku's neighbourhood children to skip, run and bicycle home for dinner. How I loathe that unobtrusive public-service announcement. It is such a happy jingle, reduced to a sad, depressing reminder when I can't even lift my head off the pillow.

Such is the state of my life.

Lately I've had no motivation to go out. I don't want to exercise. Or to wander. I don't even go out for Starbucks. I'm so lethargic I can't even read, although I try every day, scanning the same three lines until finally I return Murakami to the shelf, slotting the book next to *A History of Japan*, *Creative Visualization* and *Trump: The Art of the Deal*. All of them dog-eared, none of them complete. Then I make a cheap instant coffee with too much soymilk, and that's usually the time when the phone rings. Today it was '*Shin HOME*'. I was glad to get the call. I hadn't seen him since he'd got back from his trip to China.

Late last night Shin had left me a message in that detached, endearingly screwed-up cadence I so loved: '*Hi. I am Shin speaking. Uhh. I just back home now and I checked email. How are you now? Uh . . . Okay. Uhh . . . I will call you later. Bye.*' But it had been after midnight, so out of courtesy I hadn't called him back. I knew he would call the next day.

It was such a relief to hear his voice. I needed to speak with someone who knew how to take it all in his stride. Or at least, *almost* all of it. China excluded.

'Chinese people all look *same!*' he exclaimed incredulously. 'Same height, same hair. Same face. Same clothes! And no colour. I could see no colour! Everyone was staring. They could tell I am Japanese? I do not know. They don't like Japanese.'

Shin was looking forward to our upcoming Sunday trip to Hakone's hot springs, but he was concerned about me. 'You must bring two towels, a big one and a small one, and . . . *nothing*. You understand?'

I chuckled in response. Shin was trying to explain that bathing in the volcanically sourced waters of Japanese *onsen* was a strictly nudist affair, but I was hardly concerned, I needed to relax, swimsuit or not, and modesty . . . well, a towel would be fine. I told Shin not to worry, I knew the *onsen* rules, and he promised to call tomorrow.

'Tomorrow I have to play golf,' he complained. 'I *hate*. Then, if I'm not tired, maybe we can go tempura restaurant,' he suggested. 'But I will call you, after I buy ticket.'

'Sure thing, Shin. I'm looking forward to it. Rest up.'

'Okay,' he sighed before hanging up. 'And bye-bye.'

Thank God for Shin. My neutral ground. Now all I had to worry about was securing a decoy plan with Nori for Saturday, since even after last week's hissy fit he'd assume Sunday belonged to him. *Hah!* He was so presumptuous. However, he had given me the laptop the night I'd returned from Kyoto, and in his eyes we were 'friends' again. I was willing to give him another chance to be civil. Of course if anyone deserved time on my one day off, it was Matt, but as he was going to be sleeping all day I didn't see how it would matter if I was beside him in bed or hours away in the Japanese countryside.

So there it was. Another weekend as good as gone, and I hadn't even dealt with my knight in shining armour, galloping towards me at the reins of his gleaming white stallion. I was constantly willing Yoshi to be called away to Barcelona to deal with his father's golf course. It would make my life so much easier.

~

OH MY GOD I LOVE TOKYO. This is the slogan of my hypothetical T-shirt. I hold in my hands not only an exclusive invitation to meet Tom Cruise at the Tokyo premiere of Michael Mann's *Collateral* but also, more importantly, the many different business cards of one Fujimoto-san, whom I so wonderfully had the pleasure of meeting tonight.

Fujimoto-san was a busy and talented man: president of a production company, adviser on film distribution and marketing/sales supervisor to the Japanese divisions of major Hollywood film studios, and president of his own entertainment company. This was all very impressive, yet, promotional material aside, it was Fujimoto-san's *joie de vivre* that I fell in love with in ten seconds flat.

His timing couldn't have been better – he'd arrived as a breath of fresh air just when my perspective was becoming stale, an uplifting reminder of how it's possible to feel an instantaneous affinity with someone even in the most curious of settings.

'Chelsea-san! You are not a typical *gaijin*,' Fujimoto-san exuded five minutes after we'd raised our glasses in *kampai*. 'This is the first thing I noticed about you!'

The first thing I'd noticed about *him* was his vibrant spark of energy. He virtually exploded into the air around him. He was late into his fifties, his beard handsomely dappled with grey but his hair jet black. Lean and laid-back, he was charmingly unapologetic in stating that he was 'most famous' in his business – the business of movies. As an internationally renowned film executive, Fujimoto-san had seen over 10,000 films in the theatre. Movies were his life's passion and *more important than anything, except health and curiosity.*

I was drawn to Fujimoto-san's uninhibited joy. It seemed that every revelation of fact or feeling was followed by a contagious thread of multicoloured laughter.

He told me that at one point an illness had threatened his life and almost forced him to abandon the movies for good. At the time he fell ill, Fujimoto-san had gone *thirty-seven years* without a holiday but was still shocked to discover he could have a bad liver and fatty blood. For the next nine months his days consisted only of examinations, 1500 calories' worth of food, seeing friends and having acupuncture, all of which culminated in a triumphant return to work and a feverishly renewed exuberance. It was Fujimoto-san's one grievance that he could now seldom eat *toro* – the fatty cut of a tuna's underbelly – because he was medically limited to low-cholesterol foods.

Fujimoto-san then decided to assess my health, having talked enough about his own. After a palm reading, he asked to touch my ankle. I nervously allowed him to undertake an examination that confirmed I had good bones while he recalled the minute details – actress, movie, year, director and studio – of one of his favourite cinematic scenes of a woman's ankle coming down a grand sweep of stairs. It was Fujimoto-san's one quirk, so I obliged when he requested me to stand so he could observe my ankle from another angle.

And then, as all self-respecting reunion nights went (for this was a get-together with Fujimoto-san's former colleagues), it was time for karaoke – with a couple of simple rules. 'Chelsea-san, always you must choose two songs to karaoke!' Fujimoto-san half shouted over the music. 'One to warm up,' he elbowed me jovially in the ribs, 'two to enjoy! I have learnt this very important lesson of karaoke over many years spent chaperoning famous movie stars in Tokyo,' he grinned. But, perhaps sensing my upcoming protest, Fujimoto-san's lips drew tightly together. 'It is a must,' he said solemnly. 'No negotiations. You can try the Beatles, if you are a shy singer. Tom Hanks sang the Beatles. But Robin Williams . . . *whoa*! He very much enjoy, because he is good – how do you say it in English?' Someone suggested the word *actor*, but no, that wasn't it. 'He made many voices,' Fujimoto-san explained.

'Oh, impersonator,' I concluded, and the three men shared the new word around.

'Chelsea-san. This month I am very busy. Next week Tom Cruise is coming. Michael Mann is coming, for *Collateral* – collaboration between DreamWorks and Paramount Pictures – and then Tom Hanks again is coming, for *The Polar Express* – animated kids' movie from Warner Brothers – but next month, if you are available, I want to have dinner.'

'Gosh,' I was surprised at the sudden invitation, coming from a man who spent most of his time consuming restricted calories with mega-celebrities, and I said as much.

'No, no, Chelsea-san. Please do not misunderstand. This is my obligation. It is my job! I must facilitate the schedule for every movie star coming to do promotions for the big movie, attend premieres, and entertain everybody all night long and make sure I return them safely to their hotel. It is a great job *desu yo*, but of course, sometimes horrible,' he laughed, 'and I am like babysitter! But never mind. Tonight, are you available to join us for something to eat? Can you drink? Red wine?' he smirked, pointing at my oolong tea.

'Red wine? I don't know, I'm still a bit sick . . .' I protested, gesturing towards my raspy throat.

'It is very, *very* good red wine,' Fujimoto-san jousted back, so I conceded with a roll of the eyes while he called Nishi to enquire whether I was free to go. Nishi grimaced silently and then painfully shook his head in refusal. So Fujimoto-san lit up a cigarette and they talked. Then Nishi bowed deeply, and left.

'So what happened?' I asked impatiently.

'Nishi-san told to me he already has your time card punched until one o'clock, but I will pay a small sum for you to leave.' I started to complain about Nishi's extortionate lie but Fujimoto-san shrugged. 'Negotiations,' he chuckled, sliding a hand under the table. 'It is my job.'

—

After a brief walk through Roppongi's hectic streets we arrived outside a short high-rise hidden quietly next to Gas Panic, a bar where budget tourists flocked for cheap drinks. Once out of the elevator, Fujimoto-san pointed to a brass plate that read 'Petits Pois'.

'What does it mean, *petits pois*?' his colleague asked.

'Small peas,' I said. 'You know the small, round green vegetable?'

'Ahh! *Kirei* vegetable!' Fujimoto-san exclaimed: *pretty* vegetable. 'But this place is not a vegetable! No! It is a members-only club, and I am a member,' he smiled, opening the heavy wooden door. 'It is for men only, but you are my guest. Please, after you.'

Inside, we were the only customers in a French colonial sitting parlour with an aristocratic ambience. It was amazing that such an enclave could exist in a place like Roppongi. High-backed sofas scattered with ornate cushions were placed around large oak tables, a secret garden transformed the balcony and a small, curtained kitchen produced delicate dishes. Then Master, the short, round, old Japanese man who ran the club, emerged. Master had two young female assistants with skinny legs and jutting teeth who brought four enormous wine glasses and, just as Fujimoto-san had promised, a bottle of very, *very* good red wine.

'This wine is very exclusive,' he boasted with sparkling eyes. 'Only so many bottles have been imported. In a bar this is a hundred-thousand yen. If you are lucky enough to buy it from the distributor, it is twenty-five-thousand yen, but Master has it for fifty thousand – half price.' Master also had cheese as an accompaniment because, 'Of course you want cheese with your wine – you are *gaijin*!'

'Actually,' I retorted playfully, more to avoid being culturally stereo-typed than to disprove his assumption, 'I like Japanese food. Specifically, *natto*,' I taunted. It was a fermented soybean dish that typically scared *gaijin* off.

'Oh, please, don't eat *natto*.' Fujimoto-san screwed up his face.

'Why not? I love it, and *o-kono miyake* too. It's delicious.'

Fujimoto-san looked at me in disbelief. 'You are weird *gaijin*,' he exclaimed. As we waited for the red wine to be decanted, he went on: 'Never before have I met such a weird *gaijin* as you! Now please sing!'

'Right now? But I . . .'

'You are shy!' Fujimoto-san chuckled. 'I know. So drink up, and then choose your song.' A karaoke book was handed to me by one of the Japanese waitresses, and while Fujimoto-san sang 'Greenfields' and his friends Bob Dylan, I drank all of my wine plus three Kahlua and milks before I finally aligned myself with Tom Hanks and timidly began to sing 'In My Life' by the Beatles.

The song earned me eight calories. That was one of the perks of Petis Pois – Master's karaoke system was a super-speciality version that measured spent calories as a direct ratio of one's vocal output. Its accuracy was dubious, no doubt, and my reading below average, but I was still applauded boisterously with shouts and whistles.

'Very gooooood! I forget your face!' Fujimoto-san exclaimed, and I stared blankly back at him. 'I mean, I cannot forget your face! So *kirei*.

And your eyes, very German I think. Here is very good.' Fujimoto-san set down his *shochu* and covered up the lower half of my face. '*Ahhh! Great!* On a movie screen, the audience will need to see only this. I have met many actresses, because I take them to dinner all the time, but you are up here.' He shot his arm up wildly. 'Much better. I love your eyes.'

As Fujimoto-san continued, I marvelled hazily at his never-ending enthusiasm, but more so at the sheer craziness of the good time I was having. I swear the smile never left my face. The karaoke calories slowly piled up. The drinks flowed. The food kept coming. And the night wore on.

A FIELD TRIP TO HAKONE

Ninety minutes of toss-and-turn sleep. This was all I achieved after Saturday night before it was time to get out of bed on Sunday morning, sniffling and coughing in the shower before kissing Matt goodbye while he slept. I felt rotten but today I was going to the hot springs at Hakone with Shin, and I was looking forward to it. Sleep could wait.

Just as I slipped outside on the way to the station, Yoshi called. 'Hello, *ma chérie*,' he cooed brightly. 'Are you sleeping?'

'No, I'm not sleeping. I'm about to go to Hakone. What are you doing?'

'I am going fishing, on my boat. I'll be back at seven, so maybe we can go to dinner. What time do you come back from Hakone?'

'I'm not sure. I think maybe eight?'

'Okay, I will call you. And, *ma chérie*?'

'Yes?'

'Please be a good girl. I am a good boy, all day for you, fishing *alone*.'

—

Shin took one look at my sinus-enflamed self and led me straight to a juice bar in the basement of a Shinjuku store tower. He was dressed like a bum again, but this time his black beanie, pilled sweatpants and generic T-shirt were complemented by a grey hoody tied around the waist, rigid and stale from being dried out in the sun. I think the clerk might have doubted he actually had any money in his yellow vinyl pouch, but with fresh citrus juice in hand we made a beeline to a pharmacy where he bought nasal spray, extra-strong Halls and a multi-pack of personal-sized Kleenex for me. 'And something else?' he asked as his face creased in concern. *Well, no, Shin. I think you've covered all bases. Thanks.*

'Okay, we must go this way. This is tourist pamphlet, but maybe not in English. You can look at pictures . . . and this is Freepass – travel ticket for train, and smaller train, and cable car. You are sure you are okay?' he asked, handing the paraphernalia over.

I sniffled in response, and with a disapproving frown he led the way to the Odakyu line bound for Hakone. Waiting on the crowded platform, I injected the first squirt of nasal spray and cried out in alarm as the astringent pain seared right through to my tear ducts.

Shin was unimpressed. 'Why you cry?' he shouted. 'Is not strong one! I know! I bought it. *I* can read Japanese.'

But my vision blurred as he became a foggy shape and my eyelids went into overdrive. 'Are you okay?' I heard him say. 'Here, take this.' He found my hand. 'Is tissue! Are you okay?'

'Sure, I'll be fine.' I blotted uselessly at my eyes just as the crowd began to board. As the train pulled away, Shin drew the blind to block the sunlight and instructed me to sleep, draping his stale jumper gently over my knees. I closed my eyes and quickly faded away.

—

Historically speaking, Hakone first made a name for itself as a gateway to the Kanto region during the Edo period, a resting stop on the long road between the Shogunate's Tokyo and the Emperor's Kyoto. In modern times it has become the most popular resort region in Japan, situated in the picturesque Fuji Hakone Izu National Park.

Located only eighty kilometres west of Tokyo, Hakone's volcanic hot springs, grand hotels and scenic nature attract twenty million visitors a year to a town of less than fifteen thousand. If I had my choice, it would be a town of less than fifteen thousand *plus one*. Hakone was love at first sight, and yet the only way I had of capturing it was with a novelty camera disguised as an Asahi beer can that Shin had given me on the train. I think he delighted in the fact that I'd be walking around Hakone looking like a drunken *gaijin* all day, attracting disapproving looks from old Japanese ladies.

Regardless of my inability to capture it, the pristine landscape was irresistibly romantic. I adored the small cars of the Hakone Tozan Railway in which we switchbacked over a river, through tunnels and woods to Chokoku-no-mori station, where we found the wonderful Hakone Open Air Museum – 70,000 square metres of nature scattered with over a hundred outdoor sculptures. The museum boasts one of the world's largest collections of Henry Moore and a spectacular installation of giants by Rodin, but my equal-first prize for favourite exhibit went to a bronze naked man lying face down on the grass and 'The Hand of God', a dynamic 1954 sculpture of a man questioning the heavens by Swedish-American Carl Milles.

After more than an hour we followed the exit signs to return to the railway, passing one last installation at the bottom of a steep escalator – a pulsating red light encased in a gigantic plastic green alien. Shin boarded the escalator ahead of me and was halfway up before he turned to call back down: 'You are alien too, in Japan.' I laughed as I stopped to take a picture with my beer-can camera. He didn't know how right he was.

—

Necks craned in anticipation as the cable car crept slowly up the mountainside, but as we traversed the first ridge my attention was captured not by the steamy crevasse of bubbling pools below but by the bright pair of knickers that must have fallen from my bag as I'd rummaged for a sweater earlier. I might have been quietly mortified had everyone not been glued to the window to see whether Mt Fuji would be visible today. As we approached the next ridge, I managed to quickly whisk my florals away unnoticed.

The closer we got to the top, the stronger the stench of sulphur became, thick enough to make everyone plug their noses and giggle, until the rare appearance of Mt Fuji in its entirety made us forget altogether. The great Fuji-san was beautiful, like a faint watercolour in the distance that might disappear if you squinted too hard. Everyone gasped in reverence as cameras clicked away to immortalise the exceptional view until we disembarked at the crest of Owakudani, the Great Boiling Valley. As one would expect of a weekend retreat so close to Tokyo, the area was swamped with tourist buses, but there were remarkably few foreigners.

Shin was an exceptionally thorough guide and had me pose for pictures in front of everything: colourful shrines, steep hillsides punctuated with tufts of steam escaping from deep within the mountain, even ordinary fences and rock signs. Certain areas were closed due to high levels of sulphurous acid gas and hydrogen sulphide, but we stuck to the main trail until we came to one of the most curiously innovative tourism gimmicks in existence: black hard-boiled eggs. Cooked in volcanic water, their porous shells turn black from mineral absorption, and while they were delicious, it was probably the myth that each egg would extend your life by seven years that explained the zeal with which people cracked them open to enjoy with a bit of salt and a spectacular view of Mt Fuji.

Browsing through gift shops, we sampled sweet bean cakes and green-tea everything before Shin introduced me to *wasabi* ice cream – the best thing ever to hit my taste buds. I bought a tube of *wasabi* and Shin added an adorable black-egg keychain to my goody bag. When I held it up to the light and peered through a tiny hole, a snowcapped Mt Fuji appeared behind a billow of steam.

—

Returning to the valley at nightfall, we taxied from the main station along a river to a pair of *onsen* that could be visited by the hour. Shin chose the more expensive bathhouse since it would be quieter and 'a more good experience', but he was still concerned I wouldn't know what to do. Since neither he nor the owner wanted to tell me, they just pointed to a picture and told me to ask a woman on the women's side. *The women's side?* Yes, of course, these *onsen* were separated by sex (as I later learnt, all but the most rural were), and even though I'd been prepared to go in naked with Shin and a bunch of strangers, I breathed a sigh of relief. We parted ways in the corridor, and I entered a steamy, terraced wooden hall open to the outdoors, where three graduated rock pools sat below a stunning cliffside waterfall. It was magical. Undressing quickly, I stowed my clothes in a woven basket and stood shivering with a towel the size of a facecloth, trying to look around discreetly for what to do next. At a low row of taps there was a Japanese woman on a stool, rigorously soaping every square inch, so I waited until she finished by rinsing with a wooden bucket and quickly pranced across the cold stone floor to copy the procedure.

There were only a few women scattered among the *onsen*, so I chose an empty, shallow pool to dip my toe in. It was scalding hot, but inch by inch I submerged until the volcanic water became bearable, and suddenly the tension of a thousand ills slipped away into the cool night air. I forgot that this was my twenty-fourth hour without sleep and remembered what it was like to feel wide awake, peaceful and maybe even healthy as I lay on the bottom of the pool, staring up at the dark night sky until the soothing waters left my skin supple and smooth. After fifteen minutes it felt like I'd slept for a year, and thirty more had me completely rejuvenated. No wonder the Japanese hold *onsen* in such reverence.

Shin was shiny and glowing when I found him putting on his socks in the hallway an hour later. 'You were okay?' he asked, obviously still concerned about my foreign reaction to the naked bathing and scrubbing. 'Was I *okay*?' I laughed. 'I was excellent.'

'Okay, good,' Shin grinned. 'Me too. But let's get some snack to eat before train back to Tokyo. Then you can sleep.'

—

Can I have a 'Go to Jail' card please? I know it's in there, waiting. *GO DIRECTLY TO JAIL. DO NOT PASS GO. DO NOT COLLECT $200.* I want that card, and I want it *now*. I don't want to wait for it to randomly come up in the stack between Baltic Avenue and Park Place. I want to impose it on myself, immediately. I can't stop the flip-flop. I am addicted to attention. I am addicted to alcohol. Every time I roll the dice they come up snake's eyes, and now I'm afraid that the substances could get a whole lot worse.

Somewhere on the train between Hakone and Tokyo, as Shin read peacefully, my phone rang. I walked to the front of the carriage so as not to disturb him and agreed to meet Yoshi as soon as I got to Shinjuku station.

YOSHI-COLA

Yoshi picked me up in his Benz on the other side of Shinjuku station at 8.45 pm. I was sleepy and calm, having just said goodbye to Shin on the Yamanote platform, but Yoshi was jumpy and hyper. There'd been too many waves to take his boat out at Odaiba this morning as he'd planned, so he'd turned around and gone home.

He must have spent the day idly because he drove like a wild man through neon streets to an underground car park, racing to an elevator that took us to the top of a Shinjuku skyscraper. Inside a crowded restaurant we gorged on tempura and substandard wine while Yoshi grew agitated and cranky, complaining about everything in existence except me. Usually I would have called him on his pessimistic rant, but I was overtired and suspended in a state where I couldn't figure out whether I wanted to be around him or not. Emotionally, the answer was a resounding yes – I felt safe and adored and comfortingly special in his wake – but logically the shades of grey were building up to a colour much closer to black. When we couldn't eat any more and I was drunk enough to need his arm for stability, Yoshi paid the extravagant bill with his Amex *noir* and then turned to me as he swept the *noren* curtain aside. 'Home, or one drink?' he asked graciously.

I answered without hesitation, 'One drink.'

—

The Yakuza don't touch Charlie here. Speed. That's their thing. At least that's what Yoshi told me. It's all they bothered to run. For everything else they just took a cut: cocaine, crack, heroin, pills; they all came through Romania or Iran. Yoshi preferred the Romanians. Apparently they had a really good source, but it paid to be sure. There'd been a rumour floating around the clubs that ten people, including some foreigners, died from cocaine laced with heroin this week. No one knew where it had come from, but those with a choice were avoiding it, at least until the rumour died, which was pretty fast. Bad news never lasts very long in Japan. Especially not when foreigners are involved.

Leaving the tempura restaurant, Yoshi drove in a straight line from Shinjuku to park his Mercedes in front of a building on the Roppongi strip. Even after several drinks he was highly abrasive. 'I hate this *fucking* Roppongi,' he spat resentfully, 'but every once in a while I gotta come here.' I didn't need an explanation, so I didn't ask for one. I stayed in the passenger seat as instructed. He flashed an impish smile before jumping out to disappear into the elevator lobby, coming back down only a few minutes later, a few grams heavier than before he went in.

—

Not much later we were sitting on an elegant sofa in the Compass Rose sky lounge on the twenty-second floor of the Westin Hotel in Ebisu, drinking and listening to a chanteuse play jazz on a baby grand piano. Outside the window Tokyo's skyscrapers were a grid of blinking red dots. Aloofly drunk and exhausted I stifled a yawn and Yoshi looked my way. 'What's the matter, *ma chérie*? You sleepy? I bore you?'

'Don't be ridiculous, Yoshi. I just didn't get to sleep last night at all. I'm exhausted.'

'It's okay. I have,' Yoshi stated quickly, 'queen's drug. You wanna?'

I looked into his eyes. Small and precise. 'Yeah, okay.'

'Let's go.' Yoshi grabbed my hand and we left our drinks on the table. Out in the hallway we loitered until the doorman disappeared from sight. 'Okay, wait here. I check.' Ten seconds later he was beckoning me in.

'But that's the *men's* room!' I whispered, and he pulled me in by the arm.

'So what? No problem. Hurry up.'

I followed him into the last stall and he turned the lock behind us.

Opening his wallet he pulled out a tiny ziplock bag and poured two wayward lines onto a small silver shelf. Handing me a credit card he said, 'Here, make it pretty. I'm too drunk.' So I used Yoshi's plastic millions to even up the lines as he rolled a ¥10,000 note and placed it between my fingers. 'You choose,' he cooed. 'I am gentleman.' And his eyes twinkled for the first time that night. 'Always ladies first.'

I gave Yoshi a long look and he fidgeted. It is a terrible feeling to want something you know is destructive. But fuck it. I bent down and snorted the cocaine. I handed Yoshi the note and my heels clicked as I shuffled out of his way. I pressed against the cubicle wall watching him; there was something desperate about the way he snorted his line. He was trying to contain it, but I could see its effect, just before he turned away to sniffle and clear out his throat.

Then we heard the door open, and Yoshi turned with a finger to his lips. We heard the sound of a zipper, a pause and then the long, continuous flow of a man urinating. I found it hysterical and nearly died to keep silent. Yoshi made me sit on the toilet seat, motioning to stay while he exited the stall. I heard him washing his hands and making small talk in Japanese. As if everything was normal. I giggled insanely. Inaudibly. In a toilet stall I was on top of the world. Yoshi knocked and we scuttled out of the bathroom in stages like something from a bad James Bond film. I had to take a deep breath just to walk back into the lounge with composure. Hyper-alert and oversensitised, I quashed the feeling that everyone was looking at us, sitting innocently two feet apart on our couch by the wall.

'Ahhh, now *genki*,' Yoshi exhaled. 'How 'bout you? Okay?'

'Great. I just can't breathe again.' I put my hand on my sternum.

Yoshi frowned. 'Again?' I nodded and he slid my daiquiri over. 'Drink up.'

'It's okay, I'll be okay. Don't worry,' I smiled. Yoshi was gleaming. He was back to his alluringly confident, endearingly arrogant self and I was totally spacked. It was hard to maintain equilibrium as he began to complain about having to spend Christmas in Oahu at his father's Waikiki condo. It was hard to focus on his face without feeling panicked.

'Why do I have to go to fucking Hawaii for Christmas? In two days

I am bored. There is nothing to do. But not if you're there,' he hinted salaciously.

'I'm going home for Christmas, Yoshi.'

'Okay, okay. Why are you so difficult? I'll give you an airline ticket as a Christmas present. Then, you can come back to Tokyo in January, work at Greengrass . . .'

'What? But I don't want to hostess any more. Are you crazy?'

'Oh, what will you do? Model?' he asked casually, and suddenly the ludicrous reality of the situation I'd worked myself into hit home. Even to Yoshi, hostessing was nothing out of the ordinary. It was just another job for a woman and just another part of his culture, but I felt sadly betrayed that Yoshi wouldn't care if his hypothetical girlfriend still worked at a hostess bar. In fact, I was gutted. True, Matt had no problem with me working at Greengrass, but it was temporary and, while I still had it under control, we were in this together.

Yoshi, however, was still in the hopeless stages of trying to acquire me, and just now, just suddenly, it became clear to me. That motherfucker.

For a while Yoshi fidgeted as he told me how beautiful I was and how much fun we'd have dressing up for the opera. If I became his girl-friend, he said, he would be so proud and my life would be full of never-ending surprises, but the only surprise I'd ever have to give him was a new G-string. His mother would be surprised to find them in his laundry of course, but Yoshi would tell her to stay out of his business. I'd look good in Valentino and all his friends would be jealous. He wanted me to get a little bit of fat but otherwise I was perfect. He didn't like too skinny girls.

'Anyways, *ma chérie*, I wanna have. You wanna have?'

'No thanks. I can still hardly breathe. It was too much I think.'

'Okay, I'll be back.' And so Yoshi went solo to the men's room while I sat primly on the couch and drained both his glass of water and mine. I was sucking on my second daiquiri when he strutted back into the lounge like a peacock, and I had to endure more of his vivid promises until I made a show of looking at his Rolex. Yoshi looked me in the eye.

'You wanna get a room?' he asked brazenly. It was the first time Yoshi had ever been so direct and I felt hot and ashamed and terrible that even my being here with him was a lie.

'No,' I said bluntly, and he shrugged as if it didn't make a single ounce of difference to him. That was enough for me, and I said, 'I want to go home, Yoshi. I'm tired.'

Yoshi pressed his lips together and smiled. 'Of course, *ma chérie*, everything for you.'

We were both intoxicated to the point that he shouldn't have driven and I shouldn't have let him, but Yoshi drove through the deserted early-morning streets to the top of mine. He stopped where I asked him to and turned to look at me. 'I am serious about you,' he confessed. 'I am decided.'

'Really?' I objected. 'Am I the type of person you'd introduce to your mother?'

'I don't know yet,' he said quietly.

'Well obviously you aren't serious then,' I said flatly. 'Because I know that you know that you wouldn't, Yoshi, and this is just your game.'

'No, *ma chérie*, I care about you, but you don't . . .'

'C'mon, Yoshi,' I put two fingers to his mouth and he kissed them softly. 'Don't say any more. Thanks for tonight,' I said quietly. 'I'll see ya.'

Stepping out onto the deserted street, I gently shut the door and didn't look back. I was just a filler for the part. An understudy who got to perform the lead only after the last star burnt out. That was probably why his last girlfriend left. She got tired of the drugs, of the pitch and yaw of Yoshi's magnetism and deception and the fact that he didn't actually know you, that he didn't actually seem to *want* to know you, and that all he wanted was someone with whom he could pretend it was *all okay*.

If I wasn't here, somebody else would spend the evening getting high with Yoshi. Someone else would amuse him with her company. Someone else would listen to his perfect sentences about a perfect relationship in a perfect future that could never exist. As long as she was young and pretty and full of grace, what more could he possibly want?

I should have listened to Karolina when she said: 'We girls think that we're playing with them, but really they're the ones that are playing with us. Don't take anything they say at face value, and don't get involved, and you'll have a good time.' Well, I *wasn't* having a good time. Fuck Yoshi. And fuck this stupid place.

—

Roppongi is a cold, hard expanse of concrete city blocks, each one sublet to the devil on an indefinitely renewable lease. As a lawless entity of its own, Roppongi will hand out every temptation, every justification and every distraction on a sterling-silver plate. It will slide things into your hand when you aren't looking. It will follow you close behind, whispering in your ear. I know this, because I could hear it. I could feel it. If ever I were going to fall apart, if ever I were to completely lose it, Tokyo would be the place.

Without my darling Matt, I'd have already lost my mind. This is the only thing I know. Without him to tell me about physiology and fitness magazines when I come dazed through the door at all hours of the morning, without him to listen while I spew out the details of twenty hours lived away from him, without him to go out and buy the laundry soap when the thought never enters my mind, I'd be hopeless. Although it appears to be the opposite, every day spent in this delusion only strengthens the value in which I hold us.

I've had enough of this. I'm not sure what I'm doing any more. I'm drained. Twelve hours ago I was complete in the volcanic hot springs of Hakone, and now I've hardly returned to Tokyo and already I'm sucked dry.

I want to stop. Six more weeks. Can I really survive? I just want to sleep, but my pupils are larger than they should be. I hate seeing the glint of sunshine when I wake during the day. My life is upside down. I am looking inside every white or silver Benz that passes us on the street. Do I know that man? Will he recognise me? I feel like I shouldn't hold hands with my husband in public. I am hungry, but I don't feel like eating. I am confused; I feel beleaguered. I have accrued too many symptoms in too little time to even start to diagnose my condition. I am happy and joyous. I am sad and alone. And what about paranoia? Add it to my list . . . just another box ticked off with a fat swoosh of the red Crayola marker. I think maybe this is the craziest thing I've ever done. *Maybe.*

God help me if it's not.

MIRROR, MIRROR

Abie's eyes were sunken when I showed up for work just shy of nine. Without a scrap of make-up she looked like a little girl shivering under the air conditioner despite having an illegal cardigan thrown over her shoulders. With each day I was coming to expect this dishevelled appearance, but it was the tangled, ratty hair that made me ask, 'Abie, are you okay?'

'No. I thought I wasn't going to come back this weekend. It was so, so rough . . .'

It all started with a reckless decision – the ingestion of some hardcore drugs at a nightclub. An afterparty brought her to Benny the Israeli coke dealer's house where, anticipating a gnarly comedown, she'd refused a ride home for a reason she didn't want to disclose from a guy she didn't want to name and instead of spending money on a taxi, wandered the unfamiliar streets alone using Tokyo Tower as a guide, then lay in bed for hours talking to a pocket mirror while she stared back at herself, thinking she was dying.

Oh boy. Hadn't Abie done this before just recently and wasn't it just as horrific? Well, last time it had been LSD at a rave in Roppongi, but her laments were still the same: 'I hate Tokyo. I hate the Japanese. I want to leave. What am I doing here? Who am I?'

'Abie, you need to promise me that you're not going to touch any drugs . . .'

'Ever?' she questioned cynically, and I just looked at her. Abie had become lifeless, deeply morose and plump in only a matter of weeks. What had happened to her?

'Abie, please take care of yourself,' I pleaded, and she cried while I hugged her.

'I know,' she whispered. 'I already scared myself, it's okay.' But it would be only twenty-four hours before Abie would tell me she just wanted to go smoke dope again and sleep off her misery. Words are futile sometimes.

And human patterns ever so hard to break.

I'd heard so many stories about girls spending Saturday nights in Roppongi getting royally fucked up in order to lose themselves in a chemical reprieve. If they weren't already getting them for free, girls who'd never paid for drugs were paying for them, girls who'd never used drugs were using them, and all of them were crashing down to find themselves lost in a concrete jungle.

It was a sobering task trying to navigate the streets of a daytime, functioning society as a thrashed-out white girl trying to find her way home after a night of work and partying. Under a midday sun the Japanese who observed a *gaijin* traipsing through their disciplined neighbourhoods in clacking heels and a cocktail dress couldn't be blamed if they thought she truly *was* a foreign devil, even if they'd never show it outwardly.

And *that* was part of the problem. The Japanese didn't even seem to notice her. But she noticed them in their normal houses, among normal sights and living a normal life. Daylight was meant to be forgiving, but alone in such a state the sun only magnified her ominous feeling of hollow isolation. She was far away from home. Far away from what she knew. A plane ticket, a passport, the promise of an easy fortune and the adventure of a lifetime had brought her here but, ill-equipped and overwhelmed, she'd ended up displaced, simultaneously despising and worshipping the things that had enticed her to this city and this job in the first place. She didn't need others to label her anything; she already felt *gaijin* in every sense of the word, and it gave her an abject loneliness and filled her with a void that begged to be filled, if only artificially.

Of course one shouldn't generalise, but this was too often the reality that found girls like Abie back in their dog-box apartments during the late-morning hours of any given Sunday, sobbing out their eyes into a mascara-streaked pillow.

TAKE A NUMBER

In response to a rambling message detailing my deteriorating state of health, Nori returned my call to state that on Wednesday, he *needed* to see me. 'I want to know how you think about me.'

'*What?* What do you mean?' I asked sharply, hoping he'd be too embarrassed to repeat himself, but Nori did, word for word, and I was forced to lamely sidestep the question. 'Um, sure. Did you say Wednesday? Yeah, okay, it would be good if I could see you Wednesday. We can go for dinner and spend some time together. That would be nice.'

'Okay,' Nori sighed, 'I believe you.'

What was that supposed to mean? I didn't say anything for him to believe.

'But anyway,' he said, forcing his voice into a high-spirited tone, 'did I tell you? Yesterday my hostess friend from Roppongi came to Yokohama to see me. She spent the entire day at my house,' he laughed fakely, 'and we had so much fun.'

'That's great,' I said, starting to complain about my sinuses. What did Nori think? That I'd be jealous of a fabricated story because I secretly desired to be with him? God! I knew I was just the blank screen onto which he projected his foreign films of delusion, but when had the sub-titles gone so outrageously wrong? 'Hey, maybe you would know what medicine I should take,' I rambled on. 'I can hardly breathe during the night and . . .'

'I want you to tell me, *what* you think of me,' Nori interrupted, but no, I doubted that he did, so I made up the excuse of not feeling well, said I'd talk to him later and hung up before he could protest.

⁓

Shin dials my number every two or three days. Goro does it sporadically. Nori daily, sometimes twice, but usually thrice or more. Then there's Yoshi. He calls whenever he *feels* like it, and always with a certain tone, like he's been thinking about me for eons and just can't take it any longer. *I just wanted to hear your voice*, he'll say, *ma chérie*.

I find the inflection of my voice changing every time I answer the phone. It's the same automatic adjustment that happens every time I sit down next to someone in the club. You start adapting. Gauging the distance between his hip and yours. Anticipating reactions. Manipulating outcomes. But let me specify, I *never* flirt with the customers. I'm a conversationalist. Pure and simple.

Yet there is one exception. I still can't force Yoshi into a box and make him stay there. No matter how hard I try to keep the lid on, he keeps busting out. I don't think about how this affects my life most of the time, because I don't see this as my life. My nights and days are not my own. It's still me, but somehow not. I don't know if I can explain it much more clearly than that. There are too many questions, with too many variables. Most of the time I just leave them unanswered. Yet there is one question I know the answer to without even having to ask. If I were a single woman and Yoshi was his same self, would I consider it? *Yes.* There. I said it.

This is the kind of shit that is running around in my brain. I know I shouldn't, but I trust what Yoshi says to be true, no matter how illogical that is. I really think he might love me. Who knows why? Maybe it's just my own inflated ego. And that scares me. I know all the consequences. I know all the outcomes. But the demons. The demons are not easily quelled.

⁓

I was only a few pages into *A History of Japan* when the phone rang. I knew it was Yoshi even before I saw his number – but it was just another uneventful call from the office wherein he schmoozed and I laughed inconsequentially. As Yoshi hung up and I threw the phone aside, it suddenly struck me that I didn't even know his last name. Not his company, his profession, his age, *nothing*, and yet I'd gone to Kyoto with him with only $40 in my pocket. I'd done coke with him on two separate occasions when it was just me, him and a hotel. If you asked me the number for the police in Japan, I'd stare at you blankly. Silly girl. It should have been something to think about if I wasn't overwhelmed by the need to sleep.

I set the alarm to 7.15 pm and crawled back under the covers. When I pulled them to my chin in the artificial darkness, my lip jutted out involuntarily, but I closed my eyes before the tears could come. I am so depressed at times during the day. Raw, exhausted and overexposed.

This is how I feel.

YOSHI'S LAST NAME

Tonight, Abie was more relaxed than I'd noticed of late, but this was probably just a by-product of the excessive THC now swimming in her blood. She'd begun smoking daily since a decision to follow her true spirit and go ahead with that uncannily predictable mission of so many young Israelis: the intrepid trek through India. Until she left in four weeks, Abie was no longer concerned with money; she saw Grandpa only occasionally, never bothered to bottle and simply went home each night to smoke pot and dream of Goa. As I watched her puff on a cigarette, she thought I looked sad. 'You have this big smile on your face all the time, but I look into your eyes and they're sad,' she mused. 'What's up?'

'I just have a lot of confusion. I'm all *fucked up*.' I rolled my eyes as if to amplify the absurdity of how stupid I felt. Or perhaps to hide the weight of it.

'Yoshi?' she asked under her breath.

'Yoshi,' I repeated, and the dilemma unleashed. 'I really think he's serious. You know? What if he *is* serious? Imagine what I . . .' but Abie interjected with force.

'He is *not*. This is his game, Chelsea, and you cannot believe him. He is your fucking customer. He comes here, and he is your customer. You love Matt and Matt loves you, and that's *your* life. You don't *have* to tell him *everything*. They know it's all fake! You're crazy to think anything else.'

'I know. I just never thought that I would be this *involved*. I mean, it's not like I'm about to run away with some rich Japanese guy whose last name I don't even know. I'm not as deluded as them. But I just can't help feeling . . .'

'That he's old enough to be your dad?' Abie offered.

'I was gonna say *sorry for him*.'

'Could you really imagine being with somebody that's addicted to drugs? Chelsea, come on, this guy is. Do you know what that would do to somebody?' Her hand plummeted from a point high above her tangled mousey hair. 'You may start here, but you're going to end up on the floor.'

'I know that. I just wish that . . . well, I don't know what. It's just such an appealing daydream, but when I really think about it, I'd never want to be that person who spent my life saying *Yoshi, can I have this? Yoshi, can you buy that?* And obviously I can't tell Yoshi about Matt, but I don't know what to do until I leave. No excuse would sound valid. What do I tell him? He's getting so . . . insistent.'

'Nothing. You just play his game. He is your customer and that is *it*. Right?'

'Right.' *Irashaimase!* And who should walk in the door but the ever-charismatic devil himself. 'Oh fuck. Guess who just walked in the door.'

'Is that Yoshi?'

It sure was. He was dressed impeccably, and with a crisp shirt and tie, he looked all business. Abie embraced me in a dopey, support-group hug. 'Okay, go have fun . . . with your customer. I love you.'

'Who is this nice gentleman?' I asked coyly, standing over the low table, and Yoshi took me by the hand while I kissed him on the cheek. He was incredibly uptight. 'Last night, was it dead, because of typhoon?' he asked.

'No, it was busy.'

'Oh!' Yoshi seemed genuinely surprised. 'Did you enjoy yourself?'

'C'mon, Yoshi, it's business. Besides, they were all crazy.'

'Am I crazy?'

'You're a different kind of crazy, Yosh.'

'Good crazy?'

'Yes, good crazy. You're one of a kind.'

'Good. I just come from a business dinner. Bleh, I was supposed to stay for drinks, but I dismissed myself. Said I had an early morning and came straight to see you. I miss you,' he cooed. 'Chelsea, how are you? *O-genki desu ka.*'

'*Genki desu*, and you?'

'Fucking business. I am businessman. I hate it.' Yoshi pulled at his tie. He glanced at his watch. He was checking it every ten seconds.

'What's the matter? Have you got a hot date tonight?'

'No.' He struck the face of his Rolex at the quarter-past mark. 'My dealer is coming. Ten minutes.'

Oh, so now we're being *that* frank about it, are we?

'I'll go downstairs, but fucking drug dealers, their ten minutes is thirty.'

It was difficult to say anything after that. I was shocked he'd even come. Yoshi was playing his game, just like Abie said, and he was a master player. I was a fool to think otherwise.

'Did you get my pictures developed? From Kyoto?' I asked coolly.

'Yeah, in my car. Downstairs. What you wanna drink?' I ordered wine and Soh gave me the surprised, bug-eye look. I may have been opting for oolong tea the past week, but I needed two glasses of red just to ease the tension. Yoshi was complaining about everything.

I cleared my throat. 'How often do you do it, Yoshi?'

'Do what?' he barked defensively, and I just motioned at the Rolex. He knew what I was asking. '*What?* Come on, not every day. Only for party, with you,' he smiled coyly. I raised my eyebrows. 'Oh, *ma chérie*, not on a weekday, come on. I am working man! I am business guy. No, never.' Yoshi's phone rang and he snapped it open. 'Okay, I'll be there, two minutes.' Then he left me alone for fifteen minutes and, without a glance my way, strode back into the club and straight to the toilet. I called Soh over.

'When Yoshi pays, can you please write down his last name?'

'Okay. But why he disappear so long?' Soh asked, and I just shrugged. Another ten minutes passed before Yoshi rejoined me.

'Were you chatting up Mama-san?' I couldn't get the sadness out of my voice.

'I don't know what she's fucking talking about. She is saying something, but I don't know what she says. Why, you jealous?' I kept my mouth shut. 'Chelsea, *ma chérie*, you miss me? You think about me? No, you don't. I know. You don't care about me.'

'I don't want to hear that again, Yoshi. Stop saying that.' I slapped his hand as he tried to slide it up my thigh. He didn't seem high yet, but I couldn't be sure.

'This is going to be my booty,' he purred. 'Isn't it? Oh, I can't wait. Say it's mine.'

'Fuck off, Yoshi. Don't touch me.'

He just laughed. 'Okay, I go to toilet. I wanna have.' Yoshi's nonchalance was so calculated it seemed the thought had just casually slipped into his mind. 'You wanna?' he grinned.

'No.' I flatly refused. And so then, on a weeknight, Yoshi disappeared for a party of one in the men's room.

'You *genki* now?' I asked cynically when he came back.

'No. Okay, maybe one minute, then *genki*.' Sixty seconds later Yoshi was noticeably taller, in possession of the confidently arrogant air he usually possessed. With a long inhalation he collapsed his arms. 'Ohhhh, now I am so *genki*, because with you.'

What a crock of shit. I hadn't changed my name to Charlie. *I* wasn't delivering euphoria to his every cell after he'd just snorted me up his nasal passage. What was Yoshi talking about? He started to sniffle and called Nishi over to request a cold *oshibori*. While Yoshi poured Nishi a fresh beer, I wondered how much had gone up his nose in a lifetime.

He pulled me close in a tight shoulder grip. 'Nishi,' he pleaded, 'whatta can I do? I like her so much, but she doesn't like me. I don't want a one-way love.' Nishi said nothing and sipped at the cold froth. He laughed without noise as I jabbed Yoshi in the ribs to create more space and left when more customers arrived, leaving his beer on the table. 'You know,' Yoshi whispered, 'having sex with myself is better than a one-night stand. Am I right?'

'You're ridiculous, Yoshi.'

'Okay, maybe, but I am man, and in love with you. I need to survive. Are you going to help me move to my new apartment? You can be my first guest. We can have a party. It will be so good, my apartment so close to yours. You know before, I used to live near you.'

'I thought you lived next to the Westin, in Ebisu.'

'Yeah, there too. Many places.'

'So how many times have you gone home to your mommy?'

'Every time my heart gets broken, I go back to recover. Then I move out again. If you break my heart,' he warned, 'I will go back.'

'But you haven't even moved out yet.'

'No, but soon. The twenty-sixth. You know international supermarket? My apartment is very near there. Second floor. You can come over any time, twenty-four hours open. After work you sleepy, come over, have something to eat.'

Right. I'll show up drunk at 3.00 am. You'll appreciate it, I'm sure.

He put his hand gently over mine and intertwined our fingers. 'Zebra babies.'

I laughed and wondered how many girls he'd said the same things to.

'But I told you, I am serious! Already decided, but you don't believe me. When are you going to move in with me?' he asked.

'What?' I was shocked. 'I don't even know your *last name* and now you want me to move in with you?'

'Tokugawa. T.O.K.U.G.A.W.A. Yoshiaki Tokugawa, but people just call me Yoshi.' *Well, that solved everything. Cut me a spare key.* 'What, you don't think I love you? Oh, oh, oh!' he whimpered sarcastically. 'You don't know my name, *yadda yadda yadda.* You don't believe me? *Chérie,*' Yoshi's eyes lingered. '*Everything* for you.'

Okay. Deep breath. The only thing I believed from Yoshi was that his last name was Tokugawa, and only because I saw it embossed on his Amex when he pulled it out to pay.

Out in the hallway Yoshi promised to call me tomorrow. 'Is that okay?' Of course it was okay. I loved him and loathed him. I corralled him into the elevator. I turned my back. I retreated in haste and waved over my shoulder. At the last second I glanced back, only to see him making out with the air pocket in front of him, kissing empty space like crazy.

—

Some days are better than others. Some days are shit. I coach myself into feeling better all the time. At Greengrass tonight, Jodie thought I looked particularly *genki*. 'You look like you had a fabulous weekend,' she said. *Did I? But what did I even do?* I can no longer remember what happens from one day to the next. Each twenty-four-hour cycle in this blinding fantasy world is a totally enjoyable, totally reproachable kaleidoscope of emotion.

'That's what makes you leave Tokyo, and that's what makes you come back. It's addictive, you'll see. Less than two weeks after you leave,' Jodie said, 'you'll want to come back.' Then she paused. 'Nope, let me restate that. *First* week, guarantee it.'

Those may have been Jodie's words, but somehow I was starting to believe her. I am waiting, waiting, waiting. But staying, staying, staying.

THE SURGEON GOES MENTAL

Stunned and astonished. That's the only way to put it. How else could I feel? Only yesterday I hadn't even known his last name and today Yoshi was calling from the hospital where his cousin had just given birth. 'It's a boy, a baby boy!' he shouted proudly. 'Her second child, *already*. He is so handsome, but already he looks like such a naughty boy.'

'You know why?' I laughed, 'because he's related to you. Congratulations, Yoshi, that's really, really wonderful.'

'Thank you, thank you. I am so happy. What are you doing?'

'Just reading. I was . . .'

'What? *Reading?* Are you crazy? Look outside! Beautiful weather. Go outside!'

'Okay, okay, I know. I'll go for a walk.'

'Good. Are you being a good girl?'

'I am a great girl.'

'I know. How about last night? Busy?'

'Yeah, so-so. I went home at one-thirty.'

'Okay, *wakatta*. Anyway . . . I better go. Talk to you later.' With a casual *hai*-bye, Yoshi hung up, and I stared at what was left in my hand: *1 2 3. 4 5 6. 7 8 9. # 0 *.* Yoshi had chosen me from those numbers. Pressed connect. Waited for my voice as it rang once, twice, three times. I couldn't believe it. What had possessed him, a man I barely knew, to call *me* at such a moment of intimate family celebration? Especially when all I thought I could ever expect from someone like him was 'twenty-four-hour booty calls'?

194

The image of two hands laced together came immediately to mind. *Zebra babies.* That was the reason. I just knew it.

—

That night at Greengrass sitting with Nori felt like disciplining a six-year-old resolved to continue a week-old tantrum. I couldn't believe it, and I was tired of playing. 'You're angry, aren't you? What is your problem? Why are you so angry?'

'It is your fault I am angry!' Nori shouted back at me. 'You need me and I need you. You should know, because . . . I love you! And . . . you will be mine.'

'You blew it, Ito-san,' I said, reverting to formal address to sever any familiarity left between us. 'You're not my friend and I don't believe what you're saying. You are mean, you are childish and you are unfair.'

'No! But I really love you. I don't call to you, I know, but you are not just hostess for me. I have emotional involvement to you. Don't you think so?'

Fuck off, you psycho, I muttered inaudibly. 'Why are you acting like a child? I can't even understand why you are behaving this way, Ito!'

'Because! It is your fault I am miserable. I wanted to see you, that Sunday. Why can't you understand that I will do everything for you? I will make you successful.'

'No, sorry, Ito. Actions speak louder than words. Do you know that expression? *I. Don't. Believe. You.* You've never even taken me on a *dohan*. And you lie all the time!'

'But . . .' Nori began again and I threw up my hand to silence him. He was in a state of desperation and I couldn't stand it, but he wouldn't give up. 'Only you are for me. No one else makes me happy. I think about you always, but you upset me because I care about you. You will be mine.'

It just kept getting worse. I told Nori how I had to get up early to go to Asakusa tomorrow, so that when Fumio's inevitable invitation came to go eat with them and another hostess, my excuse was already in place.

'Uh, so now . . . you will go home?' Nori asked.

'Yes,' I said coldly, and Nori paid his $600 bill without giving me a tip. I couldn't wait for his face to disappear behind the elevator doors.

INNOCENCE FOR SALE

As a train cut through the cool air of a smoggy textbook morning, I sat in its third carriage, silently twirling the beer can that was my camera. It might not have been the most appropriate choice to take to Asakusa as the English tutor to a group of Japanese schoolgirls, but when I'd agreed to take the job last week, through the same talent agency that had got me the SMAPxSMAP job, they hadn't given any specific rules about camera choices.

It was another day without sleep. Another Tokyo extravaganza.

—

The all-girls Shinagawa Jusho Gakuin looked like anything *but* a junior high school; it was more of a Stalinist monolith that issued students with swipe cards to enter the security door. The vaulted cafeteria perpetuated the communist-era feeling, which was only exacerbated when a talent-agency member assembled our group of thirty-five foreigners inside, made a brief speech and left us in the capable hands of identically uniformed thirteen-year-olds who subdivided everyone into alphabetical and then numerical groups.

'May I please have your name?' they read from a piece of paper in perfect unison.

Chelsea Haywood.

'Chelsea Haaay-wood-o,' they said. 'You will be in Group F, number five-o.' Once everyone had been classified, we were led down stark corridors to a staircase. 'Our classroom is on the third floor,' they read. At the third floor the girls stopped again. 'Please follow us.' And soon we arrived outside our classroom five minutes ahead of schedule. Looking dumbfounded at this unexpected obstacle, their quick solution was to ban us from entering until the scheduled time of nine o'clock, when we were filed to the front of a blackboard to introduce ourselves 'with your biography' to a wide-eyed class.

I stood at the end of the line and waited my turn. First, Natasha was from Moldova – a Soviet state I didn't even know existed. Connie from the Philippines was next. She'd been in Tokyo twenty-five years on account of being married to a Japanese man. The Polish girl, Alina, also had a Japanese husband, and the last foreigner, Bill, was just a regular dude from the States.

Bill was seated first at a table of six girls who went ape shit when he pulled out his chair, shrieking in a fit of screams and giggles and causing him to turn several shades of red. He was a foreign *man*, after all, and that was pretty extreme for teenage schoolgirls in Japan.

To a less dramatic effect I was greeted by gasps, giggles and a heavily whispered *sugoi* (cool/great/fantastic), but the noise at my table was still disproportionate given that it came from only three girls. I had to ask Saeko and Reiko to repeat their names, but the third girl's name was Yoko.

'*Sumimasen*, Chelsea-san, *etto* . . . how old are you?' Yoko asked as all three girls hovered over exercise books. They held their breath with pencils poised.

'I am twenty-one years old,' I enunciated slowly, and they shrieked with delight.

'Do you have a boyfuhrend-o?' giggled Reiko.

'No, I do not have a boyfriend. I am married.' This elicited even more shrieks.

'Where are you fuhrom?' asked Yoko, and Canada was scratched into a blank space in wobbly letters. After much discussion in Japanese, the girls asked what I'd like to eat for lunch and then studied potential spots on a map of Asakusa. When enough questions had been answered to satisfy their curiosity and the expectations of their teacher (who they *very, very much didn't like because she was very bad and old, with a two-year-old baby*), they smiled on cue, announcing, 'O-kay! Let's go to Asakusa.' We left before anyone else.

The girls were dead silent as we walked to Kitashinagawa station; the only one to answer any of my questions was Yoko. The others simply giggled. Aboard the train, Saeko and Reiko stayed where they could see me, stuffing their school bags between pigeon-toed feet. Yoko kept her bag on her lap beside me, overflowing with Hello Kitties and Minnie Mice. Inside every compartment there were more containers and various cartoon *things*, the only useful one among them a mobile phone dangling with more than its weight in gizmos. I asked where she lived in an attempt to start conversation, and she answered *Saitama*. Saitama was over an hour away, which meant that Yoko travelled a long way just to get to school. So did Saeko and Reiko, but from different outlying areas of Tokyo. Already they were genuine Japanese commuters in training.

'What time do you have to get up?' I asked.

'I get up-puh at six o'clock-o.'

'And what time do you go to bed?'

It took some debate between the girls before Yoko finally answered. 'Everybody go to bed-do attuh one a-m.' *Oh my God.* Only five hours' sleep! These girls were only thirteen.

'Why so late? What do you do?'

They all knew the answer to that one. 'We watchu tee-vee,' said Saeko in a cloud of giggles. Of course, homework would be finished to perfection beforehand. You could count on that. An elementary obsession with cartoons does not necessarily replace a sharp academic intellect. Not in Japan. It just created severe sleep deficit. These junior high-school girls could probably still spout all the laws of Physics 101 at the drop of a Hello Kitty. But why did they go to a school that was so far away from home? I half-expected an answer regurgitated from the parents who paid their tens of thousands of dollars in yearly tuition. An answer like: 'This school provides good prospects for our future,' or even, 'The teachers are very nice,' but the girls surprised me.

'Because we rike zis school uniform. It is very *kawaii*, so cute-o!' Yoko giggled, and the others agreed. The sad thing was the girls weren't alone in their thinking. As one of Saeko's dark-brown knee socks slipped down her shin, she quickly bent forward to pull it back into order. Even with no teacher around to enforce the school's strict grooming policy, it was far too incriminating to be caught with *rusu-sokusu* (loose socks).

The girls' uniform, worn to establish that famously Japanese 'group feeling' from a young age, was innocent enough in construction: a floppy necktie and white-collared shirt, yellow cardigan, beige school blazer and shiny, flat-soled shoes. Apart from the deviant sock, Saeko's only misdemeanour was the length of her red pleated skirt. It was supposed to come down to the knee, but she wore it mid-thigh, probably in more of a fashion statement than anything else. It wasn't her fault the required dress code was anything but a symbol of innocence. She looked as proper as she should. As proper as one could in duds interwoven with the stigma of a nation that tolerated *buru sera* an erotic fascination with schoolgirls and their uniforms – as an acceptable part of the male sexual psyche.

Named after the crisp white bloomers (*buru*) worn under the sailor-(*sera*) inspired middy outfits of schoolgirls everywhere, *buru-sera* is only one aspect of a much larger picture: adolescence, and all its characteristics, as a commercially marketable sexual ideal. In Japan, it is completely acceptable – mainstream, at least – to promote the sexual fetish of schoolgirls with advertisements on trains and street corners, in magazines and newspapers.

It is not unusual for an adult male to pore over a pornographic *manga* comic, or just the regular old kind of porn, with no shame on a crowded train, or standing in line at the magazine rack in a convenience store. It is 100 per cent legal for pornography to be sold in street vending machines, as long as no pubic hair is visible. It can be watched in violent anime films that commonly depict the rape of minors and, more specifically, schoolgirls. In these films, and even on television cartoons, male characters suffer instant nosebleeds at the sight (or thought) of a cute schoolgirl. The stimulation apparently causes blood to rush to his head and come gushing out his nose. Weird? I think so. Just illustrations? I think not.

So why, then, do these things permeate Japanese culture so widely? Maybe because youth in a sexual partner is not just desirable but also deeply revered.

This idealised form of premature beauty is inherent in Japanese law.

According to Interpol, Article 177 of the Penal Code puts the age of consent for sexual activity at thirteen years in Japan. While most urban municipalities and jurisdictions have now imposed laws to bump the age of consent up closer to seventeen, it was only in 1999 that specific legislation was passed to forbid any Japanese citizen from paying for sex with someone under the age of eighteen. It's no wonder that Japan is the world's leader in child pornography. With such a unique set of legal circumstances, you have the opportunity for some very strange things to occur.

But still, why the off-the-wall obsession? Why are schoolgirls idealised to such an extent in this particular nation? Is it because the schoolgirl is weak? Submissive? Naive? *Childish?* The least threatening figure in a society where power is all about adult masculinity and conformity among the masses is a must? Whatever the reasons, there is no single explanation for *buru-sera*, but its influence is everywhere.

It is why twenty-something women, commonly known as *kogal* girls, hang out in nightlife districts dressed as heavily modified schoolgirls, desperately trying to exploit the uniform's allure to attract the attentions of men. Skirts are raised to skim just below the bum so that little white panties peep out with the slightest movement. Flat-soled loafers are replaced with twenty-centimetre platforms and are worn with mandatory *rusu-sokusu* bunched at the ankle. Hair is dyed in crazy cuts and faces plastered in heavy make-up, garnished with hot pink super lashes. These young women have created their own hyper-stylised caricature of the adolescent. They believe they are too old to be sexually enticing at twenty or twenty-one, so they try to hold on to the last flickers of their one perceived power before they become '*spoilt sponge cake*' on their twenty-fifth birthday. An endearing term reserved strictly for women, it is inspired by nothing less than the heavily discounted Christmas cake that goes on sale (and is rarely bought) after 25 December. That alone is a sad, sad illustration of something gone terribly wrong, but the obsession goes much further than just fashion.

How about used schoolgirls' panties for sale in vending machines? You betcha. These made their first appearance in Chiba Prefecture some time in 1993, at around $50 a pop. Previously available only by walking into speciality *buru-sera* shops, you could now spare yourself the embarrassment and just duck down to the local *used-undies-of-a-thirteen-year-old-girl* vending machine. But then, if you wanted a pair with a photo or bio, or even a vial of urine, you had to go to the shops anyway. The girls stopped in on their way to school for a new pair that could be delivered soiled on the way home.

What I wanted to know is: who ran these shops? Who determined the value of each pair? What took precedence? *Let's see. That one has traces of menstrual blood, but hooray, this one has several particles of excrement. Bump up the price!* Disgusting. At least the public were outraged about the vending machines, but with no direct statute existing to ban the sale of used panties, there was nothing the police could do to remove them, until one day they became booby, booby about u, and three traders were slammed with charges under the Antique Dealers Law, a law that requires all dealers in second-hand goods to obtain permission from the local authorities. Miraculously the panties disappeared overnight, but it was a small triumph.

In a society where female adolescence is revered, young girls are tragically aware of their sexuality and how to gain from it, *financially*. In a land of consumer paradise, materialistic worship is on the rise. With absent, overworked parents, the values of impressionable young girls can become easily skewed. The god of Dior takes over. The god of Gucci, Louis Vuitton or Chanel. These deities require their followers to undertake ostentatious shopping sprees as the mark of their beast, and that mark requires finance. Enter *enjo-kōsai*. But before anything is said, let's make one thing clear: *enjo-kōsai* is voluntary prostitution by school-age girls to raise lunch money in amounts great enough to purchase Burberry wallets and Gucci boots. (No teenager I ever went to school with was sneaking in a little jiggy on the side to raise thousands in cash while she continued to lead an otherwise normal, sometimes outstanding life. But then, no man I ever knew would have dared indulge her.)

With a literal translation of 'compensated dating', *enjo-kōsai* is one of the worst drawbacks of the mobile phone besides brain tumours. Through special telephone clubs and increasingly popular internet sites that openly facilitate contact between these individuals, schoolgirls can arrange meetings with older, usually middle-aged, men and date them in exchange for designer gifts or enough money to purchase them. A *date* can mean anything from coffee and a stroll in Yoyogi Park to dinner or sex in a love hotel. *Schoolgirls* can mean junior or senior high-school students, although some are as young as twelve. *Payment* is anywhere from ¥30,000 to ¥60,000, or the equivalent in goods, for a single tryst.

Men who actively partake in this fantasy are hard to define. They are often married, with children in the same age bracket as the girls they seek to exploit. They are salarymen, public servants, policemen, teachers, judges. Just as there is no typical profile of the girl who takes part in *enjo-kōsai*, neither is there a typical man.

The men who indulge in this fetish blame it on *tamaranai* − an uncontrollable action. Luckily the majority of Japanese people find such an explanation hard to fathom and even more outraging than the sale of schoolgirls' panties.

No matter where you turn, there is another shocking example of a warped sense of sexuality. In 1997 the *New York Times* printed an article stating that in Japan there were two legally published magazines called *Anatomical Illustrations of Junior High School Girls* and *V-Club*, which featured naked schoolgirls of junior-high age and younger. I didn't go looking to see if they still existed.

Then there are image clubs, which provide an environment for gross public misconduct in a private setting. These entail imitation school classrooms, gym change rooms and commuter-train carriages staffed with costumed prostitutes, allowing customers to live out fantasies that should be bottled and sent off for incineration.

And just while we're on the subject of wildly unbelievable stories of Japanese craziness, let's not forget *The Dream of the Fisherman's Wife*. Perhaps the first documented instance of tentacle rape in Japan, this erotic woodblock print surfaced in the early nineteenth century during the Edo period. It depicts a naked woman French-kissing a baby octopus while entwined in the tentacles of a second, giant octopus performing cunnilingus on her. The print, and its theme, had a resurgence in the 1980s when for some strange reason the male penis was not allowed to be graphically depicted. Thus, tentacle rape emerged as the *logical* alternative and spawned the development of another unique niche in the wonderful world of Japanese pornography.

So, with such a heavily sexualised identity, it is hard to view Japan's schoolgirl fetish lightly. It would be nice if Japanese men's desire could focus on women of a more appropriate age, but let's not kid ourselves. Japan is, and always has been, a patriarchal society. Women are not equal. Men dominate. The fact that women are submissive both generally and sexually is woven into the social fabric.

In a detached culture of little intimacy, sex is a commodity. Case in point? Geisha. Hostess clubs. Dating Japanese schoolgirls. Statistics suggest that 5–13 per cent of Japanese schoolgirls have tried *enjo-kōsai*, but, like anything in Japan, who really knows the truth? It is all truly, truly baffling.

THE DISTANCE GROWS GREATER

Who knew that health could be so easily corroded? While Matt has been working out regularly at the gym and becoming bigger, stronger and brighter each day, I've been diminishing like the tiny star in the sky that you thought you could see better before.

This place is an insane asylum. Delusion replaces reality, illusion masquerades as truth and fat replaces muscle tone. My arms have acquired a certain flabbiness, my cheekbones have softened and I've just recently torn a seam on my tailored cocktail dress. What is worse, the skinny jeans I arrived in now have but a millimetre to give around the thighs. It is a bleak situation. If only I were like the sun, blessed with a colossal state of energetic self-combustion, then I'd be skinnier *and* brighter. Or would I?

Oh twinkle, twinkle, little star, how I wonder where you are.

~

Chuck was a Japanese guy with an almost-American accent. He'd studied at a Californian university, spent most of his career stateside and tonight he was in the company of Rudy – a mid-life Californian of Mexican heritage who smoked noxious cigars and danced the uninhibited madman whenever 'Ob-La-Di, Ob-La-Da' came on. Rudy often came into Greengrass to appreciate Jodie's crass British humour, and already they were knee-deep in profanity while Chuck and I sat having decent, if not controversial, conversation.

'What blood type are you?' Chuck asked seriously, peering deep into my eyes.

'Blood type? I have no idea.'

'Humph.' Chuck didn't look surprised. 'That is because you are *gaijin*. Are you able to tell the character of a Japanese person straight away when you meet him?'

'Well, no, that's pretty much impossible.'

'I can. But never a *gaijin*. You know what your problem is?' he jabbed forcefully at my sternum. 'Your blood is all screwed up. It's mixed up so much, it's irrelevant to you.'

'You mean the blood of my ancestors? What, and Japanese blood is homogenous because you were isolated for so long?'

'No, not homogenous. *Pure*,' he said with distinction. 'There's a difference.'

In Japan, blood type indicates personality in the same way that your horoscope does. It's a teenage obsession, a frivolous hobby for women and a casual social lubricant from a young age thanks to painstakingly thorough physical examinations held in all Japanese schools. You can instantly judge another's character or their compatibility with you based on their blood type. You could even select the right condom from an all-too discerning vending machine. Of course, the theory of blood-type profiling, and, by extension, colour-coded condoms, is as lightweight as *Hey baby what's your star sign?* But, like many things, its history is rooted in some rather dark soil.

Blood groups were first discovered in 1909 by Austrian scientist and future Nobel laureate Karl Landsteiner, who classified them into four types: A, B, AB and O. When Landsteiner was able to show that trans fusions between like groups did not result in the destruction of new blood cells as they did when differing blood groups were introduced, it was a breakthrough in medical history, the only side-effect being that two decades later, Hitler used it to claim the superiority of the mostly A and O Aryan race over Jewish, Asian and other populations who were predominantly type B – the same blood group typical among animals. So elitist was Japan's militaristic government at the time that despite everything else, this particular Nazi theory was enthusiastically imported and used to commission a study aimed at breeding better soldiers (type Os were apparently the ideal blood group for combat).

Of course, when questioned, the Japanese will attribute their modern superstition not to the Nazis but to the innocent articles and books by psychologist Takeji Furukawa that first emerged in 1927, such as *The Study of Temperament Through Blood Type*. While Furukawa randomly assigned character traits to the four blood types, his work was later expanded by journalist Masahiko Nomi, a man who revived the theory to craze levels in the seventies and sold millions of books suggesting that just as different blood was incompatible, so too were people with different blood types.

Today the mainstream acceptance of blood-type analysis in Japan makes it a regular feature of women's magazines and morning television. More interestingly it is still used as a tool for analysis. A nursery school outside Saitama experimented with dividing children by blood type to compare how they ate snacks, cleaned garbage or took off their shoes at the door, and some Japanese companies have been known to give employees assignments or divide them into departments on the basis of blood type. The profile of every celebrity, politician and anime character always includes the individual's blood type; the anime heroine Sailor Moon is notably type O – the most 'average' and therefore the 'best' type in Japan.

'For instance,' illustrated Chuck, 'an O blood type, like me, can never lie.'

'What about Rudy?' I questioned suspiciously. 'He said he's an O.'

'No, not Rudy. He is O type, yes, but he is *gaijin*. My Japanese colleague over there, he is also O. But you can trust his character.'

I wasn't so sure about that, so Chuck changed the subject. 'Where were you last Saturday at six-thirty, during the earthquake?' he asked, and I explained that I'd been asleep.

'Do you know the Japanese bath? It's very deep, but that's where I was, submerged up to my head, relaxing, when all of a sudden the whole room began to shake. The water went crazy and suddenly I was in zero gravity. It was the strangest feeling. My wife came running in. "What was that?" she said. I said, "An earthquake, what do you think?" It's a very dangerous time for an earthquake, because everyone is cooking. Not because of burns, but because of fire.

'Luckily, in Kobe in 1995 – Japan's famous earthquake – no one had left home yet. It was morning time. Otherwise, many more than just five thousand would be dead. My friend was living in Kobe during this earthquake, and he too was in the bath, relaxing. But you know what happened to him? The earthquake was so powerful that when it came, it threw him up out of the bath water, right onto the floor!'

I could imagine the feeling. Perhaps as jarring as throwing yourself into a hostess club.

—

'If you learn Japanese to a high-school level, I will personally tutor you to a business-level speaker and give you a position in the movie business. It will take you perhaps two years, but you have such a great opportunity in Japan! You are most lucky that I have such a deep vocabulary in Japanese, and I would be the best teacher for you.'

'That's a generous offer, Fujimoto-san, but I think it would only take me six months.'

'Hah! I don't believe it, but *boku wa anata ga suki desu*,' he said: *I like you.*

'*Watashi wa anata ga suki desu*,' I shot back, and he was so impressed by my simple conversion of gender that this alone convinced him I had a great mind.

'Chelsea-san, you have a thirty-year-old mind I think, but still a young heart, and,' he laughed boomingly, 'a stunning ankle! For me, this is very important. If your ankle is ever to become fat, then *sayonara!*'

'*Hai, hai. Arigato gozaimasu. Ja mata ne.*' Fujimoto's feather-haired colleague snapped his phone shut beside us. 'That was a call to relay a message from Michael Mann. He was most impressed with the farewell dinner held for him at Inakaya by United International Pictures and wanted us to know that he thoroughly enjoyed his time in Tokyo.' Fujimoto-san nodded confidently at the announcement, glowing with pride.

'I know,' he said. 'I made sure. It is my job. I love his movie *Collateral*. So what about Tom Cruise? Did you go to the premiere?'

'No, I've already seen the movie, so when I got a call from your office to say that Tom wasn't going to be attending after all, I didn't want to pay the ten-thousand-yen penalty for not showing up to work.'

'What?' Fujimoto-san raged. 'You must pay to not come to work? I can't believe it! You are like slaves! And what happens if you have an accident? You must also pay? Humph. I'll tell you what. I will promise to take you out to dinner next week. I can give you four hours of my time and pay your slave fee of ten-thousand yen. What do you think?'

I agreed and Fujimoto-san gave me a choice of three evenings during which he could emancipate me.

Some time around midnight Nishi came over from the bar to talk in hushed tones, and Fujimoto-san turned to me with a wide smile. 'You have great opportunity now! Another customer has called for you, so get your things, casually, and let's go.'

'What? Go where? What about the other customer?' I was confused. Fujimoto-san had only recently told me of his early start tomorrow and how he had to get home soon.

'Yes, they want you, so go change and I will take you somewhere else.'

On the way out I caught sight of the 'other customer'. It was Christopher, the Korean film producer from my first night at Greengrass, his mouth agape as I waved meekly before being whisked away from under his nose. Out in the hallway I quizzed Fujimoto-san as he slid on his fedora. 'Why did they let me leave? Did you slip some money under the table?'

'No, ON the table!' he laughed. 'Money talks.' Indeed, a supplementary gratuity layered atop an already large house bill of $700 spoke like a bullhorn. I just wondered what excuse Nishi had given to Christopher.

Out at the Crossing Fujimoto-san's colleague begged our forgiveness and took a cab home, leaving us to walk through a chaotic Roppongi to Petits Pois alone. 'He has a wife waiting,' Fujimoto-san explained, 'and I do not, so let's go.' Upstairs I chose a window seat overlooking the terrace garden, and Fujimoto-san ordered a bottle of wine and abalone salad from Master, who was holding the fort all alone. He sang an old Frank Sinatra tune while we perused the karaoke book. Petits Pois was Fujimoto-san's favourite place to sing karaoke and it was fast becoming mine, as I was certain that Master had a pitch corrector on the microphone.

Whenever it was my turn to sing, Fujimoto-san became intent on studying my face. He found it funny when I sang because he thought I was 'innocent and not so cool'. He'd even move around the table to better observe me in my vulnerable, calorie-burning state, when he wasn't shouting things like '*This* face! I like it!' at various points during the evening.

'Weakness is a strong point sometimes. For you, it is bad singing, which for me is most enjoyable to watch. Especially because you have so many faces. It is good for you, but you should try a Japanese ballad.' Japanese ballads were Fujimoto-san's favourite, and by slight coincidence they also earned him the highest caloric ratings. He thought that once I came to understand a Japanese love song, I would come to understand Japan, but at the moment, while he belted out words I couldn't even guess the meaning of, I only felt appreciation for something that was outwardly beautiful but still incomprehensible. It was far easier to interpret Sinead O'Connor, and her songs earned me the highest calorie ratings I could hope for, although these still paled in comparison to those of Fujimoto-san.

'Why do you choose such difficult songs?' he objected. 'They are all hard, all hopelessly tragic and all romantic. What is wrong with you?' he teased. 'And how did you come to have such eyes? Usually *gaijin* eyes are so big and so round! But you do not have *gaijin* eyes. *WHY?* You have such a weird, beautiful face,' he mused. 'But not *gaijin*.'

Towards four o'clock in the morning Fujimoto-san and I were both thoroughly enjoying ourselves but giddily drunk and downright ravenous. Oddly enough the best solution seemed to be ramen noodles. Even though they were not particularly low in calories, and a no-no on his diet, Fujimoto-san ordered a large plate, because apart from tasting 'especially nice when you are drunk', ramen noodles were key to ending a long night of drinking on the right note. In popular opinion they diminished one's drunkenness and restored the small amount of dignity needed to make it home on two feet. Maybe that was why you could find noodle shops open until the wee hours on every block in Tokyo; we must have driven past fifty as the taxi zigzagged through the streets of Moto-Azabu to drop me off under a streetlight in Hiroo.

With a firm shake of my hand Fujimoto-san waved an enthusiastic goodbye and I stumbled blindly down the hill, through the automatic doors, up the elevator and down the hall into our apartment. Matt undressed me quietly while I chattered away non-stop, tested the temperature of the water with the back of his hand and gently put me into the shower once again. He might have rolled his eyes in good humour while he waited to towel me off, but he was growing distant. There is no snuggling any more.

I HATE YOU BUT I LOVE YOU

'Did you feel earthquakes?'

'Huh? What? What earthquake? I didn't feel any earthquake.' I yawned audibly into the phone. It was eleven o'clock and Shin was compiling reports for work at the library, while I was doing the rational thing and sleeping.

'Again? *Nothing?*' Shin cried. He'd already woken me yesterday when violent earthquakes measuring 6.8 and 6.6 in northern Kyushu had caused trains to stop and he'd been stuck in Chiba. Only then he'd shouted at me that I must be drunk not to feel them. At least today his accusations had been downgraded to a simple, 'You are crazy.'

'I was *sleeping*. How am I supposed to feel an earthquake if I'm asleep?'

'Because wake up! *Shaking!* I think so, but maybe you did not feel because you are crazy. Anyway, tonight, you want to have dinner?'

'Yeah, sure, sounds good. What time will you be finished with your reports?'

'I don't know. I will call you, okay? Go back to sleep.'

Hours later I woke to another phone call, but when I saw it was Nori I quickly smothered the phone until he hung up after the twentieth ring.

I was just drifting off when Yoshi called, and this time I answered straight away. He was at home, his parents had just left and, with nothing to do but watch TV, Yoshi was bored. Did I want to go for coffee? Sure, I agreed, but he could tell I was half-asleep and hung up, promising to call back in an hour, hour and a half – an imprecise estimate for a Japanese man but entirely typical of Yoshi. Of course he didn't mention the earthquakes – they were inconsequential.

Then Nori called again, and this time I answered. He began to drill me about the earthquakes from the time I said hello. Was I okay? *Yep.* Did I feel them? *Nope.* Was I worried? *Maybe a little.* And what about scared? *No, not really.*

'Uh, okay. If you have any troubles, then you should call to me and I will come to your house and save you.'

Right. He'd be the last person I'd want to see in an earthquake. Luckily the rest of the conversation was pleasantly devoid of anything loopy or delusional, except for the few moments right before Nori hung up, when he reassured me, 'Tokyo is safe. It is okay. You can do business in Japan and not worry about earthquakes.'

—

By 4.30 pm Shin had finished his reports and was heading to Harajuku to look at antique furniture. Did I want to meet him there at six o'clock? You betcha. Even though I'd agreed to have coffee with Yoshi, Shin won every time, whether he was going to Harajuku or halfway to the moon. He was the only one I could spend time with without any terms and conditions, and besides, I didn't want to become more confused about Yoshi than I already was. That meant avoiding him as much as possible. But there was just one thing I had to do before I left.

Ring, ring . . . ring, ring . . . I'd have to speak fast to cut him off. 'Hi, Yoshi? It's Chelsea. Look, I'm busy for a few hours, but do you want to call me later and maybe we can meet up then?'

'What? Say again? *Later?*' Yoshi scoffed. 'What time later?'

'I don't know, maybe ten?'

'Ten! Maybe too late. I have to work tomorrow.'

'Sorry, Yosh, I just . . .'

'Okay, next time,' he cut me off abruptly. '*Hai*-bye.'

Whoops. It sounded like Yoshi was driving, which meant he'd left home and was waiting for his hour to hour and a half to pass so that he could call with good manners intact. Oh well. It was better this way. Like he always said, *whatta can I do?*

—

I found Shin on the fourth floor of Oriental Bazaar, discussing the price of shipment to Melbourne with a member of the staff. He waved quietly and I wandered off to browse the antiques until he came up behind me. 'I want this one,' he pointed. 'It is handmade, Japanese style. A wedding present for my friend in Australia. Do you remember I told you about her?'

'Mmmm, your Mensa friend, right? I remember.'

'To send is nine-hundred dollars, but cabinet price only ten-thousand yen more! So expensive,' he frowned. I noticed the Starbucks in his right hand. 'You need coffee?' Shin asked, but before I could nod, he answered for me. 'Of course, you are always needing coffee. You are so bad woman. Let's go.'

—

'What you want?' Shin asked as we stared up at the menu board together.

'I don't know. I can't decide,' I said.

Shin raised one eyebrow. 'Give me hand.'

'What?'

'Hand. Give me hand,' Shin repeated, pulling at my wrist. When I stretched out my hand he promptly turned it over, smacking a ¥500 coin into my palm. 'I am outside.'

I found Shin attempting to activate an international calling card. He handed me his phone as I set a *venti* soy latte on the table next to him. 'Enter the number of your parents,' he instructed.

'But they're sleeping. I'll wake them up.'

'It's okay, try,' he insisted, so after several botched attempts I eventually reached the family answering machine and left a vague message about Tokyo's recent natural disasters. It must have been two o'clock in the morning in Canada. After I hung up, we meandered up Omotesando to find a Body Shop for a moisturiser I wanted. While I was inside, Shin called Karolina in Poland and as he examined my purchase Karolina and I chatted about Tokyo and how weird it was for her to be back home until I gave the phone back to Shin. They talked for a few minutes more until Shin snapped his phone shut and strode over to me.

'Okay, I am hungry, so . . . you want go eat Chinese? It is Iron Chef's restaurant. You know, from TV?'

—

I knew Yoshi would put in an appearance, I just didn't know when. Tonight he came in a handsome black jacket and tight black sweater with white, perfectly ironed pants, a new pair of tiny glasses and the same old inflated attitude. He sat at his usual table next to the bar and talked with Mama-san while Tehara came to my table with a wink to politely excuse me from conversation.

'Hello, *ma chérie*, how are you?' Yoshi said as I joined them. He made a comment to Mama-san and they both laughed. He was giddy and drunk, but as soon as Mama-san went to the bar, Yoshi dropped the veneer, put his arm around me and, very matter-of-factly, spat these words into my face: 'I HATE YOU.'

'What? You hate me?'

'Yes. I hate you. You are always changing your mind, like a spoilt child. *Okay, one and a half hours*, then *Sorry, I am busy*. WHAT? I was already driving. I was in Shibuya! So go home. Nothing to do,' he pouted.

'Oh, you're angry about that. I knew it. I knew you would bitch about it. Yup, just like I thought. But I can't believe that you hate me.'

Yoshi clasped my hand and peered into my eyes. 'I *hate* you, but I *love* you.' He looked down at his Rolex. 'I am leaving in fifteen minutes.'

'So you just came in here to tell me that you hate me? Isn't that nice?'

'I don't know, depends on you,' he smiled mischievously. 'You wanna make me breakfast? Let's go.' I stayed firmly seated. He lit a cigarette.

'So what were you doing up till now?' I asked. 'You are so mysterious.'

'No, *YOU* are mysterious woman. I think so. I was with my friend at another club before now. He is my customer, so I took him to a place where there are many international hostesses. We sat down, and one girl, I don't know where the fuck she came from, but she said to me, *you are so handsome.* Oh, lip service, I don't need.' Yoshi left a pause long enough for me to interject, but I stayed silent. 'Do you think so?' he probed.

'Give me a break, Yoshi. I'm not going to service you. You should know better than that by now. What do you think?'

'Oh, you are such a good girl,' he cooed. 'This hostess, she wants to know about me. She says I am so handsome.' Just his own repetition of her words caused Yoshi to puff up.

'You are just like a peacock, do you know that?'

'Peacock? Why peacock? Never mind. Thanks for the picture you sent to my email. So cute, but so baby face. How old? Eighteen? Twenty?'

'No, nineteen,' I said, and the next part just slipped out: 'Two years ago.' *Shit.* My hand shot to my mouth, but the look of surprise on his face was already complete.

'*WHAT?* You are twenty-one? Shit, no, you're at least twenty-four, twenty-five, maybe older!'

I shook my head slowly. 'In September I turned twenty-one.'

'Really? I can't believe it. I am *double* your age.' He looked stupefied. Deflated. *Old.*

'Wow, what a reaction. So what . . . does it matter?'

'No, of course not, if you are twenty-one, it is better. Because you are not a young girl. Twenty-one years old, they are stupid, their mind crazy. But you are a lady. Still, I will be so proud. Can I have a question?'

'I don't know. Can you have a question?'

'What is the oldest you have been with?' *Oh God, what a male.* 'My guess is thirty, maybe thirty-five. It was good, right? When was the last time you had sex?'

'That's none of your business.'

'Okay, then don't be mad if while I'm waiting, I have a one-night stand. Okay? I have respect for woman, sometimes six months with nothing. I cannot. I need it. But if you are my girlfriend? Never. Last girlfriend, I told you, one year and three months, not cheating. Ex-, ex-girlfriend, okay, cheat two times . . .'

'WHAT?'

'I had my reasons. Okay, maybe was not *true* love. For you, true love. I am decided, I told you. I am going to be very busy until the tenth, because of big project, but after that, all my time is for you. Every moment. We will go to dinner, to the movies, small island . . .'

'You love your small island.'

'Yes, because I want to make you happy. Everything for you. *Ma chérie!*' Yoshi stroked the back of my hair. 'Why do you think I am moving into my own apartment?'

'You really want me to believe that you're moving out just for me?'

'Yes, of course. Now, is not comfortable. I mean yes, my food, cooking, washing, everything my mommy does for me, but no space. In the new place you can come over, we can eat, watch TV. It's good. *Ma chérie*, what do I tell you? Everything for you.'

Oh God. Yoshi was so full of bullshit and I was too sober to let it slide, so just to test how 'decided' he really was I started to talk his hypothetical language. 'All right, but if I move into your apartment, I can't be working nights when you're working days. That would be impossible. I'd never see you.'

Immediately Yoshi looked worried. 'Okay, but now you are talking *later on*. Now we are only friends,' he frowned uncomfortably. As if to affirm this he set down his cigarette to give me a formal, businesslike handshake. 'We are friends first,' he repeated before glancing at his Rolex. 'So are we going some place nice for a party? I can cancel all my appointments. No problem, I don't care. I wanna stay with you, but maybe you don't want that.'

'Yoshi, why do you say that?'

'Because you never call me. What, you can't call just to say hello, that's it, goodbye? No problem. But it's okay, don't worry. You don't care about me, I know.' Yoshi stopped to return the stare of an older man who'd just walked in. 'Your customer?' he asked accusingly. I'd never seen the man before. 'I think he likes you. He is your customer. You'd better go talk to him. It's your job. You're working. I know. You have to. Go on,' he insisted sweetly, 'but if you like him, I am jealous. I *fucking kill you*.'

Yoshi reached for the bill and signed off on his trusty black Amex.

'See you tomorrow!' Mama-san called out as Yoshi left.

'See you next week!' he yelled back.

—

As Nishi led me straight to the man whom Yoshi had just threatened to kill me over, Soh spiralled a finger round his ear and whispered in mine, '*Cra-zeee guy!*'

'I am Mizu-tani,' the short, well-dressed man announced. 'I speak no English.' He then proceeded to speak exclusively in French so I replied in French . . . and he denied comprehension. 'I am sorry, I cannot understand. I don't speak French. Before, I requested to see you straight away, but Nishi-san said *NO!* You are very busy. I think you are much in demand, so I am waiting. I saw you, but you were with him, this such nice guy here.' Mizu-tani pointed to the table where I'd been sitting with Yoshi when he first walked in.

'Who, Yoshi?'

'Yes, such a nice guy. I saw you, but you had laser-beam eyes, only for him.'

'Ah, yes,' I chuckled. 'We are friends. He's great.'

'I think he really likes you. In fact I know he really likes you. He loves you. I could feel it. I get this feeling from him. I am a magician and I know. But maybe next week he will love some other girl, I don't know.'

'WHAT?'

'Someone else. I don't know. I am not him but he really likes you. I needed to meet you. You are my type. You have such brilliant eyes. I have two questions. First question: why are your eyes so brilliant? Second question: why are you so nice?' Mizu-tani suddenly slouched low on the bench, his face in mine, staring into my eyes.

'Umm, because I have a good heart?' I said. 'I think you call it *yasashi.*'

'No! Wrong answer! Tell me what I want to hear.'

'Okay, the reason I'm so nice is because I've fallen in love with you.'

'Yes! Good answer.' Then Mizu-tani proceeded to tell me I am so nice in Korean, French, Arabic, Thai, Italian . . .

'How do you know so many languages?' I asked, duly impressed.

'I am magician! I told you.'

'Well in that case, please take my card,' I offered, and Mizu-tani sprang up to study it millimetres from his eyeballs, as was the fashion with overly enthusiastic Japanese men who'd become instantly smitten with me.

'Chelsea Haay-wood-o at eee-mail-o dot com. This is you?'

'Yes. Can I have your card?'

'No!' he snapped. 'I never give my card, and you cannot have it. I *never* approve the girls I sit with. In fact I *never* request them, but you I asked to meet. Go away, go away.' He mimed to an imaginary harem of girls. 'I don't care about them. Only you, but if you don't like me no problem, I don't mind. I say things straight, and thus, I have many enemies.'

'But you must have many friends . . .'

'No! Not many,' he stopped to ponder the ceiling, 'but good ones.'

When Mizu-tani paid the bill at a quarter to three, he folded up a ¥1000 note like origami and tried to stuff it down my dress. I pulled away and he shouted. 'DON'T WORRY! I am too short. I cannot see that high.' His bouffant hair did come only to my sternum, but looking up, he could plainly see my disapproval. 'What, you don't like me?' His bottom lip jutted out. It quivered. His eyes clouded in fury. Suddenly, Mizu-tani was running wildly towards the open balcony, yelling that he must commit suicide because I didn't love him.

'Mizu-tani! *Mizu-tani!*' I shouted. 'Come back here, Mizu-tani! All right, I love you!'

Mizu-tani abruptly stopped hiking one short leg up onto the railing, let go of his grip and walked back, dusting his shoulders off as though nothing had happened. He leant far back so that he could look down his nose at me. 'Please turn around.' I turned around. 'Not so big,' he assessed. 'Maybe 88, here 70, then here, maybe 80. But up here, C!'

'I doubt it. Try a B.'

'No! For me limit is C. I don't like D. I am small guy.'

I laughed at Mizu-tani's poor hearing and pushed him into the elevator. It was time to go home.

By the time I finally stepped into the elevator, two tall, dashing Brits

218

greeted me in silence on their way down from a club on the eighth floor. They smelt strongly of sake and, as foreigners often do with each other in Japan, made immediate and piercing eye contact – a sudden confrontation that caused me to quickly turn my back.

'Oh my God. *Gaijin*,' I gasped playfully. 'Please don't look at me.'

They both chuckled and a deep, inquisitive voice came over my right shoulder. 'You work here?'

'Yeah, but sorry, I can't look at you. It's too weird seeing white guys in a place like this, if you know what I mean. I don't want to talk to you.'

'Where are you from?' asked the second voice.

'Canada.'

'Tokyo must be crazy,' they both said, and I slowly shook the back of my head.

'Trust me,' I laughed, 'you have *no* idea.'

LIVE SQUID FACE

At ten to seven the pink and white corner of Roppongi Crossing was already packed with bodies. While Japanese men sweated patiently in suits, blonde women looked at watches as the Nigerians pressed lewd fliers at pedestrians passing slowly by. I searched the sea of humanity for Shin's face, placid and serene among the chaos. I was surprised to see him in a handsome three-piece suit, with a briefcase, no less, but he smiled and greeted me like we were meeting in a quiet park. 'Hello. How are you?'

'I'M OKAY. A LITTLE SCARED,' I said loudly.

'Why?' Shin's voice was as calm as ever.

'THE LIVE FISH!' I shouted back.

'So you want to go somewhere else? We can go, no problem. Maybe tempura?' he suggested.

'NO, NO, I WANT TO TRY IT. I ALREADY AGREED. C'MON. LET'S GO!'

—

'Say hello to your dinner,' Shin smirked as he pointed to a large tank of fish embedded in the outer wall of Momiji-Ya restaurant. I stopped in my tracks.

'But they're so big! I thought you said a *small* fish.'

'No. These ones *are* small. You can kiss it!' Shin laughed. 'I told you, it's okay.' He pushed on the door and I squelched out an air kiss before following him to a bar in the middle of the restaurant. 'Look, down there,' Shin instructed, and right below us lay a shallow pool with several species of fish, caged lobster, a pair of small reef sharks and one big fat turtle.

'Oh my God!' I gasped. 'Not a turtle!'

'Of course! You can eat him if you want,' Shin advised. 'In soup. But maybe your stomach is not big enough. I don't know. I think maybe two people means too much waste. Maybe family is better. So,' Shin said, handing me a menu, 'what you want to order?'

'Nothing if I can help it.' I opened my menu to look for *Things Unalive and Grown from the Soil*, but instead I found *Live Prawn, Live Squid, Live Abalone* and even *Live Robster* for ¥6090. It was difficult to visualise swallowing any of them. To make matters worse a squid with perfect timing suddenly gave a terrible, high-pitched screech as it was lifted from a tank by the door and flung into a plastic basin. 'It's crying!' I whimpered.

'Of course! Everything cries. I cry. My cat cries. Fish cry. It is natural. Maybe they will cry here.' Shin pointed to the empty plate in front of him. 'Look, you can see him.' Shin stopped the chef as he passed and we stared into the basin at a lump of lifeless, sparkling goo until it jerked spasmodically and Shin jumped, waving the squid away. He frowned to himself and looked to me sideways. 'Okay, so small fish? Are you decided?'

'Uh-huh,' I said meekly and felt sick to my stomach. 'Small fish.'

'Okay, and I will eat lobster. That one,' he pointed into the pool. 'He looks friendly. Maybe also you can try squid. Look! Over there! Squid now dancing! *So beautiful.*' I looked back at the tank and saw the squid gliding in unison; probably a captive behaviour signalling grief for their fallen comrade. Then Shin called my attention back to the pool, where a chef was trapping a small fish in his net. 'Your order!' Shin pointed unnecessarily. 'This is your order. Look, maybe it will cry.' But the fish only flapped, so Shin said, 'No, now fish also *dancing*, like squid!' He was clearly amused, and I felt worse by the minute.

'I am sorry! I'm so sorry,' I cried out as the chef disappeared. 'Oh no.' I buried my face in my hands. Hadn't I been a vegan once? A vegetarian for longer?

'It is too late.' Shin patted my back as I languished in guilt. 'It is *your* order.'

Yes, it was my order, but I couldn't stand to picture a sliced-up fish still gasping for life as I transferred pieces of its body to my mouth and swallowed while it looked back through an eye that could still see. It was sick and sordid, not fresh as could be. What was with the Japanese and their food? For one, a whale is not just 'a big fish' as I'd so often heard. Secondly, at least on fishing shows where I am from, the hosts implement a catch-and-release policy, not a catch, hack an arm off and add soya sauce one. But thirdly, and perhaps most illustrative of all, is the name of a common item gone unnoticed on Japanese menus the world over: that of *oyako donburi*. Known to Westerners as cooked chicken and egg over rice, *oyako donburi* literally means a big bowl of *parent-child*. Now isn't that sweet?

Which is why I sat quivering in regret. In guilt. And then, in extreme relief, because by some miracle my fish came back from the kitchen as a tiny pile of sashimi on a huge bowl of ice. Shin peered at the mound in disappointment. 'Oh . . . cut up,' he frowned. 'You cannot kiss it now.' Maybe the chef knew it was for a *gaijin*, and that she would freak if he sent out a half-breathing, half-butchered fish to consume.

'Anyway. I called to Karolina after Chinese restaurant on Sunday. I told her I ate thirty per cent and you seventy,' he chuckled loudly. 'She is same, she eats so much. But *eighty per cent*! I told to her that you found her kimono at Greengrass. So thank you.'

'No problem. I'll give it to you tonight. Did Karolina eat the live fish?'

'I don't remember. We came here, but maybe she didn't want to. I ate it before, but so tiny ones,' Shin said, indicating a couple of inches, 'in water. You drink them. *Glug, glug, glug*. And then still alive, swimming in your stomach. Then I drank sake.'

'Why, to drown them?' I shrieked. 'To make them drunk and drown them?'

'Yes, what do you think? Otherwise how die? You have to kill them.'

'Wow, that's terrible. How many times have you eaten them?'

'No, not *how many*. Only once. One time. Just experience. Like now.' Shin's lobster came and he gave me the half without all the guts. 'You want more? You want to try squid?' he asked doubtfully. I looked at the creatures swimming gracefully around the tank. Then at Shin. Then back to the tank. 'You think so?' I asked.

'I don't know! Your choice. Maybe you want to try. Good experience.'

Hmmm. I deliberated for a few moments. 'Okay . . . I'll do it.'

'But *you* must eat. I will not eat. You must have it.' I promised and Shin summoned the waiter but refused to translate that I wanted a small one. 'No. He says you can choose. Over there. And you can kiss it,' he teased. Great. So I walked over to the tank and, with a long exhalation, gave the death sentence to the smallest squid I could find. It was netted and flung into the tub, but thankfully there was no crying.

While we waited for it to arrive, I anxiously sipped green tea and watched the turtle come up for air. And then there it was. The squid. I could make out the tube, a pile of legs and some orange squooshy organs on a huge bowl of ice. It was all severed into tiny pieces, but when Shin picked up his chopsticks and poked one leg: Every. Single. Piece. Moved.

'Oh my God!' I shrieked. I poked the legs and they all practically jumped off the ice.

'*Whoaw!* It is angry!' Shin shouted in surprise. 'So angry!'

I covered my mouth with both hands. I was mortified. 'Oh my God, I can't eat this.'

'You have to!' he protested. 'Your order.'

'Okay, okay. I promised, didn't I?' I started to laugh nervously and tentatively put a piece into my mouth. It curled slowly around my tongue and my eyes widened. I chewed quickly. My leg shook. And there was Shin beside me, scrutinising my face as he laughed in amusement.

'Now you have to try this one.' He pointed at the pile of rubbery arms. I poked at the smallest arm and *woosh*, the entire pile revolted. 'Whoaw! It is so *angry* with you!'

'Oh, I can't eat it. Really, I can't believe it. Ughhh. Okay, okay.' I took a deep breath. 'I'll do it. Ready?' Shin nodded calmly in expectation. 'One, two, three.' But the small arm remained clamped between my chopsticks. I looked at Shin.

'Go on, you can try,' he prodded, and so I quickly popped the arm into my mouth. There was sudden violent movement. Powerful suckers latched to my tongue, suctioned the roof of my mouth and started to pull at my cheek. I half-screamed, and then the hysterical laughter began.

'Eat it! Eat it!' Shin chanted.

'Oww! Owww, OWWW, OW! OH MY GOD!' We were both laughing like hyenas. I tried to chew but the squid's arm wouldn't stop moving. My eyes watered and I turned away. I couldn't swallow. The pain was too great. I had to pull several suckers off my tongue before I could spit them back out. It took me several long minutes to settle down.

'Good experience, right?' Shin inquired cheekily. I glared across at him and put my pinkie alongside one of the suctioned arms. Shin laughed as it glued itself to me.

'Look how strong it is! I can't believe it, and it's only a little one. Look how big these suckers are,' I said, lifting the biggest arm I could find.

'So huge piece!' Shin exclaimed. And then I had a bright idea. Maybe it was the sake, but I looked defiantly at Shin and announced, 'I'll try this one, as some kind of record. No other hostess you ever bring here will be able to eat a piece this big. Okay?'

Shin looked as if I'd gone mad and agreed hesitantly, helping to separate the arm from the head. One sucker was a centimetre in diameter, and when I dropped it in the shoyu sauce, it grabbed the bottom and wouldn't let go. 'I am going to put *that* on my tongue,' I declared with little conviction, and Shin looked at me again in disbelief. This time I counted down in Japanese to allow for more time, closed my eyes and blindly chucked the squid in.

HOLY. FUCKING. SHIT! The sensation hit like electrocution. Acute pain began at the edge of my tongue and spread across the entire surface as the arm searched for a predator to recoil at. My head jutted forward as it stuck to my cheek and constricted my tongue. I dropped the chopsticks and shrieked. '*Aaaagh! Argh! Uhh. Egh, arww . . .*' I made so much noise that Shin would have been embarrassed if he weren't preoccupied with laughing, but it was so painful I had to get it off. I pulled desperately at the end of the rubbery arm. 'A nap-kuhn! Nap-kuhn!' I cried urgently, and when Shin quickly handed over the entire dispenser, I began laughing and crying at the same time. His face was frozen in astonishment. Maybe some fear. Finally I managed to rip it off my tongue and squashed it in my napkin. Distraught, I cradled my face in my hands.

'Why are you crying? Don't cry!' Shin pleaded. 'Just experience You can write about it. *Battle of Squid and Your Mouth*. Or, *Squid Battles Chelsea*. Is good story! You don't have to eat, only try. It's enough.' Shin looked worried, but I think he was impressed. It was a good story for him too, to recount to all his future hostess friends.

Twenty minutes later when we poked it for the last time, the squid still quivered, right before we passed the tank where it had been swimming when we came. As I stopped to watch those still gliding through the water, I didn't have any revelation as to why I ate the live squid. I just did it. I couldn't resist. For all its pain it *was* a good experience, in a totally strange and foreign way. At least I won't be forgetting a single second of the trauma and absurd entertainment as long as I live.

—

Suddenly the noise around us became deafening. Everything that could ding, whiz, whirr and honk came spilling out of high-tech booths accompanied by the squeals of Japanese girls. Shin and I had been on the way to Greengrass after dinner when he'd turned to indicate with his briefcase that we should enter a games centre, and now he was feeding money into a photo booth, pulling me inside and telling me to get ready.

The booth started to count down in English. Shin counted down in Japanese, and *poof*! We were immortalised. A maniacal soundtrack played while Shin selected two photos to keep. He'd barely put frames around them when a cartoon clock began ticking and he told me to get ready again. *Poof!* Two more photos appeared and Shin raced to draw on them, lining his eyes all in black. 'What are you doing?' I yelled over the noise.

'I don't know! Ahhh! I don't know how to do!' he shouted back, dragging embellishments onto the screen: a ladybug, stars, a flowery frame and a sloppy 'TOKYO' in bubbled 3D writing. Then time ran out and alarms went off all around us. The entire experience nearly gave me a heart attack.

'It is Japanese style.' Shin started to defend himself when I gave him a look.

'And a "good experience",' I mimicked. 'Right? How old are you?'

Shin smirked and the photos came out, every bit as crazy as you'd want them to be. I started to laugh and he grabbed them from my hand. 'Oh no! Is *mistake!*' he groaned. 'I look Chinese!'

'That's your own fault. You drew make-up on yourself. Do you want one?'

'No. What will I do with them?' he asked incredulously. 'Only throw away. Look! It is *you*. Not me. Anyway, what will you do on Sunday? I am going to Kamakura, to find green-tea incense for my friend in Melbourne and you can come, if you want. Do you have plans?'

'Nope. No plans.'

'What? Why you don't have plans? Same as last week, *no plans,*' he mocked.

'No, last Sunday we met for Chinese. We went to Chen, that famous restaurant in the big tower in Shibuya. You know, Kenichi Chen, the Iron Chef? Don't you remember?'

'Oh, that's right. Okay, well, we will go only if nice weather. Did you feel earthquake today?' I shook my head. 'What? Why didn't you? So strong one! What were you doing?'

'I was sleeping,' I argued, and Shin forced air through his nostrils.

'There will be so huge earthquake one time and you will sleep through it! *Miss Lazy*. I can't believe it. Let's go now, to your club. It is time. Otherwise you will be in trouble from Nishi.'

HALLOWEEN AND THE
MASK OF KOJI

Perhaps as an ominous sign from the universe I first met Koji Osara on the one night of the year that the demons come out to celebrate. It was Friday, and Greengrass was celebrating Halloween two nights early. The club was decorated in pumpkins. I was dressed as a mummy, wrapped in long strips of material sewn onto my underwear. He was introduced with a whisper from Soh. 'Crazy guy,' Soh said. 'Crazy customer.' What did Soh mean? Crazy as in *fruitloop* or crazy as in *psycho*? From his tone there was no way to tell, but still, I was . . . disquieted.

It was nothing conscious, but I had an instinct. Maybe intuition, maybe not; but the moment I met Koji Osara I felt a deep, disturbing suspicion. Of course, it was Halloween and that was the feeling in the air, so I could be forgiven for overlooking it.

In any case, I came to know Koji Osara as an obsessive, pessimistic, blinking, swearing, international consultant with a PhD from Oxford. Of course this didn't all surface during the initial pleasantries but was a summation I'd gathered by the end of the night.

In the beginning the only thing I had to go on was his appearance: of mixed Asian descent, somewhat overweight, longish, unruly hair, chubby round face and red polar fleece; he had an iced bottle of wine, three packets of gum and a container of globulous mints. Koji was quitting smoking. I took him to mean cigarettes. He meant marijuana. A dog had smelt it in his bag at Narita airport and he'd been interviewed by an inspector.

'I am from the hippy generation. I protested the Vietnam war when the Yanks occupied their country. What do you fucking expect?' He blinked rapidly, pained as though the lids stretched too tight over eyes too open and round for his lineage. It was an odd habit, an uncontrollable reflex that kept you on edge, much like the ever-changing topics in Koji's monologue.

'I don't like American Jews. They are manipulating the world. My boss is an American Jew. I hate him. But I like the real ones. Big difference,' he smirked. 'Israel is okay. I once lived in a kibbutz for a woman, picking grapefruit as my contribution, but they wanted me to change my religion. For me, shrimp is more important, not love. I didn't want to stop eating shrimp.'

Just then Mama-san came to welcome him and offer a mint slice. Koji accepted, starting his deluge again before he'd even swallowed. A spray of crumbs rolled down his fleece to stop on his belly. 'In my culture it is very rude not to accept and say *thank you so much*, even when you don't like something. Even if it is total shit. To understand Japan would be to live here ten-thousand years, so in other words you can never understand. But good fucking luck if you want to try. Please, could I ask you some questions?'

'Why not? I'm ready for anything.' I was, after all, dressed as a mummy. With pallid matte make-up and hollowed-out eyes of black, I looked like a corpse.

'I have some difficulty in distinguishing between some pairs of English words. Perhaps you could assist me. What is the difference between *ensure* and *assure*?'

'Ummm.' Well, at least the question was original. 'I think *ensure* is more like a promise that something is correct, or a guarantee of it, whereas to *assure* someone is to give them evidence they should believe it, or convince them if they have some kind of doubt.'

Koji's expression remained unchanged at this. 'Expectation and anticipation.'

'Uh, expectation is . . . waiting for something that you *know* will happen, or at least that you believe will. Anticipation is waiting for something that you *want* to happen or, I guess, that you're really looking forward to. It's more emotional, but I don't think expectation is.'

Koji poured too many mints into his mouth and started to chew. He blinked spastically. 'Ejaculation and eruption.'

'Okay, that's a bit *weird*, but eruption is the sudden explosion of something that comes out of something, like a volcano obviously, whereas ejaculation is really only specific to semen coming out of a penis when a man cums,' I deadpanned.

'My fair lady, may I ask you another question?'

'Oh-kay . . .' I braced myself firmly. Blink blink. Then he smiled cheerily.

'Could you please move your long legs that way? I'm claustrophobic in this corner. I now have the shakes from not smoking marijuana and from the flashbacks. The fucking flashbacks. Please never smoke. You have too much potential. But anyway, you must be wondering about me. I was born in Roppongi.'

'Oh,' I said neutrally, and we spoke about culture, the French, Americans, business and people until Nishi first brought Carmen to sit across from us and then Samicah, a new girl who'd just started tonight. It was her first time in Tokyo and, although she'd never intended to work in a hostess bar, she'd already spent all her money and was now in shock. Her dress was hideous, but I breathed a sigh of relief to learn she was an Israeli Jew and not an American one, as Koji had been so emphatic in his prejudice and might have affronted her otherwise. 'What do you do?' Samicah asked awkwardly. 'Do you live in Japan?'

'No. I am a mongrel.' Koji blinked back. 'My father is Japanese. My mother is Chinese. I went to school in the States, therefore I don't know much about Japanese culture. But they are ignorant. As for my profession, if that's what you're wondering, I am a medical doctor.' Then he said in an aside to me, 'I think they are both nineteen.'

I thought they were both freaked out and afraid of him.

'I am very skilled at perception,' he divulged humbly. 'I just arrived in Tokyo at two-thirty to Narita airport. I come every month. How old are you?'

'Twenty-one,' I said.

'Hmm. Incorrect. I thought twenty-three. Maybe because you are Canadian. Such fucking cold weather. No sun but great skin. Like fucking Eskimos. But I love Montreal. It is not a typical North

American city. It is European, because of the higher culture of the French. It was their colony first. They fought off three sieges before the French army lost to the Brits. Of course it became a province of Canada during Confederation in 1867, but the Montreal people have a secret treaty with Thomas Jefferson. That is a very big secret.'

I had no idea what that meant. 'Yes, but what do you think about the need to get double approval for a green card if you want to live in Quebec? That's ridiculous.'

'Of course. In their opinion it is necessary. They want to be autonomous. Montreal refused help from the Canadian government when they hosted the 1976 Olympic Games, and they are refusing to support the upcoming Olympics in Vancouver.'

'Did you know that on our cereal boxes, when there are competitions, the small print will say, *Open to all residents of Canada, except for Quebec*? In the last referendum the vote was 49 per cent to separate, 51 per cent to remain part of Canada.'

'You are not precisely correct, but yes, I know.' Koji narrowed his eyes and for a moment looked normal. 'Listen to Jodie! She never stops fucking singing! Braying like a stupid cow. I have known her for some time, and always when I come to Greengrass she is monopolising the karaoke.'

'I think she sounds quite good,' I protested, but Koji sneered. He talked about her a lot. It was as if he were on a smear campaign; everything he said was detrimental. 'Jodie is one of those hostesses responsible for telling lies about me. Don't listen to anything she says. For some reason she hates me and spreads rumours all over Roppongi about me that are not true. I am infamous here. Ask any hostess. They know me, but none of it is true.'

'What kind of rumours?' I asked suspiciously. 'What isn't true?'

'What the fuck is she wearing?' Koji blurted, ignoring my question, and I looked over to Jodie belting out a tune. She'd taken her heels off and was singing 'Layla' in bare feet standing on the couch. The customers were going nuts. Tehara was scowling and telling her to get down.

'She's dressed up as the bride from *Kill Bill*. That's why she's covered in blood. We got ready at her apartment before work. She helped sew me into my mummy costume. Actually, it was quite hilarious. The first customer we sat with tonight thought we always dressed like this at the club. He didn't know about Halloween.'

'That is because he is very fucking stupid,' Koji shot back. 'Maybe he usually goes to pussy bars to get off on anorexic Japanese floozies in their underwear, and he thinks this is the same kind of place. This is what I mean about the Japanese. They are stupid. They know nothing about another culture. They are Nazis.'

'Um, well, I don't think . . .'

'Never mind. Please do not concern yourself with such matters. You are too smart to descend into a discussion about the fucking Japanese social condition. I can explain it to you, at a later time. Right now I just want to enjoy myself. Excuse me, sweet little Samicah,' he asked, leaning forward, 'what kind of music do you like?'

'Uh, classical,' she stuttered. By now she was alone across from us. Carmen had left and was drinking tequila shots with a table across the room. 'I study dance, so classical.'

'How interesting. I like Mozart. I love the opera, and kabuki. They come from two different cultures but they are both for people of highly developed intellect. I want to give you tickets to *Swan Lake*. Maybe the Sunday matinee. Tomorrow what are you doing? Are you working? Do you have a telephone?'

'No, I just . . . well, because this is my . . . no. I don't. Uh, I made plans to go to Hakone tomorrow, to see Mt Fuji. I'm getting up early to take the train. I might stay overnight.'

'I see. Please enjoy yourself. But if you come back early you can call Chelsea. Chelsea, please write your number and arrange to have her call you tomorrow afternoon, when you wake up. Do you know Bellini, the Italian restaurant next to Don Quixote? If you are free, please join me there for dinner. I don't like to eat alone.'

'Oh, that sounds nice,' I baited. 'Will you come to the club afterwards?'

'I know the fucking system, don't worry. I'm not a fucking belligerent idiot. We can meet at 6.30 pm, you and me. Then maybe Sunday evening we can go to the ballet and Samicah can join us, or, if I can't get tickets, then perhaps to the kabuki.'

Samicah looked delighted. 'Do you always do this when you come to Tokyo? Don't you have a girlfriend?' she asked stupidly.

'No. My first wife was Swiss. My second was Lithuanian. I met her when she was working in Roppongi, at a strip club. She has very nice big breasts and a nice juicy pussy, and I was fucking stupid and thinking only with my cock, so what do I expect?' Koji smiled insouciantly and Samicah looked stunned. I was secretly happy. I didn't want her to reconsider her plans and wiggle her way along to my *dohan*. I didn't think she could handle Koji in the right way. She was naive and obstinate, and just grated me up and down.

'Actually, I will show you something. Please be patient for just one fucking minute.' Koji whipped out a laptop to show us pictures of Oxford and his fourteen-year-old daughter. 'My fucking daughter uses my credit card to buy Sonia Rykiel without my permission. She is not of good character. If she asked me, I could buy it, but she thinks she must steal behind my back. She is fucking stupid. I don't like teenage daughters.'

The girl in the picture was white, blonde and pretty, obviously his stepdaughter. But she looked much older than fourteen.

'Oxford looks beautiful,' I commented.

'You have never been there?' he asked. I shook my head and he blinked. 'Hmm. I have a proposition for you. Please, come to Oxford and stay in my apartment. I can give you a ticket from my frequent-flyer points. Don't worry, I won't rape you. I will be in London, to extend my visa and come back. This is where you'll stay.' Koji showed me a spare bedroom in a regular-looking apartment. 'I have very powerful lawyers in Tokyo. My secretary, Betty, can help you if you have any questions while you are here. She lives here. She is from Adelaide, a friend of my ex-wife. It is a complicated story, but you can call her any time, especially you, Samicah.'

'I want to help her,' Koji said to me, gesturing towards Samicah. 'She is a new girl, not so mature, and she needs help.' Samicah started to rebut this but Koji interrupted. 'I'm sorry, did I say something wrong? You seem offended. Maybe my vocabulary was wrong. Chelsea, please correct me. It is obvious you are a superior speaker and I should learn from you to not communicate like an imbecile.'

'Yes, me too,' Samicah piped up. 'Please correct my English when it is bad. I have a lot of trouble to find the right words, and that would help me so much.'

'I'm not getting paid enough for that,' I said wryly, and Koji squinted darkly. Keeping his eyes on my face he said, 'Samicah, if for some reason you decide not to go look at the fucking boring Mt Fuji, why don't you join Chelsea and I for dinner tomorrow? It would be most beneficial for you. However, if you want to just meet us downstairs at 9.30 pm before going up to the club, I can also make sure you get a *dohan*, to increase your position.'

Samicah looked to me for help. Great. Now she was probably going to tag along and take half of my *dohan* points. That's what I get for being mean. 'Why is it beneficial for me to come to dinner with you?' she asked. 'What does he mean, increase my position?'

'I am good for advancing your position in this club. I will ensure a *dohan* when I come back again in November. This is why. Nishi! Come here please. Nishi, can I please have a *dohan* tomorrow evening with these two ladies?'

Nishi nodded and patted Koji on the shoulder. Then he placed a palm on my head. 'Chelsea-san, tomorrow I want to talk about extending your visa.'

'Oh. Okay.' This was news to me. When Nishi left, Koji stayed silent for a very long time as he stared at my face. I made wide eyes at Samicah across the table.

'I think she is smart,' Koji finally spoke. '*Very* smart. She is graceful. You should get to know her. She can tell you many things.' I smiled like a prop from *The Mummy* and he blinked in return. 'I think you are a beautiful girl, one of the most beautiful girls.'

After that Koji requested to sing karaoke and it was almost 4.00 am before I saw him out to the elevator. I pressed the button and he said, 'Well, thank you for a lovely evening.' The next thing we knew, his red polar fleece was heading towards the stairs, jumping over boxes and clutter, and then he was gone.

Samicah turned to me, stupefied. 'Was tonight normal? Are all customers like him?'

'No,' I said. 'I've never seen *anyone* take the stairs before.'

BELLINI WITH A
PSYCHOANALYTICAL
PSYCHO

'Please do not disturb me while I am selecting the wine.' Koji blinked
rapidly. 'It is the most important part of the evening. If I fuck it up now,
we might as well go home.'

And so began my second consecutive night in the company of a
nutcase.

At 6.20 pm I'd arrived at Bellini. 'Koji Osara,' I'd said to the waitress,
and she'd sat me right next to the window. From a slightly perched
height I felt like an exotic fish alone in a bowl, just barely protected
from streets awash with marines prowling in packs like piranhas. They
stopped often to stare, and to point. Oh, how I'd like to take a razor
down the middle of their buzzed haircuts sometimes.

Koji and Samicah arrived together, Koji still wearing his red polar
fleece. While Koji chose all the food, he divulged that he was in fact a
psycho*analyst* and not just a medical doctor, although now he was
merely a consultant of undisclosed genre. For some reason he hadn't
been comfortable announcing this last night, but it certainly explained
a lot of his behaviour. No wonder he was so crazy.

'Already on Friday I knew from CBC, or what is it, *CBS*, that the
weather forecast would be bad, but I wanted Samicah to discover for
herself. I did not want to impose my will onto her. I knew she would
not go to Hakone but would be joining us for dinner instead. I *antici-
pated* she would come to Bellini.'

'Well, you're very clever,' I said dryly.

'No, I am a strategist.' Koji blinked pleasantly. 'A strategic marketer. I am a famous guy in this restaurant,' he boasted. 'I want to create respect for ladies. If you want to come to Oxford, I will introduce you to some very intellectual people. My first impression yesterday was that you had a brain. Nishi-san knows to carefully select only people with a brain to speak to me. This is why he did not seat me with Jodie.' I smiled at this and looked at my fingernails. I poured Samicah some more water. She was drinking too fast, and I didn't want to take care of her later. Koji kept his eyes on me. 'You did not react to what I said about Jodie. Why not? She is your friend, but you did not defend her?'

'Well, Koji, what you said was very indirect This is Japanese custom, to avoid confrontation, am I correct? Please excuse me for my apparent indifference,' I said, raising my glass, 'but I'd prefer to enjoy the meal.'

Koji clinked his glass against mine and looked oddly satisfied. Behind his head the people passing by were still staring me straight in the face.

'I had strategically selected the best seat in the restaurant to display your beauty to everyone.' He bowed as Samicah sat chewing with her mouth open beside him. An African waiter came to refill our glasses and Koji said to him, 'She is too beautiful, impossible for me. I am a stupid inferior, but maybe you have a chance.' Koji swivelled round to me. 'He has a nice fat juicy cock.' Blink blink.

I covered my mouth and tried not to look at the waiter.

'What do you expect?' Koji continued. 'He is from Nigeria. The men of their tribe are very virile. So no need for dildos, am I correct?'

'I'm sorry,' the waiter said with great composure, 'but I'm happily married. He is right though, you are very beautiful,' and to my embarrassment they discussed details of my beauty, which somehow morphed into a discussion about the CIA, Yakuza and the decrepit state of 'underworld Roppongi'.

It was very, very weird.

'Please, don't hesitate with the red wine, young Samicah. It is from the Napa Valley, in California, so of course it is very fucking good. Please listen if you want an enjoyable future. When you meet a handsome young man, you will be so grateful to me, because I am going to tell you a secret.' Koji paused until Samicah took a sip and then said very flatly, 'If you drink really good wine, your pussy will smell very nice.'

I looked to the ceiling and Samicah almost choked. There was silence while Koji tried to make eye contact. First with her. Then with me.

I took a sip of water and he took it as his cue to speak suddenly. 'Yes, I thought you are a very beautiful woman. I am so honoured to spend time with such a beautiful lady. You are the most beautiful woman I have ever had the chance to meet. Brains and beauty is something most fortunate, but also most unfortunate. You have small demons, and you must pay attention to them. They will overcome you if you are not careful. Such a beautiful lady who is intelligent has all the opportunity in the world. You are able to do whatever you want, and you will have so much success.'

I laughed in spite of myself and gave him a patronising bow.

'Now, for first impressions. Please, if you do not mind, tell me what your first impression was of me. We can start with Samicah.'

Samicah looked up from her plate. 'Uh, okay. Can I say *nice*? I think you are a nice person, very considerate and worldly-wise, um . . . and nice,' she fumbled. 'Oh, I'm sorry. It's hard for me to speak in English.'

'Hmmm. It is my impression that you are like my sister,' Koji said condescendingly. 'You are very young and naive and just embarking on your journey of the seven seas, but they are very dangerous and I feel you need protection. I want to protect you. So there, that is my impression of you. But Chelsea,' said Koji, clearing his throat and starting to blink even faster, 'my first impression of you was Greta Garbo.'

'Greta Garbo?' Just how Koji had come to this conclusion while I was wrapped up like a mummy was questionable, but apparently Miss Garbo had the same problem as me.

'A brain! And the same eyes, but unfortunately, she started to make herself ugly with make-up so that people would see her character. I think this was her grave mistake. Eyes hold one's character.' Koji stopped blinking for once as he moulded a smile into his chubby cheeks. 'Now, if you could please tell your first impression of me.'

'All right.' I set my wine glass down firmly. 'You revel in being unconventional. You are an outcast from your culture, but it is of your own doing. You are happy not to conform to the norms of society and have developed your life accordingly. Other people think you are a freak because of your eccentric behaviour and idiosyncrasies, but I think it's just a show. For some reason you think you don't have any other choice than to act this way, but it is clear you are very intelligent. You have gained your wisdom through this non-conformist path.'

Koji looked stunned. 'Have you read my paper?' he stammered.

'How could I possibly have read your paper? I only met you yesterday.'

'My autobiography! You can view it on my website, which is printed on the card I gave you last night. I asked you to go there. It used to be my profession to be a psychologist, but now I designed a robot with sensitive technology that has enabled it to speak with very young children. It is not just a stupid hunk of metal. It has cognitive ability, although limited. But anyway. Tomorrow the kabuki will begin at 4.00 pm. Did you get my email?'

'Sure, but I didn't read all of them. You sent so many emails.'

'Yes, because I am obsessive.' Koji blinked pleasantly. 'My fucking useless shrink can tell you that.'

My eyes dropped to the three packets of gum on the table. 'And how do you find that?'

'Find what?'

'Being obsessive,' I said.

Koji ignored my question. 'Please wear something nice to the kabuki on Monday because we will have box seats.'

'Okay.' I looked at him questioningly. *What was with this guy?*

'I am choosing my words and speech in order to establish good relations with you and to show respect. My grandmother's last advice was to never trust Russian hostesses.' I raised my eyebrows at this and refilled Samicah's water glass until Koji repeated himself. 'My grandmother's last advice was to never trust Russian hostesses. Don't you think it's funny this is her last advice to me?' I shrugged aloofly and Koji huffed out a sigh. 'I must take action to establish good relations with women because I can never understand them.'

'You know, maybe you could just try being normal,' I said cruelly.

Koji set down his utensils and sighed. 'Even when you pretend to be a stupid bitch, it is still interesting to have conversation with you,' he spat, and I laughed as Samicah's mouth fell agape. 'This is why I like you. I used to go to parties in Milan where everyone wore a mask and spoke intellectually. It was very sexy not to know someone's identity, I think, because there is sex where you just want to fuck someone, and then there is the allure of not knowing who someone is.'

'How interesting. I'm sorry, please excuse me while I visit the ladies.' On the trip to the toilet I stopped to strike up conversation with the Nigerian waiter. 'Leroy,' I read from his name badge. 'How's it going?'

'Good . . .' Leroy searched my face for a name.

'Chelsea,' I smiled. 'I'm sorry about this guy. He's a little bit strange.'

'Yeah, Koji is crazy! He's one sick motherfucker, but he's got a lot of money, so you should encourage him to spend it.'

'Sure,' I replied, but I didn't really have to encourage anything. Koji had already spent over a grand on the wine. 'Oh, and Leroy? Can I get a salad? Koji didn't order one.'

'What size, sweetie? A big one?' He grinned and I nodded in glee.

Back at the table Koji was onto the more academic subject of how he loved opera, Shakespeare and kabuki equally. Having originated at around the same time, he explained, he liked to watch each art form to compare similarities. 'A performance is like our dinner, for instance. Earlier I knew the meal will be most delightful, but taste like shit. Looks are good, but taste is not. Beauty is not everything. My impression of you is that you are very smart,' he said suddenly. As I continued to crunch away at my salad, he turned to Samicah with a great degree of seriousness and said, 'She is some kind of genius.'

'Is that why you've hardly eaten?' I asked. 'Because you think it tastes like shit?'

'No. I like to spend a lot of time eating,' he protested. 'I am distracted by talking, because above all I am interested in context.' Koji blinked profusely, and not on purpose I started to mimic him.

'This characteristic of yours,' I said, blinking. 'Why are you doing this all the time?'

'I am just so amazed by your beauty, that is all.' He blinked back.

'I cannot believe it.' He smiled and I smiled and Samicah looked befuddled and we drank more red wine, until Leroy arrived with a white. 'Please ignore my stupid remarks, young Samicah. This is also very good wine, over five-hundred dollars a bottle. Once you drink two glasses, you will be very happy and will begin to enjoy yourself. You will have a good time.'

Samicah drank three glasses, but when coffee arrived she didn't drink any, so I drank hers as well.

Outside the window people went by in Halloween costume. Two guys in masks, prancing in the cold, wore pink and yellow jumpsuits. They stared through the window and pointed. Koji turned for the first time to look out the window and a group of Japanese girls scuttled away giggling.

'The Japanese are very discriminatory,' Koji sighed in contempt. 'Because I am half Chinese they don't accept me. I have never fucked a Japanese woman. I dislike Japanese pussy. Please don't ask me about it. Anyway, I am delighted to spend time with you.'

When Koji paid, he asked whether it was okay if we took a taxi to Greengrass. 'This is not okay with Jodie. She wants to walk because she is on some fucking stupid kind of diet, and it is a waste of money. Is it okay with you?'

We took a cab for two blocks.

—

'You have a most sexy dress. Very beautiful,' Koji said approvingly as I sat down beside him. Already there was French wine on the table, preceding a cheese platter and popcorn, all of which Samicah snacked on drunkenly while looking dazed. 'It tastes like shit,' Koji complained passively. 'I wanted Domino's but Nishi said it isn't possible. You'll have to excuse me. I have to make a stupid business call at 10.00 pm.'

'What, this late?'

'I am calling London,' he stated unflinchingly.

'Oh, what time is it there?'

'Eleven in the morning. Please excuse me,' and Koji stalked madly out into the hallway. When he came back, we sang for hours. There was hardly any talking. Everyone was drunk. I sang 'Steamroller Blues'. I sang the Red Hot Chilli Peppers. I don't remember what else, except that Carmen's table interluded with Spanish songs such as 'Bésame Mucho'. Then at midnight there was a delivery of two large bouquets of red roses. So that was why Koji had gone out to the hallway.

'I like to make surprises for ladies. It is important,' Koji proclaimed.

'Yes, thank you,' I said sweetly, as the underlying thought persisted, *but you lied so very well.* And again we sang until the clock read half past one in the morning.

'Now I must go to bed. I am sorry. It is already very late and I have a very important appointment tomorrow. I cannot miss it for any reason. Any last questions?'

'Yeah, sure,' I said. 'I guess I'm just wondering, not for any reason, but did you ever get fulfilment out of your job as a psychoanalyst? I mean, did you ever feel like you really actually helped someone?'

Koji's face fell at the question. 'I will not discuss this matter for a further three years,' he said curtly. 'Tonight we are only having fun, singing and drinking. Please don't misunderstand. You are a very beautiful, genius kind of lady, but it takes me three years to really judge whether I can be friends with an individual, because people have shallow faces.'

Three years? That was eons for a man who'd once made a living as a Freudian analyst. Perhaps that's why he'd quit. Koji's faith in his judgement must have been challenged somewhere along the way. Maybe it had something to do with himself.

1 + 1 = WHACKO,
OR, KABUKI NIGHT

I remember closing my eyes all right. But it wasn't sleep. If sleep is subconscious and waking is conscious, I was in the half-light between. Each time I woke from hallucinatory dreams, I'd see that it was 9.00 am, 10.00 am, 11.00 am. I was continually emerging from a bizarre Dalí dreamscape to a cruel and punishing world that wouldn't let me rest for more than fifty-nine minutes at a time.

An inflamed left tonsil wasn't helping matters. Nor were the night fevers, which began weeks ago and have been increasing in frequency. I feel languid and hardened, weak and brittle, boiled to the bone, with all flavour leached out of me. It isn't a good combination of feelings, and it's getting to the point where I don't feel like going to sleep at all any more. There's no longer an assurance that I'll wake up feeling better.

I suppose I should have asked Koji to psychoanalyse me last night, but maybe he'd have time before the kabuki today. Oh, but wait, that's right. We weren't supposed to talk about any of the psychoanalyst stuff. I still had three years to go.

I crawled out of bed well before the alarm and dressed in my blackest of black.

—

I came up behind Samicah at Higashi-Ginza station and drew my finger under the words *Kabuki-za, Exit 3* on the exit map. 'That one. That's your exit.'

'Oh, hi. It's you. You surprised me. Wow,' she said, taking in my severely formal outfit. 'You look beautiful. I don't have anything like that. Is this okay?' Her heavy brown clogs and home-made spiral-print dress were not okay; it was akin to attending the opera in your overalls.

'It's fine,' I lied.

'Where did you get that? I can never find clothes like that.'

I told her a friend of mine had bought them for me – one of my customers – and she asked if I could ask him to take her shopping too. I had to explain that it didn't work like that, as well as explaining why we shouldn't be late for our *dohan*. I felt like her babysitter.

We waited outside the Kabuki-za. The crowd had all but jostled inside by the time Koji came flying down the pavement in his red polar fleece. He was fifteen minutes late, so with a grimace at Samicah's outfit but hardly a greeting he handed over our tickets and strode like a madman into the lobby, stopping chaotically for English programs and earpieces before leading us to three seats in the middle of a large theatre.

'I thought you said we'd have box seats,' I questioned, but Koji smiled fakely and said, 'I will go get you a refreshment. Coffee or green tea?'

'Oh, can I have juice?' Samicah asked, and I asked for green tea.

According to the program, kabuki had not always been a fine dramatic art but was created by a female shrine attendant in the seventeenth century as stage entertainment for the masses.

In its earliest days the performers were all women, and quite often prostitutes, which made for unruly crowds and widespread popularity until eventually the performances were deemed bad for public morals and the women banned by the Tokugawa Shogunate to be replaced by an all-male cast.

Perhaps in keeping with tradition, some male actors also engaged in prostitution, causing the Shogunate to clamp down and insist that strictly historical dramas be performed. Standard roles became the handsome lover, the evil samurai or the virtuous hero. For the cross-dressers there was a fresh young maiden, the wicked old hag or noble samurai lady.

Suddenly Koji was thrusting two iced green teas in my face. 'Your drinks,' he announced, having ignored Samicah's request for juice. 'And this is a surprise for you. I like to make surprises. Please, give one to your apprentice and move over one seat. I do not want to sit in the middle.' I handed Samicah a green tea and one of the presents and she struck a dissatisfied *mie* – kabuki-speak for an exaggerated expression for effect. I ignored her and went back to my program.

The particular play we'd come to see was a season premiere. It began with two actors frozen in dramatic white make-up while men all in black straightened out the ornate costumes at their feet.

'What are they doing?' I whispered, and Koji said, 'Please ignore them. They are not fucking there.' Soon the shadows disappeared and the actors' antiquated dialogue began, accompanied by exaggerated, but very few, movements. The performance was painfully slow but actually quite funny.

The kimonos were gorgeous and the storytelling typically Japanese, steeped in themes of incredible self-restraint, indirect conduct and hier-archical subservience and rank. For example, the entrance of an impor-tant character on high wooden *geta* (traditional Japanese sandals) took five minutes down the *hanamachi* (catwalk) bisecting the audience, building suspense at a critical time and reminding the audience of the actor's high social position.

Today, great kabuki actors are among the most distinguished members of Japanese society, the minutiae of their lives painted colour-fully across the tabloids. Not so for the lowly kabuki musicians, hidden humbly to the right of the stage. The *shamisen* player was to be heard and not seen, making his instrument's cat-gut strings sing as though the feline's spirit were still howling in its tones.

At intermission the first play was over and we followed Koji upstairs to the famous restaurant Kicho to eat *bento* boxes, drink more green tea and open our presents. 'It is a Chinese astrological something or other,' Koji explained dismissively, gesturing to a collection of tiny porcelain animals representing the signs of the zodiac. 'I am the stupid, fucking dog,' he blinked.

'Oh! How nice!' Samicah offered. 'I am the year of the tiger. What about you, Chelsea?'

'The boar,' I said.

'Humph. Dog and cat never get along. They can never understand each other.' Koji grimaced. 'So. I have seen the next play countless times, and it will be so fucking boring for me, so I will leave you here and come back at nine. I will have a massage and you can watch the play. Or, let me put it another way. You have two choices. You can come.'

—

Samicah and I chose the massage, but afterwards we had to listen to Koji complain about how he'd tried hard not to get a 'stupid, fucking erection' during his. Then we'd taken a taxi to Tokyo Prince Hotel in the shadow of Tokyo Tower for coffee. The place was a dump. It was one of the city's oldest Western-style hotels and you could tell; the carpet looked fifty years old. The tearoom was deserted, with picture windows of an illuminated skyscape, and there was no coffee. Koji was holding forth.

'Whether you accept them or not, these are my Three Nevers, and I cannot help you if you don't listen. One: never associate with the Yakuza. Ever. Two: never associate with white Caucasians living in Roppongi more than five years. They have no reason to be here and are undoubtedly in some sort of trouble with the law, etc. *Why do you wanna know gangsters?* Three: never marry a fucking Japanese. I know many sad hostesses married to Japanese in the suburbs.'

Funny, I didn't remember asking Koji for patronising advice, although his words were directed more toward Samicah than to me. At least, she was the only one fully listening. I sat idly by, gazing out the eleventh-storey window to the silence outside.

Why had he brought us here? It was way below my standards, and it took a great measure of effort not to get ultra pissed off with Samicah's argumentative stupidity and Koji's endless complaints about his stepdaughter. Their combined effect was infuriating, but I was also mad I'd missed a call from Yoshi.

I hadn't seen him much lately, but maybe that was for the better. It had allowed me to see how easily I was enticed by him and the risk that posed to my relationship with Matt. In the limited time we spent together, Matt never talked about it, but I'm sure he could sense that something was different. If I could keep my contact with Yoshi to a minimum, the remainder of my time might just be relatively calm. Of course, I still always wanted to see him, but I couldn't risk the potential consequences. I wanted to stay married.

Oh, the dilemmas. To be out with Yoshi, at home with your husband or stuck listening to erratic statements such as: 'In the upcoming election, Bush will win. Kerry is not a leader, but don't fucking worry. Hillary is coming to be president. Only four years' patience required.'

While I sipped on chamomile tea, Koji talked about Swedish design and how a Swedish hostess he'd met at Greengrass would be designing his sushi restaurant in Brighton. In fact he was going to Sweden soon to stay on the floor of two Swedish hostesses, but it was hard to discern fact from fiction as Koji bounced all over the conversational map.

My favourite were his clinically delivered attempts to be diplomatic: 'The Japanese are a racist, backstabbing, cult society. It is because they have been so homogenous. I hate any club where you must be the same. High-class universities. The fucking marines. The Japanese. They all breed ignorance. I don't have time for people who can't get outside their own perspective. The best solution is individual action and meeting other individuals while retaining your own spirit.' Koji's smile was more of a grimace. Man, he was a psycho.

Finally, at ten to nine we left. In the back of the taxi Samicah had a hissy fit about earning only ¥3000 an hour for her first three days, the last of the month. I wanted to slap her.

'Look, Koji is doing you a favour by inviting you along at all. Most girls don't even get two *dohans* in their first month, and he's given you two in your first three days. He is trying to *help* you. Don't you understand that?'

'Okay, maybe. Sure, I don't care,' she pouted. Well, which one was it? She was insolent – and I couldn't believe she thought Koji was sane.

'I just feel sorry for him. He seems kind of lonely.'

When she started to affect niceties, enquiring about my family, I turned cold and she resorted to speaking Hebrew. It was the final straw. 'I don't understand what the fuck you are saying, do you know that?'

'Why? But it is my language,' she replied indignantly. 'It is natural to me since birth. You should be able to make out some of it, can't you?'

'What the fuck?' I ignored her for the rest of the evening.

—

Koji squinted suspiciously at me as Tehara bent over the wine to whisper in his ear.

'The conversation was that someone has requested you,' Koji told me. 'If you go now, you can't come back until 11.00 pm. However, I must make a phone call from my hotel room at 11.30 pm, so you will stay here until ten-thirty, which means we have twenty minutes. Of course this is not ideal, but I told Nishi last night we would come late. This was an exception, but it was okay with Nishi because I am the number 1 customer for him, if you understand. Tomorrow I will be leaving Japan, so, if you have any questions, ask them now.'

'Don't worry,' I said sarcastically, 'I'll email you if they're that pressing.' Koji had already spent the bulk of the evening telling me everything I couldn't possibly want to know about Russian and Ukrainian hostesses, with more obscenities than I could count.

'I have some hesitation towards British or American hostesses, because why do they need to come to Roppongi? Of course I am not talking about you – you must be here for some other reason of which I don't know – but if someone is really so smart why is she wasting her time in such a fucking stupid place with such impotent men?' Koji blinked and looked at the cheap plastic watch he'd set up on the table when we'd arrived.

'I don't know, Koji. I don't think you have to be stupid to do this. There are other reasons, you know. Life is not all about logic.'

Koji looked perplexed. 'I believe our cognitive-thinking ability is the same. That is why I like you, and thank you for speaking with me in English and listening to my fucking half-breed accent. My English teacher told me that anyone who can't bother to hear what I want to say through my accent is not worth my time. Anyway, I wish you both luck.'

'Sure. Thanks. I'll come to your restaurant in Brighton when it opens.'

'I thought you were coming to Oxford?' Koji blinked furiously. 'But now there is some discrepancy in what you are saying.'

'There's no discrepancy. You said your restaurant isn't opening for a year. You invited me to Oxford in January. I beg your pardon, Koji, but where's the discrepancy? You make too many presumptions.'

'I am sorry, that is my problem. My shrink also agrees with you, but I am not used to communicating with people who know what they want to say with the right fucking words. I apologise for the inadequacy of my vocabulary. It is my feeling that people need to say new things every day.'

'People stop learning at eighteen,' Samicah contributed randomly.

'*What?* No, they don't. It's just negligence if a person won't learn something new. Koji's vocabulary suffices. In fact it's better than most native speakers of the language.'

'That is such a *paradox*,' Samicah droned.

'Oh God, Samicah. Why don't you just have some more wine?'

'Anyway! Anyway, anyway, anyway!' Koji interrupted. 'I will remind you of your plans to come to Oxford, from the tenth until the seventeenth of January. I will try to arrange several meetings with my colleagues who are professors, and you can discuss many disciplines that may be of interest to you. Of course I will meet you in the airport. Don't worry.' Koji blinked. 'My apartment has two bedrooms, with a lock and a phone inside so that you can call 911 or the police. They know me,' he smiled pleasantly. 'Oxford is the exception. Things can happen there.'

IGNORE ME ANY TIME

It was a Wednesday night when Jessica from Sydney first started at Greengrass, and Nishi appointed her to my side like I was a geisha and she my *maiko* (apprentice). We'd met last week after Matt found her roaming Roppongi's streets for a hostess job. He'd called me during our Halloween party and delivered her to the door, so I welcomed her in for an interview while dressed as a mummy and explained all the club rules myself.

She was in Japan on a working holiday with her Australian boyfriend, but after an unqualified English-teaching job had proven hard to find, she wanted to try her hand at hostessing.

Although Jessica was tall, blonde and gorgeous, I immediately recognised the nervous apprehension that had been mine only two months ago, and did my best to put her at ease among the film-distribution executives at our table. Unfortunately Jessica was cordoned off by a yawning man who looked Indian, claimed Japanese heritage and introduced himself as T-Bone, so I did my best to keep conversation light so she wouldn't get a bad first impression, and before we knew it they had paid and were gone.

In the change room Jessica released her tension and let out a big laugh. 'You are so natural with them!' she gushed with a new-girl awe. 'How do you do it?'

I looked back at her in surprise. 'Natural?' I protested. 'Oh no, that was so forced. Can you unzip me?' I pulled down my dress and shrugged on a sweater just as a loud knock came at the door.

'Chelsea-san!' Soh called out. 'Your customer is coming! Crazy guy.'

'But it's quarter past two!' I yelled back. 'And Fujimoto-san is waiting for me!' Earlier he'd taken me out for a fabulous sushi dinner, come to the club against his will when I couldn't get the night off and had been waiting at his exclusive membership club Petits Pois for me for over an hour because Nishi had refused to let me go early. It was infuriating, not to mention highly embarrassing for me.

'Sorry, this is *your* customer,' Soh shouted back. 'Come now!'

'Arrrrrrgh!' I screamed. 'I hate it when they do this. Why are they making me stay? Did they clock you out already?' I asked, and Jessica nodded. 'Just so you know, they cheat your time here. Even if you work until 2.25 they'll only pay you until two. Usually we try to drag things out when a customer wants to pay at quarter or twenty past, because it's not fair.'

'Oh really?' Jessica looked worried. 'I was wondering if this club is very honest.'

'No, they're pretty good really. That's the only problem.' I smiled apologetically and felt bad for everything I couldn't explain but that she'd just have to learn for herself. 'Good news is you're free to go. Can you zip me back up?'

—

Mizu-tani came goosestepping out of the men's room with a glossy magazine tucked under his arm. I attempted to offer a steaming *oshibori* but he ignored me and sat on his hands. I had to pull them out and wipe each finger myself until finally Mizu-tani could no longer contain his aura of craziness and spoke. 'Chelsea, why you are so nice? I have been looking everywhere for tasty girls, but you are the first tasty girl. I have never forgotten you.'

'Where have you been?' I asked playfully.

'All over Roppongi.'

'And how many places have you looked?'

Mizu-tani held up four fingers. 'This is the fifth. But I never forget Chelsea. I called to Nishi-san, but he said someone requested you and I cannot come. He thought I was someone else requesting you. He called me Tokugawa. Who is Tokugawa? NOT ME!' he shouted in anger. 'I don't know. You are so much in demand here. When can I have time to see you? I have no time. You are such a . . . do you mind if I say? *Tasty* girl. Look at me, such a crazy guy. Look at my naughty face. I know you forget about me, but how can I forget you?'

I motioned to the magazine upside down on the table. 'What have you got there?' Mizu-tani grabbed it and opened to the centrefold. 'Dear God!' I flushed red and turned to cover my eyes.

'WHAT! You are not like them?' Mizu-tani cried. *Well no,* I wanted to say, *I'm not spread-eagled in a Japanese porno mag.*

'I don't want to see that, Mizu-tani.'

'Why? You and me, we are the same. The only difference is P and V. Okay, you can ignore me any time.' I averted my eyes as he flipped casually through the pages, stopping to smooth over various shots before slamming the magazine shut. 'Okay, serious question. I have only one question.' Mizu-tani slouched low on the couch. 'Ready? *Why* are you so nice? Please? I like you. I love you. But maybe you don't like me. That's okay, I don't mind. Because you are so bad girl.'

'*Bad?*'

'Bad means best. I cannot express you. I have no words to express you. You are unforgettable. Maybe you think of me high, middle or low. I don't care. It is your matter, but for me you are so tasty girl. Why? My tasty path is so narrow. Why you can enter? But you are so much in demand, you have no time for me. I know. Nishi tells me that Chelsea is so much in demand. She is so popular. I never request some girl to sit with me. Never. If they come, I tell them *I do not request you.* But I saw you, and I said *bring her to me.* Remember you were there, with that man? Your favourite customer.'

'You mean Yoshi?' I smiled involuntarily.

'Yes, I know he likes you. I can tell. He is tasty boy. I am thinking, how can I get you transferred to my desk? How can I spend time, only to say a few words to Chelsea, because I cannot forget you?'

'How do you know he likes me?'

'Because! He is so *tasty* boy. The outlook of him is such a nice guy. Me, in contrast, I am so bad guy. So naughty guy. So crazy guy. I have many enemies. But I don't mind. If people don't like me, I don't mind. How come you can be so tasty for me? I have no words to express. You have damaged my heart.'

'I'm so sorry.'

'It's okay. Everyone thinks I am a crazy guy.'

'Are you?'

Mizu-tani leant forward. 'Crazy for you. But I am such bad guy. I am president of the sleaze association. Honorary chairman. You can kill me. I don't mind to be killed by you. On the bed.' Mizu-tani stopped to sip his whisky. 'Do you know the government of Saskatchewan? He loves you. I talked to him yesterday.'

'Mizu-tani, I have no idea what you're talking about. Excuse me, I need to visit the restroom.' When I came back, Mizu-tani had moved to the corner table. He was slouched like a rag doll, observing Mae and her favourite customer, Akira – a producer with Koizumi hair.

'They are so relaxed,' Mizu-tani sighed enviously. 'Such good atmosphere. Nishi!' he called wildly. 'Nishi, come here! Nishi knows my character. Nishi, how can she love me? I want to know, what can I do? If you take her away, I will kill you. With my bazooka. Nishi has a very small weapon.'

'I don't want to hear about it,' I laughed, and Mizu-tani goose-stepped off to the toilet.

From behind the bar Soh, the Burmese waiter, rolled his eyes and announced there was only twelve minutes left to go. 'When do you leave Japan?' he asked. 'The twenty-eighth?' I nodded, and he started to wipe away a flood of imaginary tears. 'All your customers will cry!'

'I know,' I sighed. 'I know they will.'

WHAT IS IMPORTANT?
YOU MUST DECIDE

Shin came straight from work to meet me at the Bic Camera super-store in Yurakcho. He'd accrued extra points on a loyalty card and wanted to donate them along with a hundred bucks so I could have the latest Konica Minolta – the exact same model as his. He even bought me a second memory card and, since there were no extra batteries in stock, lent me his card so I could come back and get them myself next week. What a star.

As we passed a golf display going up the escalators, Shin deflated instantly. 'I have to play golf tomorrow,' he sighed. 'I hate.'

On the way back down I pointed to the mannequin holding a nine iron. 'Your favourite!' I teased, and Shin pulled a face.

One floor later he pointed to a poster above my head advertising beer and sake. 'Your favourite,' he smirked and I laughed until it hurt.

—

'So, Miss Lazy, what are you doing this weekend?' Shin asked over coffee and a crème puff smothered in glazed fruits. We had just finished dinner in Ginza.

'I don't know,' I shrugged. 'No plans.'

He pretended to strike me on the head. 'Why, you are crazy? I am thinking about something, which is Hakone.' Shin flipped open a small pocket calendar. 'What about next weekend and Hakone? You don't have to get up early. Maybe Friday night is late for you . . . we can leave after twelve and go straight to private hotel, by own cable car, and relax, and Sunday we must check out 10.00 am. Then go to *Ashinoko*, big lake. But at the *ryokan*, everything is Japanese. There is no restaurant. Old woman brings dinner to your room, and such big breakfast, of rice and *miso* soup . . .'

'No cereal?' I joked.

'No. You sleep on *futon*, on the floor, you understand, and wear Japanese pyjama. You *must*. Everything Japanese. Inside and outside is *onsen*, and we will share one room, but, one on one I don't want. Before, Karolina and Minko and me, was comfortable . . .'

'Okay, no problem. I'll invite my friend.'

Shin looked at me doubtfully. 'Is your friend a woman?'

'Yes, not a man. Don't worry. I'll ask Carmen – you don't know her. I can't wait. I *love* Hakone. You have no idea how much I need it. Did you play golf yesterday?'

'No, I did not. I am so glad. I hate it. How is your job? I know club is okay, but what about you? I am worried about you. You are bad hostess.'

'*What?*' I gasped in mock horror, and Shin rolled his eyes.

'No, not in *bad* way! For me you are good, but never calling, saying *please come, please come*. Never before I meet such bad hostess. I am worried about you. You need points? Do you have enough?'

I was touched by Shin's concern for my professional welfare, but he wouldn't believe me if I told him about all of the Yoshis and Noris, the Taizos and Mizu-tanis who gave me an abundance of points all through the week. 'Don't worry, Shin. I do okay.'

⎯

'I will make you a confession,' a customer whispered. 'In Osaka my friend gave me a slip of paper with a number on it. He said if you trust me, call this number when you get back to Tokyo. Of course I trust him, he is a very good friend of mine, so when I returned to Tokyo I called the number. A man answered and he said *Mr Aoki?* – that is my name – he said *are you interested in a very beautiful, very nice Australian girl?* I said I am. So he said *would you like to make an appointment with her?* I said I would. So around three o'clock, I think it was a Monday, he told me to go to a room number at ANA Hotel. Precisely at this time I knocked and she was there. We spent two hours together and then I paid her, but when I was leaving I caught sight of her notebook, by the phone, and there was not just *my* name but so *many* men's names. I asked her *what are you doing in Tokyo?* and she told me everything.

'She had gone on vacation to the United States and on her way home to Australia she had booked a brief stopover in Tokyo. She came into Roppongi one night and met a nice Japanese man, and he asked what she was doing. She told him she had spent all her money in the United States and she had no money. So he said *if you trust me, I can help you make a lot of money in Tokyo very fast in a nice way*. If she could agree to his plan, he would pay for her to stay the whole week in Tokyo at ANA Hotel. She should stay there all day and he would arrange to have four men a day sent to her hotel. Very rich, very nice Japanese men. He promised she could make one million yen in a week.

'She said to me she could never do this back in Sydney, but in Tokyo it was a very big secret. She said to me in the beginning she thought four men in one day was too much, but after one day she understood why he said it would be easy, because Japanese men are very quick,' the customer laughed.

'How much did *you* pay?' I asked.

'It was a long time ago, maybe sixteen years, but fifty-thousand yen, or five-hundred American dollars. He took a third and she kept all the rest. I don't know if this is happening all the time in Tokyo but for me it was very convenient. I am company president, and I cannot go to a love hotel. Many people know me. I have many employees. But he is very smart. Even if somebody sees me going up the elevator at ANA Hotel, I can say I am there for a conference.

'I can tell you many stories about such girls. In the late eighties I knew many wealthy young ladies. They became rich because of their sugar daddies. Men were buying Gold Coast condos for Australian girls!

'Your club is very proper, for conversation only, but many hostesses have confessed to me their secrets. Like one hostess I know. She works in a place like this, but also at an S&M club during the day. She likes her job. It helps relieve the frustration from her difficult night-time customers. She can hit and whip and kick Japanese men! One is a very important company president, and he comes to her house in the morning. He brings, how do you say it? *Tupperware*. In this Tupperware she must do a morning shit, and he takes it away. He pays her thirty-thousand yen. At first she felt bad, but thirty-thousand yen is a big amount of money. She recently told me – she's not sure – but she thinks he is eating it at home.'

Well, at least he had got something for his money. By the time Mr Aoki left, he'd paid neatly the same and gone home empty-handed. Nothing shocks me any more.

EVERYBODY NEEDS YOU

Tonight Nori's extra effort in personal grooming matched the fervour with which he campaigned for me to 'be only with him'. The more I avoided the issue, the more resentful he became. 'I think for you I am *only* customer but . . . I care about you. For me it is serious. I want you. I am lonely. But I think that you will not come back to Japan.'

'Come on, Ito, why are you saying things like that? Do you come here just to upset me? You are very mean, putting words in my mouth like that.' It was the start of a fight that even Soh could distinguish from his post washing ashtrays behind the bar. When he started shadow-boxing with the liquor bottles I nodded, letting a few left jabs go when Nori stared off at the floor.

Soon Tehara came to engage him in conversation while I sat with arms crossed, but Nori only seemed more agitated than before. 'He is a liar for me. I am important customer for them, I know. They want only my money, so they lie to me.'

'Why would they lie to you? Look, who cares? We're friends, right?'

'I want to believe you, but I think I am only customer. If I am, I will give up and go find someone new. You are maybe for me *the impossible dream*. I don't want to chase impossible dream, but you must say things to keep me beside you. Maybe I am only a good customer for you,' he muttered and I gave no response.

Perhaps sensing the discontent of his longtime patron, Nishi quickly brought Nicole to join us, and Nori suddenly cheered. At least in front of company I was no longer to blame for his abject sorrow, but I still drank too many Baileys, one after the other, until finally he left. I couldn't help it. I can no longer remain sober in the presence of Nori Ito. I have to be drunk just to cope.

—

At the end of the night Nishi came to sit at the powwow table while I waited for the change room to empty. 'Ahem,' he cleared his throat. 'Chelsea-san, you have problem?'

'No, no problem,' I smiled at him and he slowly continued. 'This month your visa will expire. Prease make extension of three months. You are Canadian, you can. Prease ask Jodie. She knows how. I need you. Partnership. If stay December, I can pay you bonus, thirty-thousand yen.'

'I'm sorry, Nishi, but I can't. I already promised to go home for Christmas.'

'I know, but I need you. Prease understand who you are. You are young girl, you don't understand. *Who* is Chelsea? You need to understand. You and me not same. You are different from me, from girls, from customers. All not same. I am watching Chelsea. First time I met Chelsea, I know. Not same. Mae is trying very hard, making customer come, come. Last month fourteen *dohan*. I see Chelsea is not trying to make *dohan*, but *so many* requests to see you at the club. Mae *here*,' he said, indicating high above, then he plummeted his hand beneath us. 'Chelsea here. Prease, make same. Prease thinking. I need you.'

I told him I'd have to think about it and left to check email on the way home.

I wondered why I hadn't just told Nishi no. After I left Japan, I was hoping to get back to normality and my life with Matt. There was hardly a chance that I would extend my visa, even if it didn't conflict with going home for Christmas to see my family. I didn't want to be dishonest; I just felt it easiest to pretend that I was at least considering the possibility rather than to refuse outright. Oddly enough, that was a characteristically Japanese tendency. I had to laugh at myself. Maybe this culture was rubbing off on me more than I realised.

At the internet cafe I found an email from Koji sitting in my inbox.

Hi, Chelsea. This is your flight:
11th/Jan/2005 Air Canada 034 Vancouver (0910) – London (0625 + 1 day)
17th/Jan/2005 Air Canada 869 London (0830) – Vancouver (1518)
I will pick you up in the airport. The ticket will be sent to your PO Box, okay?
Regards, Koji

Whoops. Maybe I shouldn't have agreed to the invitation. I'd only done so to see if Koji would actually send the ticket.

A SHORT CONVERSATION

Matt and I were walking the noisy streets of Shibuya on a Sunday evening when my phone rang. 'Nori?' he asked, and I said, 'No, it's Yoshi . . . it's probably Yoshi.' Yoshi hadn't called in over a week, but I knew it would be him.

'Hello! Chelsea!' Yoshi shouted down the line. 'Can you hear me? It's Yoshi. What are you doing now?' I told him I was in Shibuya. 'In Shibuya? What are you doing? Party?'

'No, I'm not partying, I'm shopping.'

'By yourself, *ma chérie*? Not with a friend?'

'Yes, I'm by myself. Can you believe it? I'm spending my own money. It's incredible isn't it?' I heard Matt laugh in the background.

'Oh. Well, why you didn't call me?' Yoshi pouted.

'You're not my sugar daddy, and besides, you told me you'd be busy until the tenth and couldn't see me because you had some big project . . .'

'Yeah, but why you didn't call me all day? I was fuckin' bored, all day.'

'Boo-hoo. I went to Kamakura with my friend Shin. Why didn't *you* call me?'

'Oh, okay. Kamakura is nice place. So what are you doing this coming weekend? You wanna go to Hungary?'

'*What?* You want to go to Hungary? Are you crazy?'

'No, really. You wanna go somewhere? I miss you, *chérie*.'

'Yeah, sure, but not Hungary.'

'Really? You sure? You'd better be sure,' Yoshi threatened playfully, and I paused to think about his implications.

'Yeah, I'm sure.'

'Okay, I'll think about where. Maybe Guam. Nice beaches. Anyway, I'll see you this week, some day. *Hai*-bye.' And with that Yoshi was gone.

Great. I couldn't believe how easily I had welcomed him back in. Just as I was thinking my time in Japan would come to a calm conclusion the water was about to become turbulent. God help me.

SUBJECT:
TAKE A DEEP BREATH...

I read the first two lines of my mother's email on a Tuesday night before work. '*Hey Kiddo, Dad's used up another life . . . he'll be okay.*' My chest tightened, and a single word resonated like a dead weight: FUCK. I couldn't look at the screen. Nicole was beside me.

'What, Chelsea, what?' she pleaded. 'What is it?' But I just started to cry, and Nicole volunteered to read the rest of the email for me.

He was coming down a hill just east of here and saw a deer on the road and then another one jumped up on the highway and hit his plough and he lost control and slid. An eighteen-wheeler was coming in the oncoming lane. He said it happened so fast he thought his time was up especially as the cab caved in around him . . . He was pinned in there upside down. At the hospital he kept saying he was so glad to be alive . . .

Jesus Christ. My dad is always almost dying. Once he caught his sleeve in the sawmill conveyor belt and was dragged to the end to dangle for ages before someone happened to drive by and see him. Another time a huge tree fell on top of him when he was logging. Then a small-town redneck assaulted him, for no good reason. This time Dad's chest was damaged. He was on oxygen to assist with troubled breathing, but his heart was okay. He was stable. He had cracked ribs, a possible fracture in his lower back and bruised muscles that had released an enzyme into his blood that could damage his kidneys if he didn't get enough fluid.

What time was it in Canada? We were sixteen hours ahead. Mom would have fallen asleep from exhaustion by now. I didn't want to wake her or she'd never rest. It was better to call in the morning. I tried to call Matt but he wasn't answering. I was helpless and scared and I didn't know what to do. So I went to work.

'Look, Chelsea, your dad is okay, right? He's in the hospital, but he's fine,' Nicole soothed me. 'You can call them after, when they're awake, but if you don't come to work Nishi will fine you a hundred bucks. I know it sucks, babe, but c'mon, it'll be okay. C'mon.'

I don't remember anything that happened at Greengrass that night.

—

My dad is okay. This was my first conscious thought as I woke in the late afternoon. I'd talked to my sister in the morning, when Mom was out bringing Dad a Big Mac and a milkshake in hospital. Apparently he'd been high on morphine, cracking jokes to the nurses and generally being a rascal. Leave it to Dad to find amusement in the situation. He would be discharged tomorrow, so at least my life hadn't totally fallen apart.

I suppose as a positive I wouldn't be forced to leave prematurely; on the flip side I would just be left to wonder whether I should or not. This seemed to have become a question I asked myself every single day. Was it even worth it any more?

I dragged myself out of bed. Matt woke eventually, still tired from paddling a surfboard in his dreams, and we walked up to Roppongi so he could clock in at work before we took the subway to Shibuya to eat our favourite salmon balls and watch the people going by.

After that we found some clothes I liked at Shibuya 109 and Matt said, 'Buy them.' It felt strange purchasing something for myself. Somehow unusual. Not right. But as I handed over the cash, a Japanese pop song with an English bubblegum chorus was playing: 'I'm in love with a man nearly twice my age.' It was catchy. I sang it going down the elevator.

Matt scowled from two steps above. 'No, you aren't.'

'No, he's *more* than twice my age,' I joked, and Matt broke out into song.

'I'm in love with a man nearly twice my age, he has a black credit card and he probably has AIDS . . .' I started to laugh. And laugh. Until

Matt told me to spit out my gum, because I chewed it like a spack. What was that supposed to mean?

I knew Matt disliked Yoshi, but I always spoke about him just like any other customer. I never disclosed the feelings or conflict within me. I would be ashamed to, because most of the time I saw them as merely a by-product of this distorted environment. They were distorted feelings, and they would pass. I needed Matt. His love and support. I needed his trust. And even if he did suspect my turmoil, he was *always*, unfailingly, there for me. To listen. To cook breakfast. To put me in the shower.

After a frappucino at Starbucks we took the Hanzomon line back to Roppongi, transferred at Aoyama-itchome, kissed goodbye and went our separate ways to work.

—

'Hey, Jodie,' I said, waving her cigarette smoke out of my face at the powwow table. 'Did I tell you that I'm going to Oxford in January?'

'What? Why the hell are you going to Oxford?'

'Didn't I tell you? He sent the ticket. It arrived at my parents' house yesterday.'

'That's not with *Koji*,' she stressed, 'is it?'

'Yeah, it is.'

'Don't fuckin' go.'

I knew instantly why she'd said it. '*Why?* Is *HE* the scuba-mask guy?'

'Yup.' Jodie retold the whole story – her friend accompanying a Japanese customer to Hawaii, the adjoining rooms, the man masturbating in her room wearing only flippers and a scuba mask and how he'd tried to persuade security that she'd been the one attacking him. Only this time I noticed Jodie blinking her eyes erratically and I knew it was the same guy. *Koji Osara.* He'd even emailed her the same copy of his life story as a Word document. So that was why Koji had made such a fuss about denouncing Jodie every single night. He'd had reason to be on the defensive.

At the end of it I sighed heavily and said, 'Well, it looks like I won't be going to Oxford after all.'

MIZU-TANI THE MANIAC

I nervously put in a call to Yoshi on the way to work. 'Hello?' he answered.

I had to shout over traffic. 'HI. HOW ARE YOU?'

'So good, *ma chérie*. How are you?'

'TERRIBLE.'

'Why? What happened?'

'UM, DID YOU MAKE PLANS FOR THIS WEEKEND?'

'What, say again?'

'YOU DIDN'T ALREADY MAKE PLANS FOR US TO GO ON A TRIP SOMEWHERE THIS WEEKEND, DID YOU? REMEMBER YOU CALLED ME IN SHIBUYA AND SAID YOU WERE GOING TO THINK OF PLANS FOR THIS WEEKEND? DID YOU?'

'Why?'

I told Yoshi about Dad's accident. The worry. The deliberation about whether I should stay or go. As expected, Yoshi was a gentleman and entirely sympathetic.

'Wow, okay. Are you going to work now? Okay, tomorrow daytime I will call you. Thanks for calling me, and please don't worry, all right?'

No, I wouldn't worry. Dad was walking around. I would see him soon, but that wasn't where I found solace, because even before Dad had flown into a snowy ditch, I'd already decided not to spend another weekend with Yoshi.

According to Nicole, however, I should have just taken him up on the offer. 'Chelsea, hanging out with Yoshi is a great opportunity! Matt trusts you, and Yoshi respects you. You can trust him. Just go have fun while you're still in Japan.'

But what Nicole didn't understand was that any agreement I made to Yoshi now would mean more than just having fun. It had got to the point where I couldn't lie to him but I couldn't tell the truth either. Just seeing him was becoming impossible. I didn't want to go to Guam, to Hungary or to the small island, and I'd intended to get out of this trip. I just hadn't figured out how until Dad became my excuse.

At least now I wouldn't have to explain. That I really cared about him, but that I wasn't who he thought. That I didn't want to live that life.

That I wanted to keep my nose clean.

—

Mizu-tani locked onto me like a laser beam. As he sat talking to Mama-san across the room, his pint-sized hands gestured wildly. When I was finally transferred to his table, he slid off the bench like a Dalí-esque clock until his head formed a right angle, and then recovered himself to remark as if normal, 'You are much in demand here. I am so shy, especially for you. I am very strict. They know me here. I never request girls. Only you. I come here only to see you.'

I laughed light-heartedly and said, 'I don't think you are shy, Mizu-tani.'

'THEN YOU ARE A LIAR!' he shouted, sitting up in a fury that subsided just as quickly as it had come. 'I am sorry. Please forgive me. You are too nice for me to yell. I promised to a friend that I would be going to another club, so I can stay only one hour. Normally I never go to clubs for only one hour, but I cannot forget you,' Mizu-tani said, bringing his nose close to my nose, 'because you are so nice, and there-fore, I come.'

Two hours later I had to remind Mizu-tani that he was still at Green-grass. 'Oh no!' he cried out. 'I must emergency call my friend . . .' and he ran out into the hallway, only to come running back in soon after-wards, collapsing beside me like an abandoned marionette. 'I made can-cellation!' he breathed heavily. 'Why? Because I cannot leave you. Chelsea, please believe me. I like you! You don't like me? *I don't care.* I disgust you? *I don't care.* But I am thinking only about you. My strike zone is so small, my strike zone is so narrow, but *you* hit a strike.'

'Three strikes and you're out?' I laughed.

'Exactly. That is why I must sing for you,' and he was quickly standing on the couch, launching into a booming Italian love song. I gave him a standing ovation and he sat back down.

'Whatever I do, wherever I go, my heart will always belong to you. Why you are so nice? Your beauty I have no words for. I forget any words to describe you. How can I express myself in English when I have so few vocabularies? It is impossible. I am amazed. You don't believe me? I'll kill you. I don't like the average. Your beauty is so high, up here, this is where you are floating, and I am swimming, down here in the sewer. Why I cannot touch you with my broken wings? Why must I pay so much money just to see your face? My tax accountant tells me not to use credit cards, but how can I stop to come to see you?'

'That won't be so hard. I'm leaving on the twenty-eighth.'

'So soon?' he choked. 'What will I do? I will make tears.'

Mizu-tani lit up his face with my lighter so I could see his imaginary tears and then excused himself to go to the restroom, only to come back ten seconds later. 'I go to style my hair, up here, and down here. Okay, you can ignore me, no problem. When do you come back? January? If so, it is too long absence. My heart will break. Please, make shorter. Then we will go to Thailand, in February. Okay? I'll arrange economy for you, executive for me. Hah! Only joke.'

Mizu-tani finally left at 2.30 am, ushered into the elevator by a transsexual from across the hall while I stood back and waved in sheer delight.

AN ANGRY NORI

Tuesday night at Greengrass: psycho Nori left me three messages. (1) 'Oh, hi. How are you? Uh, I call you to say hello, and uh . . . I wanna see you. Umm, yes, I will call you. Bye . . . You call me please.' Beeeeep. (2) 'Hello, this is Nori. I called you to say hello, and uh, okay I will call you later. Bye.' Beeeeep. (3) 'Hello, Chelsea, umm, I just called you to say hello, and I want to know how you are, and uh, I will call you later. Bye-bye.' Beeeeep.

I erased all of them. He knew that I was working.

—

Wednesday night at Greengrass: psycho Nori was sulking by himself in a dark corner when I arrived. I sat down next to him and stiffly shook his hand. 'How are you?'

'I left you messages,' he replied without eye contact.

'You called me only when you knew that I was working. You know I can't answer my phone when I'm working.'

'I told you to call me,' he sulked.

'I had other things on my mind. I wasn't trying to ignore you, but my father was in an accident. I thought I'd have to leave. I didn't know if he was okay. I've been stressed out, I've had no sleep, I'm worried and I've still had to show up to work. I'm sorry, but there are more important things right now. Okay? Can you understand that?'

Nori was completely taken aback. 'Okay, I understand you now. I was worried, and confused. I thought you didn't call me and I didn't know why,' he confessed, but when Candy, a new Australian hostess who lived in Japan and was bilingual, came to join us only minutes later, Nori continued to sulk, even glowering at me.

'*What?*' I snapped at him. There was no point in concealing my anger. It was a relief to know I would be leaving Japan soon, and there was no longer any use pretending.

'Nothing,' he pouted.

Candy's face registered concern. 'Is everything all right. *Genki?*'

'No, everything is not all right. Ito is angry because when he called last week, when he *knew* I couldn't answer my phone, I didn't call back because my dad almost died and for some reason I wasn't even thinking about him, a customer from Greengrass, so now he's mad.'

Nori's jaw dropped. His eyes bulged. Had I said something so direct? You bet I had.

'Well, it's the truth,' I insisted, and Candy went cross-eyed as Nori started to rapid-fire in Japanese. He was trying to verify my story, and while she explained, Nori listened intently, the information sinking in for possibly the first time.

'Okay,' he sighed. 'I understand you now, but I think you should come back to Japan and do something with *me!*'

Unbelievable. I ignored him and asked Candy to pass the karaoke book. I needed to sing. When I'd vented all my frustration, the entire club broke into applause, with my old friend Goro prolonging his clapping unnecessarily. I smiled and waved.

'That's better. Let's pick another one.'

Nori glared at me. 'Before, you told to me that you didn't like to sing sad song.'

'Yeah, well, my situation has changed.'

'Why don't you drink something?' he suggested. 'Some Baileys?'

'I don't want to. I don't drink,' I rebuked icily.

'Yes, but before, you used to drink . . . sometimes.'

'Yes that's right, but now I'm getting too fat so I quit. I haven't drunk in two weeks. But you wouldn't know that, would you, because you've barely been around, have you?'

'Yes,' he said weakly, 'but before you used to have some drinks.'

'Well, now I don't. It's my song now, can I have the microphone please?' Not much later I began to frantically signal Tehara that I wanted to move, and soon I was listening to Goro describe the Ferrari he'd ordered. Then Tehara interrupted: Nori was leaving, and would I please accompany Candy to see him to the door? *No, I would not.* My song was next, and so I made Nori leave without saying goodbye. I didn't even bother to glance his way.

On a trip to the restroom I ran into Carmen. 'Chelsea, I am worried about this guy, Goro. He invited me to go for sushi, but he is asking me all these personal questions, saying, "Are you serious about me? I am serious about you." He wants to be my boyfriend . . .'

'Hah! No he doesn't. He's said the same thing to almost everyone here, so just play along. He's harmless. Go with him and his friend and you can eat as much as you want and then they'll let you go home. There are no strings attached to Goro. He might even take you shopping or to a concert if you lay it on thick, but be quick. He's got a short attention span, so grab him while you can.'

—

Before the night was through, Nishi sat me on a table with Taizo and his boss, Misaki. At one point, when Misaki spilt cold *shochu* across the table and onto my ankle, everyone expected me to clean up the table first, but I just sighed and mopped my ankle instead. I was tired of catering to unreasonable customers.

Soon Abie came to sit with us, and Misaki asked where she was from.

'Israel,' she replied, and in one fell swoop he opened his suit jacket within inches of her face, and 'BOOM!' he shouted.

It was Misaki's favourite pantomime to blow up Israeli hostesses like a suicide bomber. It was always inappropriate, but tonight he seemed to relish the timing.

'You should be happy,' he quipped. 'Arafat died in Paris.'

THE WEEKDAY FLU
MEDICINE

Starbucks brought out the Christmas cups today. Another typhoon originated in the north-west Pacific. Koji rang me from London: please say hello to Mr Nishi. He violated my ear with the things that he said. For breakfast I ate a pint of Häagen-Dazs.

These are the day's headlines that scroll across the bottom of my BBC life.

And now, we cross to a table with nothing but a watered-down Scotch and a pack of cigarettes: the sign of Yoshi's imminence — off powdering his nose in the bathroom. We see the young hostess lingering at the bar until he emerges and they exchange kisses, right after he slaps her on the ass and she calls him a bastard.

Yoshi was in a thick turtleneck. He'd been sick for four days, but I shouldn't worry, his mommy was taking care of him. She'd been bringing him soup for three days.

'What? Get your facts right. Have you been sick for three days or four?'

'I don't know! I am busy, but you don't care about me. I know. Did you miss me?'

'Of course I did.'

'Humph. How's your boyfriend? I *know,*' Yoshi glared at me, and I froze in a panic. 'How is he? Huh? *I'll kill you.* I'll fuckin' kill you.' He laughed, and I relaxed. Hopefully not too visibly. 'I am waiting, *ma chérie*. Why don't you ever call me? Come on.' He left briefly to make a call from the hallway, and without asking either of us Nishi sat Carmen at the table.

'Oh, hello,' Yoshi grinned on return. 'Where are you from?'

When Carmen said 'Me-hico', Yoshi spoke fluent Spanish back to her in a perfect accent. I sat staring at him with mouth open. 'You didn't tell me you spoke Spanish.'

'Why? Of course, I had a girlfriend from Brazil.'

'Brazilians speak Portuguese,' I argued, but they kept talking in Spanish. 'Excuse me for one minute,' I interrupted, and I stormed to the change room to regain composure. I was actually jealous! What was the matter with me? Why did I care?

'You know, Spanish is like French,' Yoshi explained when I returned. 'Sixty per cent is the same. Station is just a different pronunciation. *Statione*. Like Chelsea, she's my final station. I like her so much, but she doesn't like me. Whatta can I do? See ya! *Je t'aime beaucoup, beaucoup, beaucoup,*' he cooed in my ear. '*Furie.*'

'*Furie?* What does that mean?' I asked, but he pulled me in close without telling me, and Tehara came to take me back to Fujimoto-san, who was in with some clients. I was barely into my first song when Nishi came to say that Yoshi was paying his bill.

'Prease come.'

'Hey, Yoshi . . . why are you leaving? You just got here,' I protested. He was signing off on his credit-card receipt.

'Come on. I've got to get up in the morning. I've gotta go home, I'm tired, but it depends you,' he grinned wearily. 'I can call my secretary, cancel everything. Let's go.'

Yoshi reminded me I still had to come to his new place for dinner before I left. What, he could cook too? No, no, no. He could call a cook, for catering. How typical. I wanted to tell him that he couldn't buy everything with money, but he was stand-offish until the elevator doors closed on him, silent as he signalled for me to call him.

Just like his phone would be.

—

Nishi had Jessica the Australian and me join Shin for orange juice tonight. According to Jodie, Australians were Shin's favourite – tall with room for fattening. Jessica shared an apartment in Shin-Okobo near

Shinjuku with her Aussie boyfriend. The only detail that changed about her situation when talking to customers was that her name was a pseudonym, and her boyfriend became her female friend who hostessed at One Eyed Jack.

'Hi, Shin. I called you today, but your phone was busy,' I said in mock accusation.

'No. I had no missed call,' Shin insisted plainly. 'No message.'

'Yes, that's because it was beeping. What does beeping mean?'

'I don't know.'

'All right, fine. Well maybe you can tell us, what is Shin-Okobo like? Jessica just got an apartment there with her friend and we're wondering.'

Shin frowned deeply. 'Shin-Okobo is bad place to live. In Shinjuku there is Russian mafia, Japanese mafia, Chinese mafia, Korean mafia. There are many prostitutes in Okobo. People go there when they want to find them, so standing around in one place, walking down the street, is maybe not good idea. Maybe someone will ask you how much. Maybe someone will misunderstand you, so be careful.'

Jessica was white as a sheet. She'd just signed a one-year lease.

'Do you have Vegemite with you? I can bring you some, when I go next month to visit my friend, in Melbourne. How much you want? One? Five? Twenty? I don't know. It will be my first time, so what you recommend I eat in Australia?'

'Oooh, have a barbeque,' Jessica advised. 'Just with everything. Throw it all on. And always wear sunscreen, SPF30, or you'll burn like a lobster.'

'Did Chelsea tell you about live squid yet? She kissed it. She loves it!'

'Right, we're going to get married,' I joked.

'So who is Carmen, your friend for Hakone?'

'Over there, with the long hair.' Shin squinted and Jessica excused herself briefly.

'I don't think Jessica will do well as hostess,' Shin frowned. 'It is not her style, her type of job. Anyway, do you want a ride home? I am going by taxi, my friend I told you about. His taxi. I think maybe Jessica should go by taxi too, to Shin-Okobo.'

Outside it was raining. 'Is he safe?' Jessica mouthed quickly, and I nodded while Shin offered his umbrella to me.

'No, you two share that. I have a hood, it's okay!' Shin looked at me like I was crazy and I stuck out my tongue and started sloshing along in the rain behind them. I could hear Shin asking Jessica what her hobbies were, whether she liked surfing, but no, she liked waterskiing. And what about him? What did Shin like to do?

'GOLF!' I yelled out from behind. 'Shin loves golf.'

'Oh, you like golf?' Jessica asked earnestly. 'That's a good sport.' I was walking through puddles when Shin swooped around to scowl at me furiously.

'I *HATE* GOLF!' he shouted, and we both fell deep into laughter while poor Jessica was left lost in translation.

1095 DAYS MAKES IT
ALL GO AWAY

Koji Osara has been playing on my mind. He rang me from London today, inconsolably upset, and I'd had to counsel him for over an hour because, oddly, his shrink was unavailable at the time. I just couldn't imagine what he'd done to have the Swedish girls throw him out of their apartment in Sweden, where he'd just been to visit. They'd accused him of things he'd never done, he said. 'Those fucking stupid, perpetual rumours. How had they found out?'

'Found out what? What rumours, Koji?' I didn't mention that I knew the man in the scuba-mask story was him. It didn't seem like the time.

'Do you think I am a sad, pathetic creep addicted to hostesses? That's what they said to me, that I am like a fucking stupid child with no brain to believe what hostesses tell me. They said women only pretend to like me so they can get money and presents. They said only men who are pathetic fucking perverts had to pay money for girls to pretend to like them.'

—

The Koji stories kept on coming. Jodie told me that he had recently put in a similar call to her that had lasted for hours. She was shocked when I said all he'd done during his last visit was criticise her relentlessly.

Then a blonde girl named Betty came back to work at Greengrass after a long hiatus. She was from Adelaide but lived in Tokyo. The name Betty from Adelaide rang a bell.

'Oh, are you Koji's secretary?' I asked.

'Koji *Osara*! I do NOT work for *KOJI Osara*! Oh my God, did he say that? The crazy motherfucker. I haven't seen him in over a year.' Her tone was steeped in hatred.

'Is this your phone number?' I asked, producing the card Koji had written on for Samicah and me some weeks before.

'Yes! Oh my God. That's my phone number, but I would never work for such a psychotic creep as Koji Osara. That's so fucking unbelievable!'

After these two strange events I thought I'd better hurry up and tell Koji I wouldn't be coming to Oxford. So I sent him an email.

Hello Koji,

I have received your emails. Sorry I missed your call the other day. My dad told me I received the ticket from the travel agent. I am sorry to say that I won't be coming to Oxford next month. A lot has changed and I am no longer comfortable with going. I hope you can cancel the ticket. Thank you very much for the offer but I just don't want to go. I hope you can understand.

I will not be at my parents' house, please do not phone their house, they have no knowledge about my plans. I am planning on going back to Australia from Vancouver.

All the best, Chelsea

Koji wrote back:

We have just met a couple of times in Tokyo. Actually I don't know you and you don't know me not so much. So you need not feel guilty about this cancellation. I wish you would have a good luck in Aussie. Koji

Koji Osara. What a fucking psycho. Wait a minute. Koji Osara. Joji Obara. Koji . . . *is this the same fucking guy?* Both customers of Greengrass. Both freakin' psychos. Both about the same age. Why had Koji claimed to be Nishi's most important customer? Why was he so paranoid about all the rumours circulating in Roppongi about him? What could someone have possibly done to be so notorious in a place like this?

I needed to find out more, and so I googled around a bit. First, I found a paper written by Koji describing how, according to Jungian theory, the subconscious can split and a person can reinvent their identity in three years' time. I got a chill down my spine. Could this be why Koji had said he couldn't trust anyone for three years, or, more accurately, was it why Koji couldn't be trusted?

Three years ago was the exact timeframe when Lucie Blackman had gone missing. Was it just coincidence? Or was the person known as Koji Osara the product of this 1095-day metamorphosis? And what about the masks? According to a police source of *Time* magazine, Joji Obara wore nothing but a mask in many of the videotapes showing him assaulting apparently unconscious women.

Then I read several media reports that noted Joji Obara *appeared fidgety and blinked nervously* in court appearances. That was an odd thing to report: blinking nervously. It was one of the first things that struck you about Koji. I also read that Joji Obara had undergone eye surgery (popular among mixed-blood Japanese), to make his eyes rounder than the distinctly narrow Korean eyes displayed in an early photograph – one of only two available on the internet despite the enormity of the case.

Had Koji gone to such extremes? It would definitely provide an explanation for his unnatural blinking, as this is a common result of eye surgery. The retinas need moisture because the lids have been cosmetically stretched.

Could it be a possibility?

To: Koji@addresswithheld.com ('Koji Osara')
Subject: no subject
Koji Osara. . . . are you better known as Joji Obara?
Why did you say that there were accusations about you that weren't true, that you had a bad reputation in Roppongi from stupid hostesses and that you didn't do anything? I am curious to know. The reason I cancelled Oxford was because the description of the Lucie Blackman case I discovered and the transcripts of interviews sounded remarkably like you.

To: . . . ('Chelsea Haywood')
Subject: RE: Casanova's affair

276

Dear Chelsea

Hello, how are you?

I am now in Brighton to start sushi bar project.

Anyway I thank you for giving this information.

From a news resource of newspaper:

Joji Obara was graduated from KEIO Univ.

I was graduated from KEIO Univ., too.

He was 44 years old at that time.

I was 44 years old at that time, too.

He is Japanese Korean.

I am pure Japanese, not mongrel.

He came to Casanova (right now Mr Nishi changed their name from Casanova to Greengrass) a lot of times.

I also went to Casanova often, too.

He was managing a real estate business.

I am a consultant.

The initials J.O. and K.O. are comparable . . .

Yes, the profile data looks very similar between me and him.

The very big difference is that he was addicted English hostess but I am not. I don't know why, but I feel some hesitation for high educated British or American hostess, because they need not come to Roppongi.

Actually Lucy (and her friend Jessica) used to work British Airways. They needed not to resign from BA.

Next this is the secondary information from Mr Nishi:

Mr Joji Obara is very shorty and miser.

He is very gloomy.

Koji is very open minded and cheerful.

It is impossible for anyone to confuse between Joji and Koji because they have huge discrepancy.

Are these information enough to make you feel better?

Finally I apologise to let you not come to Oxford cause of this gossip.

I am sorry. Finally I wish you might have a good luck in Aussie.

See you someday, Koji

Wow. The response was not what I had expected. The factual similarities he delivered were clinical, yet his defence lay only in matters pertaining to the comparison of the psyche. He also attributed these discrepancies in the third person, as if he were talking about Koji as a removed identity and not as himself.

There was at least one blatant lie. Koji wasn't pure Japanese. He had told me he was half-Chinese (but perhaps half-Korean in actuality?). It was also pretty creepy that he had renamed the email 'Casanova's affair'. I wasn't sure what to make of that.

If Koji was Joji Obara, maybe he considered himself a new person now that he was being watched, getting help from a shrink and taking medication. Is this why we were not allowed to bring up the subject of his previous career as a psychoanalyst? Had Koji been stripped of his licence, or, more importantly, the access to psychotropic drugs such as those that Joji Obara was alleged to have used to drug and rape at least nine women?

And who said that Joji Obara was still even in jail? Sagawa the cannibal still walks the streets and is a minor celebrity in Japan, putting in guest appearances on TV shows and occasionally spending Saturday nights at One Eyed Jack. In 1992 the man even starred in a movie called *Sisenjiyou no Aria* (*The Bedroom*) as a sadosexual voyeur! This is the brilliance of the Japanese legal system, at least as far as wealthy and rumoured mafia-linked families are concerned.

Joji Obara was the son of extremely wealthy parents who were also *pachinko* parlour owners – a business commonly rumoured to be linked to money laundering and the mafia. A 2003 article quoted Obara's lawyer as saying, 'My client is looking forward to getting out of prison,' and it also stated that Joji Obara could go free if they failed to find evidence. It had been a long time. The trial had been postponed. I could find no mention in the English media of whether Joji Obara was still behind bars. Had they let him loose?

I read that Joji Obara attended Yokohama High School. Koji had said his mother lived in Yokohama. He'd also mentioned his apartment outside Tokyo, in an undisclosed location. He later invited a friend of mine there to meet his 'mother and boss' but she thankfully bailed at the last minute. Who the hell invites someone to their apartment outside Tokyo to meet their *mother* and *boss*?

By chance I discovered a press release from the Foreign Correspondents' Club of Japan advising seat availability for foreign media in the recently resumed Joji Obara trial, and the dates of his court appearances matched up almost exactly with the weekends when Koji had been, and disclosed he would be, visiting Tokyo. And there had been all those important phone calls at scheduled times, days when he made it clear that he *had to be* somewhere and was contactable only at night. It was chilling.

Then there were the odd things. Nowhere in the news reportage had I found information that Lucie Blackman had been working at Casablanca with a friend named Jessica. So Koji must have known Lucie somehow. Much later Koji claimed he'd never met Lucie, but then Nishi reminded him he'd gone on one *dohan* with her, although he couldn't remember ever doing that or who Lucie was. Funnily enough Joji Obara first claimed never to have met Lucie Blackman. Then he admitted to having met her in Casablanca, and then finally to having met her one time outside the club.

Great. Am I just paranoid? Is this place making me crazy? I didn't want to judge him outright, but somehow I think Koji had managed to incriminate himself.

ESCAPE TO HAKONE

The estimated waiting time to board the second train up the mountain was over an hour. That was the problem with novelty tourist trains; even the Japanese couldn't engineer their efficiency, especially on a Saturday when Hakone's hillsides were afire with the changing of autumn leaves. It was hot, it was sunny and it was as crowded as Shibuya on a Sunday, as evidenced by the millefeuille of holidaymakers and Tokyoites waiting peacefully to be transported to the summit. Shin turned to observe the line building behind us, and then silently disappeared into a sea of black hair. It wasn't until I spotted him off in the distance, leaning patiently on an open car door, that I realised where he'd gone. Breaking Carmen's count of the Louis Vuitton bags around her, I nudged us both out of the line. 'What? What's happening?' Carmen asked as our place was immediately filled.

'Shin says we're taking a taxi to the top.'

—

From the unassuming roadside office of Hotel Taiseikan there was only one way to our room – a small tram that descended three hundred spectacular metres to a hidden valley below, where a wide stream flowed through lush forest at the foot of a looming rock wall covered in moss and natural *bonsai*. On top sat the *ryokan*, a breathtaking collection of enormous whitewashed buildings studded with red balconies, accessed by a stone-flecked path that led through Japanese gardens. Shin had completely outdone himself.

Our room was simple, a tiny entry leading to six *tatami* mats framed by a large window overlooking the stream below. Laid out in three neat piles on a low table were our mandatory *yukata* – a lighter, cotton version of kimono – two in patterned red and white, and one in blue. For our feet there were disposable slippers, which we'd personalised in felt pen. Shin had drawn happy faces, Carmen a sun, and in a fit of inspiration I'd outlined a snow-capped mountain under a single star, to which Shin reacted suddenly, '*Whoa!* So good choice!' before frowning at the simplicity warming his own ten toes.

Picking up the blue *yukata* Shin briefly demonstrated how to wrap it left over right, tying a wide belt before leaving to change in the communal bathroom. Under the strict hand of the matronly innkeeper Carmen and I were dressed flawlessly when he returned, earning a nod of silent approval. With dinner at six there was just enough time for a dip in the *onsen*.

Tucked away at one end of the inn the two separate baths were rotated twice daily to allow women to enjoy the extravagant, historically male quarters. With a wave Carmen and I said goodbye to Shin and passed under a curtain. Finding the *onsen* deserted we left our *yukata* in baskets and ran bare-skinned across the slate, hurriedly lathered on tiny stools and rinsed with a bucket. Sliding open a partition we raced into the outdoor rock pool, steaming in the cold dusk air, and lazed in the rejuvenating water.

Suddenly I remembered Shin's warning that we had only forty-five minutes until dinner. 'How long have we been here?' I asked, and we jumped from the bath, scuttling across the slick floor through clouds of steam to chaotically tie each other back into our *yukata* and run like wild foreign women through deserted halls to our dinner.

—

We found Shin sitting at the open window, calmly reading a book when we flew through the door. He looked up sternly. 'It is okay. I changed dinner time already. I have been waiting, *sooo* long time. When you did not return, I was worried. I *was!* Maybe you fall asleep in hot bath. In five minutes I was sending old woman to look for you!'

He set his book aside and gleefully observed our skewed appearance.

'Oh, *no, no, no*. Is not okay! Turn around, you so silly woman.' He grabbed roughly at the bow in my belt. 'Should be double knot! Not *bow*. And here,' he lectured, spinning me around. 'So bad one. Always you should wear *left* side in front. You are now dead body, at funeral,' he laughed, and I quickly slipped into the entry to try again. As I re-emerged, Shin's gaze reflected my incompetence. He straightened my collar, pulled at the arms and untucked my belt to lie flat against the waist. 'This is better. Maybe you are hopeless as Japanese person, *hmmm*? I think so.' As Shin proceeded to inspect Carmen's attire, there was a soft knock at the door and a woman's voice calling out, '*Sumimasen*.' Dinner had arrived.

After a huge Japanese dinner we were ready for another *onsen*, and this time Carmen and I found other pink-edged slippers beneath the curtain at the newly rotated baths. It made us laugh to see our suns and mountains among perfectly executed Japanese characters – it was meant to be names and not artistry that identified one's slippers from another's.

Inside we found the larger, more extravagant male baths full of women, the steam so thick it masked bodies from head to toe. After a symbolic cleanse in the cold water Carmen and I shyly held square white towels to our navels and scampered outside, followed by the discreet glances of women curious to see the novelty of stark-naked *gaijin* bodies. Even in the cool evening air the deep pool was scalding hot, as if the volcanic spring were directly underneath, and we quickly sought respite near a pipe that brought water in from the stream on the other side of a bamboo fence. As we stood half-submerged, steam condensed into a slick layer on our skin, and in twenty minutes we were hot, dehydrated and thirsty.

A few litres of water later we towelled off to tie ourselves back into our *yukatas*, accessorised by the distinctive glow that one gets from natural hot springs. Across the room a Japanese woman was drying off her young son, a boy more preoccupied with waving to us than aiding his mother in her task. As she lovingly scooped him up, Carmen's eyes widened. 'Look!' she whispered, and I turned to see a menacing patch of purpled blue spreading up the little boy's buttocks.

'Don't worry,' I quickly explained. 'Those aren't bruises. It's just a birthmark.'

More specifically, it's the Mongolian Blue Spot. Common in Asian babies, Mongolian Blue Spot is the name given to the dark pigmentation found primarily on the bum and sacral region. Present at childbirth, these spots are nothing more than dense groupings of melanocytes – melanin-containing skin cells – and usually disappear completely by age five. While the spots have wrongly led to suspicions of child abuse overseas, in Japan they have merely led to the idiom *shiri ga aoi*, or 'his butt is blue', a favoured expression when a person is behaving like a child.

It was after midnight and Shin and Carmen lay asleep on futons on either side of me as I got up and quietly slid open the partition to slip down empty halls to the lobby. Only the light of a small Shinto shrine illuminated the large room, a rear-garden waterfall spilling over the rhythmic knocking of a *shishi-odoshi*. Back in Roppongi Matt would still be up, passing the time in an internet cafe or wandering the empty streets alone. With no mobile reception I dropped all my ¥100 coins into the public phone and waited as it rang. 'Hello? It's me.'

It was nice just to hear Matt's voice, a comforting reminder that I was still in fact in a real-time relationship, and when the money ran out I sat alone in the shadows, thinking about him and me and smiling. *I am still so in love with him*, I thought, before padding back down the hallways, slipping onto the thick futon and into the first deep sleep I'd had in months.

Early in the morning, Carmen and I awoke to a room without Shin. Yawning, we plodded off to the communal washroom to brush our teeth, and when we returned he was sitting on the ledge, staring down at the stream, skin slick with the shine of just having been to the baths. 'Good morning to Miss Lazies! I have already been to the *onsen*,' he boasted. 'You should go. Breakfast is in one hour.'

~

Outside, Mt Fuji floated in the sky, severed by dense cloud that made it hard to distinguish just where the snow-capped mountain began. It was surprising how quickly it had been blanketed since Shin and I had last been to Hakone, only one month ago, and how much cooler the air was as a second cable car swung us back down the hillside in the direction of the majestic Ashinoko.

Created over three thousand years ago when the eruption of Mt Kamiyama blocked off the river Hava, Ashinoko's waters filled a caldera criss-crossed by boats. Sitting at the prow of a replica pirate ship we sailed across under a wide blue sky. We could see the distant red *torii* of the Hakone Shinto shrine on the water's edge, and a sprawling hillside resort nestled among acres and acres of forest displaying the colours that came only briefly right before winter fell.

We steamed into the dock like seafaring explorers and were soon on a bus, arriving in a straw-coloured field on the edge of a wood. In true Japanese style a cluster of vending machines greeted us on the roadside, and Shin bought us cold green tea before leading the way to a path through the swaying blades of *susuki* – Japanese pampas grass – blowing head height in the breeze. Without warning Shin would turn and disappear as the long grass closed behind him, leaving Carmen and me to run to catch up. Finally we ascended to the edge of a thin, reed-like forest. After posing for more photos, Carmen and I flew down the steep gradient like schoolgirls, laughing and shrieking, refreshed and totally alive. Shin spread his arms and ran down behind us, losing a year with each step until he crashed into our hastily thrown barricade as young as a child. The three of us spent an eternity in that field of long grass. We hardly talked, breathing in moments like they might run out if we stopped to exhale.

OH MY BUDDHA

Oh my Buddha, I am trying. This is something my customer Kenji says to me. It is one of two things he says every time he comes in to drink sake mixed with soda and lemon and sing Bob Dylan or Bob Marley or even 'Bob the Builder' – God knows, he would sing it if we had it. Kenji sings so many songs, and he makes me sing them too.

The first thing he habitually says is right after I ask how he is and he is always 'very bad'. The second is when I say 'oh my God' and he echoes 'oh my Buddha' very quickly, like a chaser after Early Times whisky, which he never drinks but sometimes one of his friends does when they come in together. I think his friend's name is Zushi, but no, maybe Zushi drinks Suntory. I can't really be sure. I would usually remember but I was too busy trying to guess what Kenji did for a living. 'You can have five guesses at my profession!' he shouted. 'If correct, then nice dinner. But if wrong . . . LOVE HOTEL!'

But *oh my Buddha* I am trying.

I am trying to soften up the sadness so it doesn't hurt every single day. I languish over so many things. That maybe I am having an emotional affair, or that maybe I am not. This environment is just so fucked up I can't even tell any more, and that kills me. Every day that just kills me.

I am trying to add sugar to the bittersweet taste that is Yoshi, but every time I think I've made it better I realise the recipe is only becoming more and more unsalvageable. And still I add another cup. I am trying to medicate the uncertainty and the confusion and depression that come from not having figured anything out yet but only fucking things up more and more as I try.

This is not an easy project. What do they call those people – social commentators? Am I a social commentator? Is that what this book is about? I don't know. I am trying to be academic about it all but that thing called being a human being keeps getting in the way. I am trying to be the worker and the supervisor and the CEO and the eight million shareholders all at the same time. I am trying to trade stocks in a foreign market but there are too many of them and I am unlicensed and they just don't equate and I am coming up short and red and flying by the seat of my pants, just hoping that the JASDAQ won't come crashing down all around me. Oh my Buddha, this is not just a project any more.

Oh my Buddha, this is my life.

—

Esther sat down next to me and started to ask about my visa. When did it run out? When was I leaving? Would I consider staying? 'They really like you, Nishi *and* Mama-san. They want you to extend it,' she said. 'They really do.'

'Yeah, I know. I just don't think that I could.' I didn't want to come back to Tokyo fourteen times like Esther had. She was thirty years old. Between three-month stints spent hostessing in Tokyo, Esther travelled to India, where she studied holistic therapies with the goal of opening her own practice in Israel. She was only planning two or three more trips.

Esther had saved her money, and she knew how to maximise her potential. Every night Esther came in on a *dohan*, and when Greengrass was quiet she donned a long black coat and brought customers in off the street. By some miracle she'd figured out the Japanese psyche, and she honestly enjoyed being a hostess. The first few times had been tough, she said, but she could find something good to say about everyone, even the foulest of customers.

'But tell me about Yoshi,' she prodded. 'I have known him a long time. Maybe five years now. I used to be good friends with his friend, Suzuki. They were crazy men together. They came here so often. They went everywhere. Partying, partying. The drugs. The alcohol. The women. They couldn't get enough. They were real playboys, both so handsome.

'You know, Suzuki is one of Yoshi's only friends. It's difficult being in his position. He can never trust anyone's intention. He has so much money, but you know it wasn't all given to him. He took over from his father but Yoshi has grown the business so much. He's really worked hard. But now he feels so isolated. I haven't seen Suzuki in a long time. He doesn't come any more. But occasionally I see Yoshi. When he gets lonely, I think. Chasing the girls that don't belong. The unobtainable ones. How do you think he feels about you?'

'I don't know. He'd have me believe that he loves me, but it's just a big lie.'

'I don't think so,' Esther said. 'You know, I don't think Yoshi falls in love very often, but when he does I really think he means it, in his own way. I think he really cares about you. I can see that when you're together. You're what he wants. A light at the end of his tunnel. He's just been doing this so long I think he's lost, that's all.

'He has an unusual life. He's addicted to the drugs but I wouldn't say he can't love you. Don't take that away from him. You have your husband, I know, and he's a beautiful man. He has a beautiful soul. I think that's right for you. You're so young, but what you're going through, it has its place too. Life is so much more complicated than we'd like it to be.'

'I don't want it to be complicated,' I whispered.

Esther grasped my hand. 'I know. But just keep your heart open. You've got so much love to give.'

—

Oh God, I don't know what to do. I thought life would be easy if I didn't call Yoshi, but I was wrong. Postponing the inevitable hasn't made the feelings subside. It's just brought them to critical mass. What if Yoshi didn't come to the club again? I only have three nights left. I'd turned him away, but now I couldn't just leave. Rationally, would seeing him solve anything? Or did I even want to see him? Maybe I just wanted the high of being what I was to him.

This bullshit craziness going on in my head isn't fair. Not to Matt. Not to me. And I have to confess I did the worst thing in my life the other day. I did a Google search. It said: *Australian divorce law.*

But doing that didn't solve anything either. I just felt violently ill. And then I knew. I wanted to see him for sure, and I wanted the choice to be mine. One way or another, this had to stop. So I went to the internet cafe on my way home. I opened a new message. I typed:

Yoshi, my Yoshi . . .
I know you are very busy. So am I. I know I hardly ever call you. You have your reasons and I have mine. Even so, I would love to see you before I go. Even if it's just for breakfast.
If you wanna call me, you know my number.
Love Chelsea

I stopped to consider that I was drunk again. But then I thought, fuck it.
I pressed SEND.

THE MALE WORLD OF
GINZA GIRLS

If you stacked money into skyscrapers and drove around them in blacked-out Benzes, shiny bright Bentleys and sleek BMWs, it would be called Ginza. The place had exclusivity as its birthright and currency as its blood, circulated by a pulse of affluence that began four hundred years ago when the Shogun designated the area his 'silver mint'.

When a fire devastated a wooden Ginza in the 1870s, Tokyo's first brick housing, department stores, asphalt pavements and other Western novelties superseded the manufacture of coins and the area became the fashionable place to be seen. Little more than a century later it exploded into a skyline that shimmers in wealth, and today Ginza remains the epitome of elite Tokyo society.

From the corner outside Ginza's Sony building I scanned the crowd at Sukiyobashi Crossing for Fujimoto-san's trademark black fedora until an arm shot up and he emerged, striding confidently towards me looking his trim, vibrant self. 'It is so easy to find you!' he boomed. 'I just look for the *gaijin*, and *whoa!* So tall,' he laughed, repositioning his hat. 'Wow, you look great! Nice dress. Okay, back across we go. The restaurant is over there.'

⁓

After dinner I rang Greengrass from the silence of the restaurant lobby. 'Hello, Nishi?' I croaked ever so weakly. 'This is Chelsea. I won't be able to come into work . . .'

'Oh? *Dohan?*' Nishi interrupted.

'No, not *dohan*. I'm sick, so I'm not coming. Okay? I can't come tonight.'

'Oh. Uh, prease try, Chelsea-san. You come.'

'I'm sorry, Nishi, I am *sick*. In bed. No coming. I'll see you Friday, okay?' I gave a few feeble coughs and whispered hoarsely, 'Bye-bye.'

Fujimoto-san looked suspiciously sideways. 'Why did you tell Nishi that you are sick? I already said I would pay your slave fee. Didn't he know you weren't coming?'

'No, it's best just to say I'm sick or they'll get mad if I'm out with a customer. This way they don't ask questions. I suppose it doesn't really matter, though. Usually you only get fined twenty-five-hundred-yen for being sick, but because it's the night before a public holiday they decided you have to pay the ten-thousand-yen fine they charge you for a no-show.'

'Nazis,' Fujimoto-san muttered as we started down the stairs. He fumed to the bottom and then surprised me with a thunderous outburst of laughter.

'*What?*' I exclaimed.

'You are such a good actress!' he accused, and held open the door.

～

As Fujimoto and I walked along the immaculate sidewalks among thousands of others, Ginza felt like an anime megalopolis minus the hovercars. Located in the heart of Tokyo, Ginza actually glowed from a distance, thanks to the sheer ostentation of its galactic neon. Yet still, it had good taste. If Roppongi was Tokyo's pleasure room, Ginza was where the jewels were kept, on double-digit floors behind the doors of thousands of matchstick bars and impenetrable, inaccessible, Japanese-only hostess clubs.

It is simply impossible to waltz into a Ginza hostess club as one does in Roppongi. Invitations and introductions are required. Japanese is spoken, and honorific, patriarchal and disciplined behaviour is mandatory. Customers are screened for suitability and monitored by an inscrutable, sweet-faced *mama-san* quick to throw out anyone who threatens the reputation of her establishment. As standard protocol Western men are seldom allowed into Ginza hostess clubs unless accompanied by a regular patron who can act as translator and cultural guide, and a young, white Western woman *never* enters a Japanese hostess club alone as a customer.

It was a rare occurrence, then, to receive the welcome of a Japanese hostess in fine kimono and lightly powdered skin as she bowed deeply from her lookout in the polished shadow of the Maruyoshi Building. When Fujimoto-san acknowledged her gruffly, she shuffled to a tiny elevator that was barely wide enough for one. On the third floor she bowed and exited backwards into a plush hallway. A tiny sign – 'Club Yumi' – hung above the doorway.

'*Irashaimase!*' came a female voice, and the *mama-san* emerged to welcome Fujimoto-san with delighted recognition. She extended me a serene demi-bow.

'*Komban wa*,' I said, bowing politely, and four women in kimonos swept around to inspect me.

'Never mind them,' Fujimoto-san huffed with stiff nods. 'They are just curious. Never are *gaijin* coming here, especially women! You are very lucky,' he clucked.

We were made to wait briefly before Fujimoto-san's hostess, Yuki, floated out. She was stunning – her make-up exquisite, her skin a fine porcelain, her features delicate. I was embarrassed when she bowed deeply to me and uttered all sorts of unwarranted compliments, enthusiastically translated by Fujimoto-san. I was equally flustered when Yuki escorted us into a small, stiffly formal room lit much more brightly than Greengrass, and several tables of men stopped smoking cigars to watch us before resuming their conversation.

Immediately Fujimoto-san commanded Yuki to mix his drink and sat back. He began a presentation of my attributes to her in Japanese, and a counter comparison to me of how Yuki fell short of them, to which she'd giggle, or nod in affable agreement. In fact, from the moment Yuki appeared, Fujimoto-san acted brusquely towards her. When he spoke, it was with affection, but curtly. Astonishingly, Yuki seemed to provoke him to belittle her. They seemed comfortable with their roles, but perhaps most fascinating was how Fujimoto-san kept this previously unseen behaviour exclusively for Yuki; he continued to treat me with the same level of respect and equality he always had. It was clear that Yuki was indebted to Fujimoto-san's long-standing patronage. Hostessing was Yuki's professional vocation and he'd been coming to see her for over twenty years.

The subtle flair with which she whisked her delicate fan or a long, classic lighter from deep within her *obi* was enviable. She hardly moved in the constriction of her kimono, but she didn't need to. All the expression Yuki needed was in her eyes. And yet this beautiful, humble and exotic woman was Fujimoto-san's subordinate, and she knew it.

'Is there anything you would like to say to Yuki?' Fujimoto-san asked as he blew smoke out grandly across the table. He looked entirely patriarchal.

'I *love* her kimono. It's exquisite. She looks absolutely beautiful.'

'No, no, we can't tell her that. Yuki is too tall for kimono. It exposes too much of her lower neck. It doesn't look good. Yuki could explain to you *why* the neck is most important in kimono, but unfortunately she never bothered to learn English. She is too lazy sleeping until lunchtime or going to the spa before calling her customers every afternoon.

'It is very hard work to come to Yuki's position in such a club of high standing as this, but she has been lucky to fall into it. She is one of the most senior hostesses here, which is why she can wear kimono even though it doesn't look good. Young apprentice hostesses can only wear cocktail dresses, because they have not yet learnt the proper techniques with which to entertain customers.'

Fujimoto-san eyeballed the depressed level of his sake and threw a disdainful glance at Yuki. She bowed microscopically and giggled, folding her kimono sleeve back to rest a flask delicately on her fingertips, exposing the inside of her wrist. With the other hand she gracefully poured the sake into Fujimoto-san's glass so that neither surface met, stopping just below the brim. This innocent gesture seemed demurely artistic, but I'd read *Memoirs of a Geisha* and I knew the sensuality this simple act possessed.

I caught Fujimoto-san's eyes glued to Yuki's naked wrist, and it was strange to be so close to such a private, erotic exchange. Then Yuki was called away to entertain a group of luxurious suits at an opposite table, but not before introducing her protégé, Kiko.

Kiko was new. She was young, 20, and a university student. Working at Club Yumi was a secret part-time job, because although hostessing was common among her friends, Kiko faced the possibility of being discharged from school or attracting parental shame if her risqué activities became public. As long as the job was kept discreet, Kiko was fine. Fujimoto-san found this highly amusing. 'So what do you tell your parents if you are not coming home until after midnight?' he laughed, and the jittery Kiko wavered slightly. 'Karaoke, with my friends,' she answered, 'or the disco.'

Unlike senior hostesses who could have passed for geisha, Kiko was a complete disaster. She splayed her legs, fidgeted constantly and wrung the hem of her dress. She failed to light Fujimoto-san's cigarette when he paused, and I had to light it myself. Her nervous uncertainty reminded me of every new girl at Greengrass.

After we'd been at Club Yumi for exactly one hour, Mama-san brought Fujimoto-san his bill and made small talk until Yuki was free to accompany us to the deserted side street with Kiko. The two of them bowed us off, giggling and waving from their anonymous nook, dwarfed by a humming expanse of glass towering into the night.

—

Fujimoto-san finally found the entrance to Kentauros hidden within the Creglanz Ginza Building. It was a tiny dark room illuminated just enough for us to see the reflection of the liquor in a buffed mirror. With two suits drinking under fine smoke at the bar and four pinstripes occupying a low table, the bar was almost full when Fujimoto-san and I perched at one end to be welcomed by a *mama-san* who seemed oddly familiar, and for good reason.

The *mama-san* of Kentauros had worked at Club Yumi with Yuki until very recently and shared the same elegant grace. At a similar age to Yuki, Mama-san had retired from the rigours of her profession to open a shot bar, likely with the help and fortune of a long-established customer or two. Instead of visiting their favourite hostess at a club, now the men came to drink at her bar. It was a maturation of relationships forged over the years. She could retain the admiration of men who'd become part of her life, yet had gained a level of authority behind the bar, shedding her kimono for classical tailoring.

'It is very important for a hostess never to fall in love with her customers,' Fujimoto-san lectured. 'If fall in love, disaster! Then it's finished. One customer can see a particular hostess giving special attention to another man – it is easy from just the way she looks at him – and he becomes jealous. It is a very fine line. In Japan this kind of relationship is not about sex. The best hostesses can give the same illusion to everyone, yet shut off their own emotion. Then eventually, if they are lucky, they can open their own business because of generous sponsors.

'I know so many bars in Ginza like this, run by retired hostesses, because I am always in charge of making sure the movie stars have a good time, but this is one of my favourite. What do you want to drink, something expensive? How about some whisky – McCallan?'

'Um, no thank you, Fujimoto-san. Whisky is a bit strong for me.'

'No! Not this whisky. McCallan is so smooth you would be surprised. It is Nicolas Cage's favourite. At a bar it costs fifteen-hundred dollars a bottle, or two-hundred dollars a glass. He loves it. Are you sure you don't want to try? Okay. I'll make it a present for you then, for your father, to say *gomen nasai* because you are such a bad daughter for him. Three years away from home! I cannot believe it! How about rum? Mama-san has a very, very fine rum.' The twinkle in his eye was impossible to resist.

'Okay, fine,' I conceded. 'I'll try the rum.'

THE DEVIL'S DEMONS

When I walked into Greengrass on my last Friday night in Japan, Tehara was right there waiting. Slouched against the table with arms firmly crossed, he shifted only his gaze, like a chameleon lizard too disaffected to move, and let out a weary puff of air. 'Chelsea-san. Ito-san called to me. About you. Did he lend you his computer?'

'What? No! He didn't *lend* me his computer. Is that what he said?'

'*Hai*. He said to me to remind you he wants it back.'

'Oh, does he?' I seethed. 'Well, why didn't he call and tell me that himself? He knows my number!' Tehara shrugged indifferently. 'I can't believe it! But he . . . argh! All right. Don't worry about it. *I'll* deal with him.'

This was ridiculous. It was so underhanded for Nori to resurface from silent exile just two days before I left, and one night before I was to be paid an entire month's salary. Who did he think he was, demanding that Tehara deliver such a preposterous message?

I was fuming, but as I changed in the humid back room my anger slowly crept into bed with anxiety. Nori was a valued customer of Greengrass, and I couldn't presume this little act of vengeance was anything but well timed. The laptop was probably worth more than I was owed in wages, and Nishi would rather not pay me than let a hostess allegedly run off with one of his best customer's computers. What a jerk.

Nori had manoeuvred expertly to attempt to force my hand, but I couldn't exactly give the laptop back — I'd given it to one of Matt's friends who could actually use Japanese Windows. So now I was screwed. And what if the stupid thing was worth more than my wages?

If I didn't pay the balance, it was possible Nori would complain to Fumio, his best friend and top brass in the Yokohama Police Department, who in turn could report me to immigration. Then I'd be arrested, imprisoned or deported, all because I'd accepted an expensive gift from a man whose irrational affections I'd shunned.

I needed a solution, and after discussing the situation with Nicole around the powwow table, we decided I'd have to call him.

'Just call him like nothing happened last time between you, but you *have* to be nice. Do you understand me, Chelsea? Really, really nice. Even nicer than you've ever been before. And don't mention anything about the computer.'

'Well, then, what am I supposed to say?'

'Easy.' Nicole picked up an imaginary phone and dripped honey from her voice. 'Hi, Ito-san, how are you? I am so sorry I haven't called you all week, but I've been so stressed and unhappy. I miss you. I haven't seen you and I'm so sad. I really want to see you before I leave. Can you please come into the club? I would hate to go without saying goodbye.' My face crumpled in disgust and Nicole looked at me sternly. 'Do it, Chelsea.'

'All right, fine. He's not going to answer when he sees it's me, you know.' But Nori did answer, after two rings.

'*Moshi moshi?* Hello?'

So I swallowed my pride and did my best to regurgitate Nicole's putrid speech.

'Oh, yes, hi!' Nori interrupted hastily. 'Chelsea. Uh yes, thank you for calling, but uh, I am very busy, now. I am happy that you called to me and maybe, if before you leave Japan and I have time, I will come to Tokyo to see you.'

'Oh.' I didn't know what to say next. 'Okay.'

'Yes and uh, I am very busy, so see you later. Okay? Uh, bye-bye.' And Nori hung up while my mouth fell open.

'So does he still want his computer?' Nicole asked with a smirk.

'He didn't even mention it.'

'Exactly,' she said. 'How do you say it in English? He just wanted to take back the upper hand. It's Japanese. They're spiteful,' she smiled lovingly. 'And you're off the hook.'

—

Three days after our Ginza escapade had concluded with karaoke at Petits Pois until sunrise, Fujimoto-san laid aside his strong opinion of Nishi's 'Nazi' ways to greet me with a radiant smile and make a formal effort to bid me adieu on my last Friday night in Japan. It was a gesture I highly appreciated, because he hadn't come alone; I was a one-hour timeslot in an evening of film-industry entertainment. In my honour Fujimoto-san sang a familiar Japanese ballad that would have garnered a hundred-calorie reading at Petits Pois, and I reciprocated with a song from Oasis, in between his good wishes for my future, a thousand compliments and a warning not to get any fatter or I'd lose my cheekbones. To top it all off, Fujimoto-san had brought along a large, paper-bagged sayonara gift – a crated bottle of twenty-fifth anniversary McCallan whisky. 'Nicolas Cage's favourite! For your father, remember. I told you. Instead of sake. Very good! Fifteen-hundred dollars per one bottle!'

'Fujimoto-san! You shouldn't have!'

'No! It is my duty. You are so bad girl. You must apologise to your father, three times. One time for every year you have not gone home. *Gomen nasai, gomen nasai, gomen nasai*. Terrible *desu yo*! Never have I met such a terrible daughter as you.'

It was sad to see him go, but ours was a happy parting. At the end of the hour we shook hands, bowed in great appreciation and cordoned off a little piece of our hearts.

Then it was time for Yoshi.

—

He strode through the door late into the night. The first thing that struck me was that we matched. We were both dressed in head-to-toe black. Handsome and glowing, he caught my eye and a smile spread across my face. My heart jumped. Here it was. The final countdown.

There was something different about him. He was so relaxed, so comfortable and yet – could it be? – so sober. We settled in comfortably for an hour until we were both languidly drunk. With Nishi's permission we left the crowded club just past 1.00 am and walked to a nearby Indian restaurant, supporting each other's unsteady weight. Apart from statues of Ganesh and Shiva we had the little place to ourselves. A single waiter catered to Yoshi's loud demands for beer and food and came running when he spilt beer all over the garlic naan. Complaining of being drunk, Yoshi retreated to the bathroom and I sighed while he blew his nose among other familiar sounds through the thin bathroom wall. Yoshi was sobering up.

After he paid, we stopped into a convenience store to fill a basket haphazardly with wine, snacks and Kahlua before hailing a taxi to his apartment in Hiroo. Just as I'd imagined, the taxi stopped outside a colossal building and we took the elevator up to a grand hallway where he unlocked an imposingly large door.

Yoshi's new apartment was a work of tasteful design. Dark woods. White and black. It was excessively spacious for a bachelor pad in Tokyo, but Yoshi wrote it off as an impersonal rental while we unpacked the bags in the kitchen.

'I'll show you around, leave that,' he said, and I was given the tour of a bedroom separated by a large sliding *shoji* screen, a walk-in closet overflowing with Gucci and Prada still dumped in piles from the move, and a massive bathroom, all mirrored and dark-marbled luxury. In the corner of his sumptuous pad, next to a long white couch, I held up a picture of Yoshi with a trophy-sized fish onboard a boat. 'Mmm,' he hummed proudly. 'My boat.'

'It's a great picture, Yosh. Hey, have you got the Kyoto pictures for me?'

'Yeah, in my car. I'll get them later.'

'Can't you get them now? I want to see them, and you might forget.'

'Okay, okay. I have to go to garage. You stay here.'

As soon as Yoshi shut the door, I slid around the floor gleefully in my socks. I pulled out the McCallan and inspected the bottle for the first time. I mixed another Kahlua and milk and simultaneously tried to quell my extreme drunkenness. When Yoshi came back, I was sitting at the table, legs crossed, shaking my foot. He passed an envelope with a wide grin, and as I flicked through shots of sinewy rickshaw porters and ancient Shinto shrines, Yoshi put on some music. I was surprised at how happy I looked in the photos, how refreshed.

Then Yoshi was standing across the table. He was bent over a silver tray. He was cutting two lines of coke. Two big, fat powdered lines, like leeches swollen with blood.

'*Yoshi* . . .' I protested.

'*What? Ma chérie*, I am drunk. I need to sober up. You too . . .' he grinned, but before I could shake my head he'd expertly snorted the snow up his nostril. I watched him as it began to course through his veins, as the narcotic medicated him to normalcy, as it took the edge off his alcohol saturation, jump-started his psyche and sucked the absolute life out of him.

Silently he handed over a thousand-yen note, turned his back and left the room. I watched the note uncurl as I released my fingers and let it fall to the polished wood, stopping next to a photo of me smiling in the dappled sunshine next to the Oi River. When Yoshi came back, there was still a single line on the table and I was on the couch. He looked at me like something was wrong.

'*Whaaaaat?* You don't wanna?' he pleaded. I looked away. 'Fine, but if you don't wanna, I don't wanna.' Somehow, I thought, it was too late for that.

But then he was next to me. His hand was on my waist, and then it was on my breast, and then Yoshi kissed me. As his lips pressed into mine, I suddenly had the answer I had come for. I felt it completely, like a big iron curtain descending between what I'd imagined I wanted and what I actually did.

I felt sick.

'I feel a bit weird, Yoshi. Maybe I should . . .'

'What? Fever? You look flushed. You wanna bath? Shower?'

'No, it's my stomach. I feel kinda queasy. Maybe it was the Indian,' I stammered. But it wasn't the Indian. It was purely psychosomatic. 'I think I might have to throw up.'

'Go run some cold water on your face. There are facecloths in the bathroom.'

With a deep inhalation I locked myself into Yoshi's bathroom, leaning heavily against the door. I stared at myself in the mirror. Shit. I turned on the tap and let it run at full pressure. The water splashed into tiny liquid hemispheres on the counter, landing in a fine spray next to a cup with two toothbrushes.

I tried to focus my mind and stop the fuzz of drunken judgement clouding my vision. What the fuck was I going to do? I was going to have to carry this fake sickness to the end. I shouldn't have come here. I couldn't keep my hands from shaking. I flushed the toilet and ran the water again. There. Sonically speaking, I'd just thrown up.

I waited several minutes and then slowly emerged with an arm around my waist. The television was on. Yoshi was on the couch, watching it. *Bzzzt. Bzzzt. Bzzzt.* What was that? It was my phone vibrating in silent mode on the table. I picked it up. It said: MATT.

Oh, my dear Matt. Thank God.

'Hi Nicole,' I sighed with feigned exhaustion. 'How are you? What, you're still in Roppongi? Oh, you just finished work. No, I'm with a friend, with Yoshi, but I'm not feeling that flash, I think I'm gonna go home. Soon, yeah. No, I don't think I can meet you guys, I feel like puking. I think I might have food poisoning. I don't know. Yeah, I'll call you tomorrow. Don't worry. I'm fine and everything will be fine. Sorry. Okay, see ya.'

Matt must have wondered what the hell was going on. I'd answered all his questions so he knew I was safe, and while he was used to false phone conversations when I was with customers, this was one degree stranger than usual. I sat down next to Yoshi on the couch and dropped my head in my hands. 'I'm really sorry, Yoshi, I . . .'

'What's the matter, *chérie*?' Yoshi looked at me sadly. 'You don't like me? You don't like my apartment?'

'That's not it,' I pleaded, but when I looked up Yoshi wouldn't meet my eyes. He had something beside him. He brought out a lighter and lit up a glass sphere. As he exhaled a mushroom cloud of frosty smoke in one long, elegant breath, he sighed deeply and I coughed. 'What is *that*?'

'Ice,' he said flatly. 'You want some?'

'No.' I pulled back to avoid the brainfuck dust swirling around us. 'Yoshi, I really feel sick. I think I might have food poisoning from the . . .'

'You need sleep,' Yoshi said. 'It's okay, c'mon,' and he led me around the *shoji* screen to throw back the quilt. 'Have a rest. I'll wake you up, morning time.'

And so I lay in Yoshi's bed while he tucked me in and left the room. I heard the TV come on. It flickered off the wall. I stared at the ceiling. Caressed in the luxurious folds of a white down quilt, I'd never been in such a comfortable bed in all my life, but mentally, emotionally, I was petrified. This was my preview of life with Yoshi, and boy did it suck. How was I going to get out of this? I stared at the ceiling for what felt like forever before slipping off the bed and sliding the *shoji* screen open.

'Yoshi . . .?' There was silence as he looked up at me from the couch, standing like just another pretty feature of his designer bachelor pad. There was a naked Japanese girl writhing on the screen. Yoshi said nothing.

'I'm gonna go home, I don't . . .'

'Okay,' he interrupted, and that was all he had to say about it. No emotion. No protest. He just mechanically saw me to the door. He looked so old as he held it open, so weary. Only his nostrils swelled slightly. 'I hope you feel . . . better, soon. Go home and sleep. I'll call you. Tomorrow . . . make sure you're . . . okay.'

Yoshi meant to smile but only the edges of his eyes creased. I didn't want to leave him, but how could I stay? He was lifeless. He was fucked.

I was heartbroken. Hollow as though I no longer existed. But I did. I'd come here with him. I had been prepared to do whatever I felt was right, whatever that might entail, but I'd thought no thoughts. I had only reacted, and that was exactly what I'd been looking for. I was still drunk. Way too drunk for reason. And now I was leaving.

And I realised that it *didn't matter*. This, right here, was the only thing that could happen. I valued Yoshi more than he knew, but the sobering reality of seeing him like this, in the place where he lived, made it utterly clear. This just wasn't my life.

I hesitated at the doorway, lips formed into unspoken words. Yoshi didn't look at me. I clutched Fujimoto-san's paper bag tightly, feeling the weight of a McCallan whisky that I would never drink. The bottle was heavy, but not that heavy. Not as heavy as leaving him like this. For the last time.

I hit the empty sidewalk and ran. And ran. And ran. And sprinted. The cool air of empty streets lapped at my face. It stung my eyes and stole my breath, but still I ran.

WHERE YOU GO I WILL GO, WHERE YOU STAY I WILL STAY

Life can be so complicated and yet so basic too. Everyone just wants to be loved. They want that love to matter to somebody, specifically, for reasons special only to them. I have seen this every day for three months. In the mundane. In the absurd. The breathtaking. I have not simply been a hostess. I have loved people, in some fraction of the meaning, and I still do love other people. To these men I feel connected, empathetic and entangled in loose strands of another time and possibility. But I am *in* love with Matt. He is my reflection.

Today is our third anniversary. Tomorrow we are going to Canada so that I can introduce him for the first time to my family. Tonight we are going to Roppongi Hills for dinner before I go to Greengrass for my last night as a hostess. It is the first meal that will cost us more than $20 the entire time we've been here. Matt is ecstatic. I suspect, considering the posh restaurants I have become accustomed to, that I will be a snob. But I'll get over that.

You know, Matt, you are so very ahead of your time. This comparison of you to these emotionally absorbing relationships I have been having with middle-aged Japanese men is completely unfair. If I were able to look into their eyes when they were only your age, I doubt I would have seen the incredible sensitivity that you now hold within you. Your shell is not so lacquered, but I trust in your soul. Know that.

If there is one thing that I know, it is that I will miss this place. I will miss everything I didn't get to write about. I will miss Takatani, the eccentric blues guitarist who didn't make the cut because he wasn't linear enough, but he took me to dinner and he gave me the golden seat at his concert and wrote me a song he called 'Chelsea', and then called at 2.00 am from his studio to play it live over the phone while Matt and I drank frappucinos at Starbucks. Takatani has sold over 13 million albums in Europe. I suppose he is famous, but to me he is wonderful. I will miss our conversations about music and the arts and philosophy. I will miss listening to his sporadic bursts into song when we strolled past a temple in the middle of Tokyo.

I will miss all of the incidentals. Singing karaoke. You know I will miss that. Meeting a stranger one night who was already a friend by the next. Stem-cell researchers from Beijing. Hearing about men's lives and their dreams and their loves. Drinking late into the night with Takeru Kobayashi, six-times world champion hot-dog eater, courtesy of Coney Island, NY. For such a shy, self-effacing man, he had the largest biceps I had ever seen.

I will miss Shin, my dear Shin, and his kindness and humour, and I will miss Nishi and Soh and their antics. I will miss a country that loves An-Pan Man, a comic-book character with a regenerative bread-roll head who lets people eat his face because he is '*so generous*'. I will miss the voltage of Fujimoto-san and the way he shouts 'terrible!' over a glass of red wine and another delicious story. I will miss the cigarette smoke, although I don't know it yet, and I will be partial to the memories interlocked with the smell probably forever even though I know it is bad for me.

And Yoshi. Of course I will miss him, although I don't know how I will feel about him for a long time to come . . . but that is okay.

LAST NIGHT IN PARADISE

You'd think that if you breathed in through ninety days of your life, you might be able to articulate them well enough to convey an accurate sense of what really took place. You might be able to throw enough vivid colour onto a canvas, or draw enough ink from the well to squeeze the passage of time into an alphabet of black and white, a collection of words that could capture fleeting moments, at least if only in pieces. If you could do that with sufficient sincerity, it might be enough, if you weren't faulted from the beginning – because how can you do justice to a story that even *you* don't fully understand? The best you can ever hope for is an imperfect evocation. Anything else is impossible, and you simply have to accept that. You just have to leave it there and leave everything else open to interpretation.

—

Shin came through the door at half past nine. Phil Collins was singing. Girls were laughing. Cigarettes were burning. He glanced my way and waved. Someone shouted a bilingual toast. Drinks flowed, relationships continued and minds played at games as complicated as they wanted them to be. I waved back and joined him without waiting for Tehara or Nishi or Soh to escort me. They were too busy with other things.

Shin was slightly dressed up, but only enough to be able to deny the fact if I pointed it out. I could see that his hair was combed and he'd ironed his shirt, but he still looked like he didn't belong, as though he'd stumbled into Greengrass by mistake and would be left eating ramen noodles for the rest of the week.

When I ordered orange juice for both of us, he laughed at me. We slowly sipped two more, sharing an ordinary conversation interspersed with long silences and the occasional jab at each other's character. 'You are *soooo* bad hostess.' Shin shook his head in disbelief. 'How did you survive, all this time?'

When he requested the karaoke book, I knew what was coming.

As the Japanese words of 'Sayonara Song' scrolled out one by one, Shin sang them so incredibly off-key that it was beautiful. His eyes glistened. His voice wavered. And yet over the speakers he remained indistinct to everyone in the room but me. I'd finally unlocked the key to karaoke's heart; it wasn't about showing off, being good or bad. It was an impersonal group activity that allowed emotional expression behind the safeguard of someone else's words. Hidden behind a song familiar to everyone, you could be as personal as you wanted. That was why it was never an issue whether someone sang or not. It wasn't about yes or no, but rather it depended on the mood.

When he was finished, Shin requested that I sing him a song, as a token gesture traded between us. At first I was embarrassed. I'd never sang with Shin, and I wasn't keen to break the tradition, mostly because I didn't trust my voice not to splinter through my smile. I finally caved in when he called me a baby, and he got what he asked for.

I sang him 'Leaving on a Jet Plane'.

The truth was, none of my bags were packed and still, even at this last moment, I wasn't sure if I really was ready to go. But tomorrow my visa ran out, and I had a non-transferable ticket across the Pacific. I had no choice. My passport would be stamped. I was leaving, whether I liked it or not. If I could decide whether I liked it or not.

Shin paid after two hours, and we meandered out into the hallway, him telling a joke and me laughing. He pressed the button and it illuminated for the millionth time, the elevator slowly ascending from six storeys below.

As Shin gave me one of his paradoxical, tranquilly playful smirks, I couldn't find an expression to put on my face in return. We both just stood there, in what was probably our first uncomfortable moment together, until he raised his right hand.

'Okay,' he said simply. 'See you.'

'See you, Shin.' And then the elevator doors closed. On him. On a lot of things. Standing alone under the dim candescent light of a well-worn hallway, I remembered how I had first stood here all those nights ago, sentiments diametrically opposed, and I felt, in some way, exactly like that.

THANK YOU

To Matt, for everything. To my family—my mom, my dad, my little brother Kenton and my big sister Carolyn for always being there. To my editor Jessica Case at Pegasus, for absolutely getting it, and for a tremendous job well done. To Claiborne Hancock, for running a brilliant publishing house and supporting this book. To my agent Stéphanie Abou in New York, *vous êtes superbe.* To my agent Pippa Masson in Sydney, one million times over. To Alison Urquhart and Maaike le Noble, because they are wonderful. To Monica Catorc, a mentor and inspiration whom I treasure. To Monsieur Candela, for his magical way of being. To Fred and Pam Pitzman, whose generosity first opened up the world to me. To Aunt Trudy, who was the first sounding board for this book. Again to my sister, for doing my website for free (you know I will pay you one day!). To everyone who ever helped me, consciously or not. And particularly to those whose sunshine has lit up my life: James Prichard, Yeva Glover, Lara Kkafas, Robert Blaauboer, Sam Cascone, Liza Jenne, Jean Christian, Mark Blankestein, Rachael L'Orsa, Sandra Holmqvist, Juliet Bennett, Guillaume Catala, Andrew Candela, Matt Booy, Shamkhun, Toshio, and, of course, the unforgettable Shin.